TRANSGRESSIONS: CULTURAL STUDIES AND EDUCATION

Cultural studies provides an analytical toolbox for both making sense of educational practice and extending the insights of educational professionals into their labors. In this context *Transgressions: Cultural Studies and Education* provides a collection of books in the domain that specify this assertion. Crafted for an audience of teachers, teacher educators, scholars and students of cultural studies and others interested in cultural studies and pedagogy, the series documents both the possibilities of and the controversies surrounding the intersection of cultural studies and education. The editors and the authors of this series do not assume that the interaction of cultural studies and education devalues other types of knowledge and analytical forms. Rather the intersection of these knowledge disciplines offers a rejuvenating, optimistic, and positive perspective on education and educational institutions. Some might describe its contribution as democratic, emancipatory, and transformative. The editors and authors maintain that cultural studies helps free educators from sterile, monolithic analyses that have for too long undermined efforts to think of educational practices by providing other words, new languages, and fresh metaphors. Operating in an interdisciplinary cosmos, Transgressions: Cultural Studies and Education is dedicated to exploring the ways cultural studies enhances the study and practice of education. With this in mind the series focuses in a non-exclusive way on popular culture as well as other dimensions of cultural studies including social theory, social justice and positionality, cultural dimensions of technological innovation, new media and media literacy, new forms of oppression emerging in an electronic hyperreality, and postcolonial global concerns. With these concerns in mind cultural studies scholars often argue that the realm of popular culture is the most powerful educational force in contemporary culture. Indeed, in the twenty-first century this pedagogical dynamic is sweeping through the entire world. Educators, they believe, must understand these emerging realities in order to gain an important voice in the pedagogical conversation.

Without an understanding of cultural pedagogy's (education that takes place outside of formal schooling) role in the shaping of individual identity–youth identity in particular–the role educators play in the lives of their students will continue to fade. Why do so many of our students feel that life is incomprehensible and devoid of meaning? What does it mean, teachers wonder, when young people are unable to describe their moods, their affective affiliation to the society around them. Meanings provided young people by mainstream institutions often do little to help them deal with their affective complexity, their difficulty negotiating the rift between meaning and affect. School knowledge and educational expectations seem as anachronistic as a ditto machine, not that learning ways of rational thought and making sense of the world are unimportant.

But school knowledge and educational expectations often have little to offer students about making sense of the way they feel, the way their affective lives are shaped. In no way do we argue that analysis of the production of youth in an electronic mediated world demands some "touchy-feely" educational superficiality. What is needed in this context is a rigorous analysis of the interrelationship between pedagogy, popular culture, meaning making, and youth subjectivity. In an era marked by youth depression, violence, and suicide such insights become extremely important, even life saving. Pessimism about the future is the common sense of many contemporary youth with its concomitant feeling that no one can make a difference.

If affective production can be shaped to reflect these perspectives, then it can be reshaped to lay the groundwork for optimism, passionate commitment, and transformative educational and political activity. In these ways cultural studies adds a dimension to the work of education unfilled by any other sub-discipline. This is what Transgressions: Cultural Studies and Education seeks to produce—literature on these issues that makes a difference. It seeks to publish studies that help those who work with young people, those individuals involved in the disciplines that study children and youth, and young people themselves improve their lives in these bizarre times.

The More of Myth

A Pedagogy of Diversion

Mary Aswell Doll
Savannah College of Art and Design

SENSE PUBLISHERS
ROTTERDAM/BOSTON/TAIPEI

A C.I.P. record for this book is available from the Library of Congress.

ISBN: 978-94-6091-443-0 (paperback)
ISBN: 978-94-6091-444-7 (hardback)
ISBN: 978-94-6091-445-4 (e-book)

Published by: Sense Publishers,
P.O. Box 21858,
3001 AW Rotterdam,
The Netherlands
www.sensepublishers.com

Printed on acid-free paper

Cover art "Ahm" by Jacob Mundell, SCAD 2011

DEDICATION

Every inch of the way, every step, every text, every read-over, every time: my deepest thanks to Marla Morris. The extensive library inside her head and outside within her bookshelves helped make this book on myth more pedagogically alive. I dedicate it to her.

ACKNOWLEDGMENTS

I am grateful for the Presidential Fellowship Savannah College of Art and Design awarded me. This grant enabled me to travel to southern Ireland, where I attended a workshop on Celtic mythology, which aided my research into this area of my study. I am grateful for the careful line by line commentary offered me by Dr. Bernard Ricca, of Saint John Fisher College. His corrections and suggestions helped strengthen the chapters on new science. I am grateful, too, for the support given me by Shirley Steinberg and Michel Lokhorst, who saw this project as worthy of publication. My students are always a source of inspiration for me. I use their comments throughout my chapters with respect and appreciation.

TABLE OF CONTENTS

PREFACE

The "More" of Myth: A Pedagogy of Diversion

Creation stories most often begin in some sort of fluid. This creation story is no different. The idea for a book about myth, myth's extraordinary reawakening of our senses and sensitivities, together with the teaching of myth to art students: these ideas have been simmering at a slow boil for a while in my thinking. It was during a hot July afternoon, however, in the briny shallows of the Atlantic Ocean off of Tybee Island that the idea germinated. I was swimming with Marla, my partner. While bobbing in the brine I suggested titles for a book I wanted to write about myth in the classroom. "Early Teaching, Later Learnings," I suggested to Marla.

"No," she replied. "Too connected with a specific strand of curriculum known as Teaching and Learning. Too specific for you."

"Okay," I tossed back, "how about "The 'More' of Myth"?

Marla took a stroke or two, then came back with the subtitle: "A Pedagogy of Diversion."

So was born the title of this book.

I begin with titles. And to begin a book on myth while paddling in salt water with teeny fishlets nipping at my shins seems right. Creation, as I said, begins in fluid.

I began teaching "Introduction to World Myth" knowing little about the "world" part. I knew and had written about Greek myth, but myths of Africa, Asia, Norway, Egypt, North America, with few exceptions, were beyond my reach. My students in some cases were more advanced in some areas of myth than me. I did not grow up in the age of digital gaming and was not much of a comic book fan, two areas that use mythic motifs heavily. In one class I had a small precocious boygirl student who wore thin ties and would usually slip into class late. She had schooled herself on Egyptian linguistics. She would take a certain sadistic pleasure, it seemed to me, in correcting my pronunciation of Egyptian gods—always with a quick smile and characteristic duck of the head. By then, three years into the practice of teaching this subject, I had begun to feel more familiar with my world tour of myth, so her corrections did not bother me. Much. I was talking in class less about charts and categories and correct pronunciation and more about wonder and energy. It is with that latter emphasis that I write this book.

In some ways my exploration of myth could be called ecopedagogical, in the manner of David Jardine's (2000) splendid collection of essays. Like him, my profession is teaching. Like him, I am interdisciplinary in mind, seeking to connect, always connect. This is especially important when a modern mindset still evident today seems to have forgotten the connection the human being has with other beings on the planet, else why would the world be facing ecological disaster? As David Jardine puts it, "[ecopedagogy] is an attempt to find ways in which ecologically rich images of ancestry, sustainability, interrelatedness, interdependency, kinship, and topography can help revitalize our understanding of all of the living disciplines in our care" (p. 3).

The pedagogy of ecology seeks to find ways of discovering, uncovering, and confronting the issues of any discipline that bring back concerns about the planet.

Educational classrooms are spaces where talk holds sway, certainly. But it can also be a space of hearing other soundings, of hearkening and heedfulness (Aoki, 1990, p. 375). My students, some of them, are musicians. Composing songs for a particular myth or drumming to the spoken word are different kinds of speakings that I encourage my student musicians to try and all of us in the space called class to attend to. Myth is also a different kind of speaking that asks the reader to slow down the eyes and tune down the ear so as to appreciate nuance more deeply. Myths, originally an artform within an oral culture, are meant to be heard, not read solitarily. The ear can hold two opposites together nicely, and myth if it is anything is para-doxical (what the modernist would call irrational). The "irrationalities" of the mythic universe, however, are a given, considered equal with reason (Shlain, 1999, p. 139). Holding two opposites together in the cup of the ear is a gift from the far past that no longer surprises quantum physics. (More of that interesting connection–myth and science–later.) For now, the thought of "talk" in the classroom is what gives me pause.

The human voice changes register when it tells stories.

Storytelling is not talking. With this in mind, I read to my students, not only because I love to read out loud, am a very good out loud reader, but also because in reading out loud the human voice can't help but dramatize, take on different tonal pitches, and engage the whole body with arm swings and head turns. I have witnessed my sleepy students lose their cool when I read. They bend forward and slowly, slowly their mouths open. It is truly wonderous to watch this transformation when talk turns to voice.

Besides being ecopedagogical, mythic exploration can also be called ecopsycho-logical. Psyche, as we know, is the root of psychology: psyche, not mind; soul, not brain. The story of Psyche and Eros teaches that the soul, Psyche, loves love, Eros. An erotic classroom is one of relationship and warmth, of seeking connection. And, as in the first of Psyche's tasks to be reunited with her lover, the soul needs helpers, who emerge from nature. Remembering the story, Psyche is set on four tasks by her future mother-in-law, Venus in the Roman version, to see if she is worthy of being a goddess. All of the tasks are impossible and Psyche, being young, despairs at the thought of never being reunited with Eros. Psyche suffers for love. It is important to see this aspect of the tale, for the soul's terrain is the vale of suffering and of moods; these are deeply psychological areas. But Psyche is aided by ants, reeds, and voices: these are the stirrings within the natural world. She learns discrimination: to sort, select, and listen more closely. Indeed, erotic closeness is the place of the soul: not in large categories and meta abstractions or mega churches but in small, seemingly insignificant arenas. The tasks of Psyche are of an entirely different order from the labors of Herakles, as ecofeminists would aver.

Ecopsychology pays attention to the small. The word "attention" is like "a tending" and "a tension," the paradox holding two things seemingly opposite together. Tending to the small is giving care; allowing a tension to exist is energizing. Psyche attends while yet feeling the tension of impossibility. The wisdom of this simple story leads to the honoring of images and honoring the tiny helpers who lead Psyche to new ways of figuring her dilemma: not by figuring the figure *out*, as in cognition, but by attending to the details at hand, the figure. Each dilemma requires a different solution, one more imaginative than the next, none alike.

Mythic plot lines have been appropriated by story tellers of all times. I think the broad sweep of plot used in comics and video games puts emphasis on action rather than thought. This book is not interested in plot lines and outer action. Those serve as backdrops for the figures at hand. We must leave narrative and linear progression if we are to attend ecopedagogically and ecopsychologically to the dip down points of image and voice. So I leave you, the reader, with the invitation to read the amazing images that myth offers and to ponder the messages as I hope to offer them.

INTRODUCTION

Moreness, Myth and the Pedagogy of Diversion

I have wanted to write this book for years. It has been growing within me as I have been teaching world mythology to undergraduate artists for more than several of their graduations. This is, in a sense, my graduation. Let me share with you, those of you in education particularly, how mythology and folk stories have seasoned my thinking. If I can be half as wise as these stories, I will have succeeded in passing along some gleanings from the hours.

Like Dwayne Huebner, I am fond of the word "moreness." Huebner (1999) terms myths "symbols of moreness, of otherness, of the transcendent—symbols that life as lived can be different" (p. 344). That which is different, or more, takes us by surprise, Huebner continues, and infuses our imaginations with new images. That definition serves my purposes exactly, for I teach artists and this book is about images and the startling new ideas that come from reading images mythologically. What does this mean? What I try to teach my students is that the images we come across in the fantastical tales called myth are not just weird, although they are that. These images deserve more than our delight in weirdness; they deserve to be taken seriously as truly different ways to propose truly important ideas.

Most of the images I will be discussing in this book are the ones that grabbed me. This book offers the occasion for me to grapple with how I have been grabbed, and to express as best I can the idea in the image. The idea is, in all cases, startling to a twenty-first century person accustomed to the convenience of electricity and battery-operated remotes. So let me take "moreness" to consider electricity and batteries differently, in the manner of electromagnetism, where the littlest sub atom has more energy than I can see or feel but vibrates constantly beneath surfaces. Quantum physics meets the Quantum Daimon, the mythic subversive spirit that has been there radiating long long before Niels Bohr.

Image consciousness, then, is my intention. To quote Dwayne Huebner again, "A new image must be articulated or described so others can move within the landscape as they did in the past, but with greater freedom and new awareness" (p. 404). One new set of images I will introduce are those that are weird. I draw on images of the body in myth, configured differently. Mouth, eye, lung, thigh, thumb: we know these members of our bodies. But perhaps we know them too familiarly. To know them weirdly introduces a whole new universe of ideas about how our bodies are connected to the cosmos in ways we have forgotten or ignored. Peter Appelbaum (2008) gives other meanings of the word "weird" to include "the strange, the odd, the bizarre, the peculiar, the uncanny, the eerie, the creepy or the unusual" (pp. 43–44). But Appelbaum warns against getting too cute with weirdness. To mistake the weird for a "wow" is merely a kind of zip zap strategy to keep boredom at bay. This, he insists, is not what is intended when curriculum is weirded: "I am inviting you to establish a kind of intimacy that requires a suspension of incredulity and an imaginative acceptance that there is indeed something to this. Such an embrace is a sign of the weird" (p. 41).

A second set of weird images moves a delight with weirdness into an appreciation of the profound. Always, that is my gleaning from myth. The stories are wisdom stories because they delight and inform at the same time, if we are awake. Oddly, I teach myth at 8 AM, to young artists who have been up all night working on their other courses in graphic design, illustration, sequential art, film, sculpture or the like. There, they learn technique and problem solving. With me they are also learning problem solving but of a different sort. The biggest problem to confront is that which stops the thinking at the level of the weird and does not go beyond and below. That is my challenge. Mythic images challenge us to open the landscape of our minds, to probe beneath surfaces, to re-think, and perhaps, even, to re-member. Not only "can" life lived be differently because of an engagement with mythic image, it "must" if we are to stop endangering our ecosystem. We must awaken a new dispensation.

And so I offer myth as a pedagogy of diversion. "Diversion" is a felicitous word, all meanings intended throughout my discussion. Diversion, first, is a way away from the way, "the act of turning aside, as from a course or purpose." Diversion is also a "channel made to direct the flow of water" (Webster). "Way" is a word used by Lao Tzu to describe respect and to differentiate from "the usual." It is in the former sense of respect that Lao Tzu cautions against *losing* the way:

When people lost sight of the way to live

Came codes of love and honesty,

Learning came, charity came;

Hypocrisy took charge. (in Bynner, 1980, p. 35)

Did Lao Tzu intuit the march toward measurement in education today? How perfect a rebuke he offers to those who would codify life and learning. Carl Jung says, "in a standardized milieu, it is easy to lose the sense of one's own personality, of one's individuality" (in Sabini, 2005, p. 155). The way that seeks to channel the flow or to turn aside from hypocrisy, *this* way which is Lao Tzu's way, seeks diversion from institutional codes and purposes. Instead, a pedagogy of diversion in the first sense of the word eschews all that would institute props and stats that interfere with a natural energy flow.

Diversion also means a distraction from business or care; recreation, entertainment, amusement; pastime (Webster). Recreation is formed from the teeny prefix *re* meaning "again" or "back." With recreation we can create again. The fun we have in class with myth's weirdness is, certainly, amusing. But always I want to draw us back to the profundity offered by our diversions. We have, with our meditations on mythic images, the opportunity to create new meanings, to re-create understandings of our proper place in the larger scheme of things. Twenty-first century sensibilities have not been groomed on mythic meaning and so we must create anew the meanings long understood by the ancestors. This is not to suggest we must do as the ancestors did, our culture and world being so totally different. But it is to suggest that we cannot just dismiss ancient wisdom, calling it superstition, as if it is so much nonsense, "merely" myth. Our re-creation with images allows the opportunity for us to be explorers in an old landscape. A student once said, "This story confuses me but that is why I am so intrigued." The diversion into confusion is a path into intrigue.

To explore with understanding requires mentoring. Joseph Campbell's (1974) interpretations of mythic images suggest the two meanings of "diversion" I intend in my book when he writes,

> my thought has been to let the spirit of the pictures rule... yet there is also an argument developed.... The argument is, briefly, that through dreams a door is opened to mythology, since myths are of the nature of dream... and [of] life, along with the paradoxical mystery of the waking. (xi)

Campbell ends his statement with the word "waking," which resonates with my teaching. It is appropriate that the unacceptable hour of 8 AM becomes the threshold to my classes. The students are barely awake. I have been up since five and am not a night person. But I must bring night awareness into the daylight if the students are to awaken to the mysteries of the image.

I will confess that when I first started teaching world mythology I was flummoxed. There was so much, so much to cover; so much to conquer (I thought). I would be up nights drafting charts and cramming before class. Oh, it was bad. I was not having a good time, afraid in front of all the material I thought I had to "cover." Even after so many hours and years in the classroom, I was behaving like a first year apprentice. I was going after myth the wrong way. You see, I am attracted to the subject because I need it to unlearn how to learn. Myth will not fit into charts. The boxes I drew spilled over with names and events that just would not squeeze into the categories I was devising. So much for devising. I needed diversion. I needed an other way.

I am not sure when I became comfortable, if that is the right word, with mythic material. But when I turned the corner of my pedagogical approach a world opened to me, the classes became my delight and my treasure, and the students learned— not the stuff of scantrons—they learned to see and hear! One student recently wrote that I am a walking myth. I do not think I have ever been so flattered and touched as by that remark.

So I talk in this book about different sensing. We are accustomed to the sense of sight, so much so that we overlook what hides in the seemingly obvious. I try to educate the ear, reading out loud passages from Ovid, Virgil, and Homer (I am, as I said before, a good reader. Dramatizing the word with good voice brings a depth dimension to understanding). I encourage students to work their ideas with their hands, to give texture to their ideas, to introduce textures to the class so we can feel and touch what the image was saying. This is folding ideas into things, which, as Eve Kosofsky Sedgwick (2003) writes, is "a tropism toward the image." To bring other senses into discussion is to reawaken them, to "interleave" them (p. 106). My biggest obstacle in teaching computer-savvy students is that they think they "know" the stories because they have played myth games, seen the Disney films, accessed the websites and links. But, oh! What danger a little knowing is. For the smoothed-out, glammed-up, hyped-out versions of myth that many students bring with them to class are not what myth teaches. Not at all. My other problem is with the hero stories.

It was when I began to step back from the well-worn hero stories of myth that I became comfortable in critiquing the hero tradition with its patriarchal bias and began inserting goddess material into the readings. Then I found a way, a diversion, a texture, a deeper text.

This book is also a launching of a new idea: the bringing together of old myth and new science. The last section of the book contains chapters that extend the discussion from Part One on psychology and Part Two on ecology to Part Three on cosmological gleanings from mythic image. String theory, eleven dimensions, force fields of energy: these terms are not the exclusive domain of science, since Orpheus and Taliesin anticipated the strangeness of cosmic energies long, long ago. That these two seemingly disparate disciplines should actually share common ground is not only interesting, it is testimony to the wisdom and foresight of ancestral knowledge.

I divide the discussion into three parts, where I see myth teaching us knowledge about the psyche (Part One), about the ecosystem (Part Two) and about the larger universes that surround us, the cosmos (Part Three). Myth has always felt the surrounding worlds above, below, and within the surface skin of things – as enspirited. I hesitate to use the word "spiritual," a word that has acquired new-age connotations for me. What I want to suggest is that a natural light shines, which we cannot see in the usual sense but is there, nonetheless. This light can be called the spirit, some call it the soul, myth calls it both and also "the gods" or "the deities." These forces cannot be petitioned without thanks. The enspirited power that precedes our existence takes residence within us and to it we owe thanks. In this sense myth is religion, but a religion that has nothing whatsoever to do with dogma or social norms. Myth is *re-ligio*, a linking back to understanding that our short time on the planet is our visit; as visitors we need to learn the customs and rituals that have kept the planet spinning.

And so myth, like new science, is a constant: the stories are about surfaces that shimmer, life that is liquid, a mesh. Go below, the stories urge. Seek deeper, they whisper. You understand nothing until you let go, they taunt. There is teeth in thatthar wind. Life forms exude diverse pleasures and paradoxes in their ecological interdependences. All is symbiosis, the living together of different organisms. Just there is a different pedagogy, for sure. Still, the only surety is that our cherished beliefs and hallowed truths will be disturbed. But take heart: these subversions, diversions, and extraversions are sheer ecstasy for those who dare make the plunge.

PART I:
MYTH AS PSYCHOLOGICAL PEDAGOGY

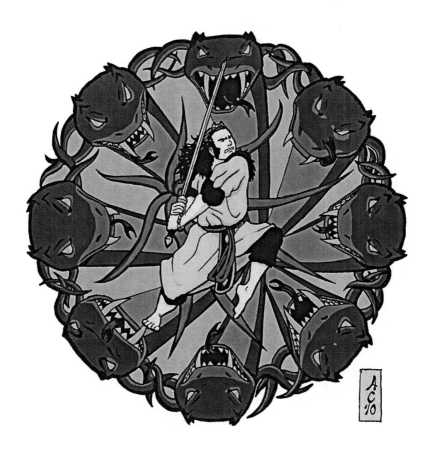

ARTWORK "SUSANOWO" BY DREW CLARK, SCAD 2015.

CHAPTER 1

STRANGE WOMBS

What is not strange to mythologists (the title I like to give to my myth students) is the symbol of the cave as womb of earth. Gaia, after all, is the Earth goddess who lives and dwells in and from the Earth and is the original birth mother of the Greeks. She is the ground out of which the early goddess figures emerge (Downing, 1989). The shape of the cave shelters emptiness and replicates the shape of other ova: bud, chrysalis, shell (Griffin, 1978). The Greeks called the center of the earth "the omphalus" or navel, the centerpoint of the human body suggesting a connection between Earth and human. The Hindus "conceived" of their creator god Brahma as emerging from the lotus flower which emerged from the navel of a sleeping Vishnu. A double birthing occurs in this story: Vishnu birthed from sleep, Brahma birthed from Vishnu's navel. We could think of ourselves, our very bodies, as having been formed from earth matter just as creation myths describe the creation of earth as from the body parts of divinities and divinities from natural forms.

At the time of the Olympian god stories, after the goddess cultures' demise, the omphalus was attributed to the beautiful male god Apollo. Earlier goddess cultures, however, claimed the navel of the Earth as belonging rightfully to Gaia and was either a grave mound or a mound symbolizing the goddess's genital center (in Malory, 1961, 1, p. xxi). Tomb and womb, death and life: what comes from the Earth returns to the Earth, as death does from life. The idea of regeneration is key to the goddess-worshipping cultures, so it is no wonder that objects and places with round shapes would offer themselves as metaphors for the powers of birth, death, and rebirth: the powers of the nature-worshipping cultures of the goddess.

Another round symbol of birth from early cultures is the cauldron. Usually described as the source of life, wisdom, inspiration, and understanding, the magic cauldron with its round shape has been variously imaged in a world-wide cycle of myths. As an image of the cosmic mother-body, the cauldron could be located "in heaven, the earth in the sea, even in the moon" (Walker, 1985, p. 101). The Babylonians, for instance, thought the dome of the world was a lapis lazuli cauldron of the Fate Goddess Siris, who "mingled the elements for generation and regeneration of living things" (*Assyrian*, 1901, p. 308). The Celtic goddess Cerridwen was sometimes pictured as a sow that ate the dead, but more often she was seen as the keeper of the boiling pot, or cauldron. While the cauldron has more widely been associated with witches' brew, such an association reflects the denigration of the earlier cultures of the goddess, whose powers over life and death clearly challenged the notion of "power" as might and fight, introduced by the patriarchal nomadic tribes. Think instead of the cauldron's round shape containing a marvelous stew of energy, a place of replenishment, nourishment and regeneration for all species. Think womb.

Readers of modern fiction might recall the many descriptions by Ernest Hemingway (1968) in his *For Whom the Bell Tolls* of the nourishing food that came out of the boiling pot. There, in the cave of a forest in the Spanish mountains, Pilar, the crone figure, and Maria, the maiden, stir stew for the hungry soldiers in a great round pot. Food, as much a part of the storyline as war, offers nourishment inside the cave-mouth for the hungry Revolutionaries. Hovering below the surface of this war story is Hemingway's reminder that the human condition is revived by sensual pleasure, the most basic besides love-making being what comes out of the cauldron: "cooked rice and meat, saffron, pimentos, and oil, the tarry, wine-spilled smell of the big skin hung beside the door, hung by the neck and the four legs extended, wine drawn from a plug fitted in one leg" (p. 68). Hemingway balances Robert Jordan's death dealing mission to blow up bridges and trains with cave-womb scenes that contain the regenerative healing powers of the cauldron.

The search for my own regenerative powers brought me back to a big dream I had more than thirty years ago, with its womb-like significance. I dreamt of taking a boat ride with an oarsman as guide:

> Leaving my moorings, we were in the water when suddenly a heavy fog descended. The oarsman asked if I could see through the fog. When I replied I could not, he instructed me to look harder. Before my eyes the fog parted and I saw a fiord with a narrow, narrow entrance and thick fur-lined cliffs going straight down to the opening. I realized we were not in water at all. We were rowing in air. My oarsman took me through the opening, having hard time keeping ballast. Penetrating the inside of the fiord, I saw an empty structure, barnlike, in the afternoon sun, rays slanting through old panes, revealing a quiet, perfectly preserved, wondrously empty room. I saw a rolltop desk with objects—a pen, a few clips—neatly left in the desk cubicles. And I caught my breath in sadness and joy for a world new found but long lost. (Doll, 1995, pp. 25–26)

It is fascinating to return to this dream as I now sit at my "rolltop desk" in a very messy room, my head percolating with new-found long-lost images. At the time, I interpreted the dream to signal a connection with my mother who was dying and my desire to write in honor of my mother from whom I had been estranged. Now I interpret the dream differently. Although I still see the dream as urging writing as recovery, I see the writing motif less in personalistic terms, more in mythic terms, as a birthing into new consciousness about ancient wisdoms. The mother I thought was mine I now think is what Christine Downing (1989) calls the "fantasy creature behind the personal mother" (p. 135) – never identical with her. I see this re-cognition of the mother as a reawakening from my literal mooring. And I respect the oarsman's instruction to look harder, for I had been swirling in a fog of patriarchal mindsets. Nor can I overlook the mixing of male language ("penetration," "hard") with female desire to re-cognize opposites, male with female, personal with cosmic, mother womb with goddess womb.

The open mouth is another womb image found in commonly carved objects in Ireland and western Romania. According to anthropologist Mariya Gimbutas (1989), who discovered Neolithic relics in the tombs of old Europe, the open mouth symbolized the generative Divine Source. As the spout of a water container, the mouth served a useful function as well as a symbolic one, for the Divine Source of the goddess was that from which sacred moisture gushed. Her Mouth opened from the vast hidden depths, "earth as the realm of soul" (Downing, 1989, p. 147). The prevalent belief of the Early Neolithic period was that all life came from water. The aquatic sphere, including water birds, were imaged on walls and pottery to give honor to the miraculous power of the goddess' uterine moisture, the magical source of life (Gimbutas, 1989, p. xxii). Geometric lines and carvings were further identifying signs of the goddess, whose open mouth was the source of nourishing liquid (pp. 64–65). That water containers were found in burial sites gives further evidence of the womb-tomb connection of the goddess: indeed, as Source she was that to which life came and would return.

Thirty years ago I wrote a mythopoetic study of strange mouthings in the work of Samuel Beckett, Irish poet and dramatist (Doll, 1988). My frame of reference at the time was primarily Greek from the Classical period. Now I see Beckett drawing on his own Irish background, perhaps even on the findings from Knowth, Boyne Valley, County Meath, where Marija Gimbutas did some of her excavations. I was fascinated at the time of my writing with the circumscribed voids of Beckett imagery: the blind eyes of Hamm and the unseeing eyes of Clov (p. 43), the ruined eyes of a statue of Demeter (p. 57), the gaping eye sockets and open mouths of his women characters uttering snippets of things heard, unfathomable to them (p. 63) and even a famous photograph of Beckett with sunglasses that seem to replace the eyes (p. 13). All photographs of Beckett characters were taken by John Haynes, who like me seemed to intuit the mystery of the open mouth and repeated round shapes. My search for the open mouth led me to the British Museum archives, where I located a Roman tragic mask of the second century C.E. showing a heart-shaped open mouth and wide eye sockets staring as in horror (p. 30). I saw then, as I do now, the draw of Beckett's characters to a source about which they "know" nothing but which "speak" to them in images "ill seen ill said" (Beckett, 1981).

If Beckett's figures themselves seem like relics (they are often inside jars or urns or are variously disembodied), I now think that Beckett's mythic imagination goes back farther in time than the Greek Classics, back to the open mouth pots of Ireland's earliest inhabitants. The pagan Celts placed a mystic significance on words (Ellis, 2002. p. 6); Beckett's characters seem not to understand what the world presents to them, certainly not the words they yearn to recognize. Beckettian women "know" the speakings they hear are significant somehow, but their ears and mouths are no longer wombs for ancient utterings.

In Beckett's most tortuous play *Not I* (1976), a female character is shown only as a disembodied mouth, called Mouth. According to his biographer, Beckett had this to say about the woman:

> I knew that woman in Ireland. I knew who she was—not 'she' specifically, one single woman, but there were so many of those old crones, stumbling down the lanes, in the ditches, beside the hedgerows. Ireland is full of them. And I heard 'her' saying what I wrote in Not I. I actually heard it. (Knowlson, 1996, p. 522)

She/It spews phrases as if from a burst dam. The wellspring that would connect the modern soul with its ancient roots has long dried up but now begs to be let back in. To further emphasize a modern audience's distance from its mythic sourcing, Mouth is reduced to a machine, powerless to respond, numbed, until "all that moisture" simply flushes out meaning, "half the vowels wrong... no one could follow" (Beckett, 1976, p. 22). Beckett's plays featuring women demonstrate this lack of connection to the once divine mouth as source. Even so, the urge to listen is always there, heard/felt/intuited as "stirrings" in the stillness (Beckett, 1988).

While the mouth, cave, or cauldron may not strike one as "weird" for womb symbols, a visit to any number of other myths about strange birthings will most probably cause a few gasps of wonder. Such is the famous birthing of Athena from Zeus's head. Yes, the head as womb! There was even, once, Celtic belief in the severed head as container of the soul. Here with Zeus' miraculous birth, the head was thought to contain the seed, the stuff of life, which was stored in the head and believed to issue by way of the marrow in the spine (Onians, 1973, pp. 109, 111, 182). The story of Athena's birth is so familiar that it often is simply accepted as mythic nonsense. Consider the impregnation of the Virgin Mary through the ear and a different reaction is most likely. Few believers consider the virgin birth as religious nonsense. Following the image of the impregnated ear—without assigning a symbol to it– can be a very intriguing quest. It might take one to hearing double entendres, murmurs, the not-said. Beckett captures the wonder of such listening with one of his characters typically groveling in the mud and therefore closer to Earth: "I surrendered myself to the beauties of the scene... and I listened attentively to the sounds, faint and clear, borne to me on the air. For an instant I fancied I heard the silence mentioned, if I am not mistaken, above" (1958, p. 145).

Unlike the mythic head as womb, the Virgin's ear as womb raises intriguing questions. Thomas Moore (1994) comments on Renaissance paintings that depict a golden stream emanating from the Holy Spirit and flowing into Mary's ear as spiritual seman. I have often thought that the strange manner in which the Virgin was impregnated harkens back to the mythic mortal, Danae, who also immaculately conceived. As an image, the "golden stream" is reminiscent of Zeus, the patriarchal birthgiver. Recall the impregnation of Danae by a shower of gold, a pregnancy that resulted in—not Jesus, but a major hero figure of the Greeks, Perseus.

As for Zeus' other strange womb, we should not overlook the second birth of Dionysus from Zeus' thigh. His thigh! This particular detail does cause comment in class, and wonderment. Thigh as womb! Explaining the origins of this idea, Onians writes that the thigh bone, *femur*, means "that which engenders" (1975, p. 182). So the *femur* was also considered life-giving, especially since it is the largest bone in the body with the most marrow. I prefer the ancient beliefs about the body and misconceptions (pardon the pun) about pregnancy to the scholarly explanation offered for Zeus' strange thigh womb: Thigh, we are told, was "a euphemism for the genitals" (Leonard & McClure, 2004, p. 192). I think the move to symbol, in the above explanation, removes the power of the original image. To have thigh symbolize or stand for genitals is not nearly as weirdly wondrous as to have the thigh *be* the womb. The move away from metaphor intellectualizes the image, making it more accessible to the thinking mind but less interesting to the imagination. Another thigh womb from another male god is fascinatingly seen in the image of Nishada born out of the left thigh of Vena, while Pritha is birthed out of his right hand (in Onians, 1973, p. 198).

Liquid is the element of most birthing, but liquid in what form? Myth presents images of birth from the froth of Uranus' testicles; birth from the swallowed semen of the masturbating Atum-Ra; birth from the sweat of Ymir's armpits; birth from the mating of Ymir's feet; birth from the urine of Izanami; birth from the blood of Medusa; birth from tears as well as vomit; birth of the world from the sucked toe of Vishnu; birth from the cosmic egg; birth from Purusha's mouth, arms, and thighs; birth from the dew of the East Wind. I suspect there must have been sweat of some sort that birthed, too, Mwindo (Hathaway, 2002, pp. 8–16, 321). Like other divine heroes, he emerged from the finger of his mother, the hand or finger thought to contain procreative power similar to that of a womb (Onians, 1973, p. 198).

Dirt, too, has been a substance that births new life. I think my favorite birthing of all these marvelous mythic images is the birth of two creatures no bigger than flies from the dirt under Enki's fingernails (Wolkstein and Kramer, 1983, p. 64). In class I like to pick at my fingernails, making a click sound, and name the creatures "Pffnf-Pffnf," a variation of the Sumerian word *kurgarra*. The creatures are THAT tiny! Recalling another scenario, the priest's intonations on Ash Wednesday, I remember being thrilled on that day at that moment of those spoken words, thrilled to be a part of Earth: "Remember, man, that you are dust and unto dust you shall return."

So how are we to think of these marvels? What might the variously strange wombs suggest about the cosmos that we, in our sophistication, do not know or have forgotten? The first response of the skeptic would be that it all is mere superstition; amusing, yes, but nonsense. One needs explanations! Common sense! Science! Are we so jaded, so indifferent to the weird, that weirdness never comes our way? Rather, with Ralph Waldo Emerson, I believe in "the inextinguishableness of wonder" (in Mack and Mack, 1998, p. viii). That a womb can be more than a female organ suggests, at the very least, that the capacity for newness exists on more than one plane, in more than one biologic. The birth of new ideas or awareness or consciousness is, I could say, on the tip of my tongue or from the sweat of my brow.

THE EYE IN THE WELL OF MEMORY

And for all this, nature is never spent;

There lives the dearest freshness deep down things;

And though the last lights from the black West went,

Oh, morning, at the brown brink eastward, springs

— Gerald Manley Hopkins

Somewhat in the manner of the Sumerian goddess Inanna, Odin of Norse mythology, father of the gods, travels to an under region in humility, having shed his outer garments. His venture takes him to Mimir's well without his usual golden armor and adornments. He goes on foot, not on his mighty eight-legged steed, and he travels anonymously so as not to draw attention to his status. His purpose is to seek wisdom that lies at the eastern base of the great ash tree of the world, called the Yggdrasil, from a well named Memory (Mimir). Like Inanna, Odin humbles his appearance, since he is a suppliant and a stranger to the land below. Along the way Odin encounters a wise giant from whom he seeks answers. Riddles are the stuff of myth: if the seeker can answer correctly the question posed by the riddler, he (usually a "he": think of Oedipus) will gain an answer; if not he will lose his head (or in the case of the Sphinx from whom Oedipus queries, he will be eaten). The head as sacrifice is indeed a mighty exchange, since Celts and possibly too the Norse believed that the head was the seat of the soul; Mimir, after all, is the name of the giant who lives in the well as a severed head. Asking questions of the head was thus a sacred enterprise of the highest order from which a sacrifice was to be expected.

What price, Odin asks, must he pay for a drink from the Well of Wisdom that Mimir's head guards? The answer: Your right eye.

I introduce my myth classes with a riddle of my own: What is the meaning of Left and Right symbolism? It is uncanny that the specifics of exactly which side of the body, which hand, arm, or eye, is an integral part of mythic storyline. Artists, too, are uncannily specific in depicting exactly which side of the body is emphasized. In his Creation masterpiece, Michelangelo, for example, has the mighty Yahweh extend his right arm to stir life into a groggy Adam. An opposite image is offered by the artist of the Celtic Dagda, also a creator god, but not an authoritative one. Dagda is pictured with his left arm gently resting on a harp, seated on the ground, smiling. And he is fat. How unlike Yahweh who emerges from the sky, scowling and muscular! That Odin must offer his right eye is consistent with left-right symbolism, giving to the left the aspects of compassion and intuition and imagination (we now know that the right brain rules the left side of the body) and to the right the aspects of intellect, reason, and control (which we now know the left brain rules). Odin, then, sacrifices the eye that sees rationally and literally: he must strengthen his intuitive powers of imagination, his left eye, which presumably had been underdeveloped up to now and which he had been unwilling to exercise.

Odin drinks from the well. And as he drinks all the future becomes clear to him. He sees what will happen to the gods of Asgard and the humans of Midgard. He sees the great battle between good and evil that will take place at the doom of the gods and he sees that evil will be destroyed so that a new era can emerge. Then Mimir ("Memory") lets the sacrificial eye sink deep into the water of the well. "And there the Eye of Odin stayed, shining up through the water, a sign to all who came to that place of the price that the Father of the Gods had paid for his wisdom" (Colum, 2005, p. 84).

Odin underwent another sacrifice, this time in order to learn the secrets of the runes, the earliest alphabet used by the Northern nations, the characters of which signified mystery and were used in divinations (Guerber, 1992, p. 33). The motifs that describe this other sacrifice are familiar in Christian, Egyptian, and Greek lore, for they include a tree, a piercing of the side of the god, the number three or multiples thereof, and the promise of regeneration or resurrection. Odin hung for nine days from the Yggdrasil, gazing into the "immeasurable depths of Nifl-heim, plunged in deep thought… ere he won the knowledge he sought" (Guerber, pp. 33–34). Thus did Odin gain power over all things.

For their final project, students in my myth classes create a painting, a story, or a digitalized short film or image from one or more of the myths studied during the quarter. Meredith chose to paint the Yggdrasil on a five foot canvas made from elephant dung, which she located on the Internet. Interestingly, the dung is ideal as a canvas: it does not smell, is durable, and is the result of recycling. She painted every corner of the five foot dung piece, highlighting the recognizable aspects of the Yggdrasil, including the squirrel Ratatosk that runs up and down the trunk, connecting upper with lower realms; the Midgard serpent, encircling the Earth underwater; and the Fenrir wolf tied to a rock with a magic ribbon made from the roots of a mountain, the spittle of a bird, the breath of a fish, the sound of a cat's footfall, the beard of a woman, and the spirit of a bear (Hathaway, 2002, p. 57; Rowlands, 2009, p. 117). Meredith was unable to paint the ribbon, I am relieved to say, since magic need not/should not be re-presented. (In class I refer to it as "The Ribbon," which I meta-phorically elicit from time to time. "I need to tie 'The Ribbon' around this discussion," I say.) So complex and colorful was Meredith's painting, with rich browns, reds, and blues! But what spoke to me, caught my eye, turned my mind around was … Odin's eye. Meredith did not overlook the small detail of the eye gleaming from the depths of the well of Mimir. Up to that point in my teaching of this myth, I confess not to have paid attention to Odin's sacrificial eye, referring to it only as the cause for Odin's eyepatch. Teacher can explain and explain away, but artist restores memory.

I will not forget that moment in class. I was both delighted with Meredith's portrayal and dismayed at my own "intelligence," having overlooked this signi-ficant mythic motif. Allow me, now, with the forebearance of Meredith and Elise, who also painted the tree, to suggest how the eye in Mimir's well offers the sense of the diversity of earthspace in the world of myth.

Carl Jung referred to Odin's two sacrifices at the well of Mimir, recalling the words of the *Voluspa*: "What murmurs Wotan over Mimir's head? / Already the spring boils...." Commenting on the connection of water with the unconscious, Jung continues, "a secret unrest gnaws at the roots of our being.... Whoever looks into the water sees his own image, but behind it living creatures soon loom up" (1977, p. 24). Jung goes on to describe the quality of the unconscious as "spontaneous," "something that lives of itself," "a life behind consciousness," "an unconscious life that surrounds consciousness on all sides" (p. 27). Do not these descriptors sound like the features of the Yggdrasil tree itself: the snake that surrounds the tree, the well water beneath the tree, the gnawing wolf at the root of the tree, the scampering squirrel delivering news from below to above, from above to below? This is not just a tree. The details of the Yggdrasil are so many and various that they attest to its psychodynamic quality. Indeed, of the many possible topics open to art students for their expression, this tree captures interest. Students have sculpted it, painted it, dramatized it, and modeled it in 3D programs. The mystery of the tree does not escape twenty-first century art students. As Ross wrote,

> In my portrayal, the ash tree that Odin is reclining against is dead and rotting. I am creating a dead tree to show that even the heavens, represented by the upper branches of the great ash tree, will be destroyed in the forthcoming war. The scene is textured to look unrealistic, with leather and iron on Odin's armor and with brown painted on the bark of the tree. I want to give a timeless feel to the scene. To do this I textured it to look as if it has been cast out of bronze.

While the story of Ragnarok, the Norse apocalypse, is thrilling to my students because of so much clash and doom, I think something more draws them to this tree. In class we did not discuss the tree in metaphorical terms, unpacking for instance the meaning of all the multiform aspects of the tree; so it is even more surprising to me that so many students picked it for their final project. The tree with its streaming movement and texture is a prime example of what ecologists might call "the conservation of variety" (Carson, 2002, p. 117) reflective of the biological sophistication of our ancestors. Within a single tree we see energy itself: though still, it moves; though solid, it is fluid; through grand, it is ominous.

Elise caught this other-worldly aspect of the tree with her portrayal of mysterious droplets hanging in the air around the tree. She pictures the tree with a highly textured, thick trunk and upper branches balanced with lower roots. She, too, intuited the multiform nature of nature, connected and dependent. The result is of spell-binding beauty. And there, in Mimir's well, she too paints Odin's eye.

The eye lies in the dark, without distraction, facing east where the frost giants lie, waiting. Its gaze fixes on the doom that will come, as Odin discovers through his sacrifice. That this is the right eye means that the eye sees only the literal end of Odin's reign, not the beginning that will also come from out of destruction. Apocalyptic stories with their highly visionary quality contain the element of rebirth, reflecting the cyclical nature of all cosmic forces. For instance, in the Book of Revelation, the last book of the Bible, the Queen of Heaven descends to earth and remains, glorifying matter in her role as *mater* (Quispel, 1979, p. 133). In the Norse apocalypse, too, rebirth from matter is foretold, as would be expected since the east is the place of the rising sun, or dawn of newness.

But the doom of the gods is certain after three winters; it will be announced by a cock's call, which stirs the lower worlds; another cock's call stirring the land of the giants; and a third cock's call arousing the sleeping heroes in Valhalla. Then a dog will bark, the great tree will shake, the giants will move their ship of dead men's nails, and The Ribbon will break, setting free the Fenrir wolf. The hound dog Garm will bark twice more. At the third bark of the dog, the battle will begin and the reign of the gods will end (Colum, 2005, pp. 188–192).

The specifics of the number three is striking. So too are the specifics of the signs of the apocalyptic event coming out of the natural world: the call of the cock, the bark of the dog, the scream of the eagle. Nature knows. Consciousness is all around and within, under and over. And since the Norse apocalypse is specific about the eye facing east, we see the new day dawning **as** the promise of a new world:

> The two humans who hid themselves deep within Yggdrasil will be called Lif and Lithrasir... Lif ("life") and Lithrasir ("thriving remnant") will have children. Their children will bear children. There will be life and new life, life everywhere on earth. That was the end; and this is the beginning. (Crossley-Holland, 1980, p. 167)

I am interested in the survivors from Ragnarok, Life and Thriving Remnant. In the passage above, the two hide themselves *within* Yggdrasil. In other passages, the two lie concealed in a forest: "Lif and Lifhrasir, still they will conceal themselves/ in Hoddmimir's forest,/ The morning dews they will have as food for themselves,/ From them people will be nourished" (in Lindow, 2001, p. 209). In either case, the new race will emerge from tree-space. This is a fascinating apocalyptic parallel to the creation story of the Norse. The first created humans are named Ask ("Ash tree") and Embla ("Elm Tree" or "Vine"), signaling the tree as container of emergent matter. Encountering the tree is indeed a strange experience (Morris, 2009, p. 151), if one waits long enough. Relate these mythic living trees with the apocrypha sayings of Jesus in the Gospel of Thomas, and a wisdom encircles: "Split a piece of wood, and I am there; lift up the stone, and you will find me" (in Pagels, 2004, p. 53). Consider, too, the more generally famous saying of Jesus, "I am the true vine, and my Father is the vinedresser" (John 15:1). For those with ears to hear, Christ is a vegetation deity living within the wood. Nature is not only consciousness, it is divine. And it births new life.

Perhaps today we see only "remnants" of this connection, if we see them at all. But even "remnants" have a strong pull on the waking mind of memory, as my student artists seem to intuit. Dreams, of course, are thriving remnants, which is why we must pay attention to their coursings through the night mind. While writing this chapter my dream was telling me not to get too intellectual about the eye that sees from below. I dreamt that I was swimming in a lake with a stony bottom and a stony beach. I was in the shallows but I could see that animals were swimming in the distance, possibly antelope or deer. I was not worried; in fact, I was rather pleased with myself that I could swim in the shallows and not be disturbed by the animals out in the deep. Suddenly, I turned, and with my left eye I caught a glimpse of an animal head very near to mine. It seemed to be chasing me. There I was, one head in water being eyed by another head in water from a different species. I was both afraid and astounded.

I think this "thriving remnant" was reminding me of a modern tendency of having the experience but missing the meaning. Writing about myth, I need to remember that these powerful images from early cultures are not just there for my tinkering but are there to strike awe. Indeed, the dream left me feeling awe-full, as in the original meaning of the word, full of awe; for I knew it was big and I knew it related to the images I was working on, putting me back there among root and water. It put me in the well. Perhaps in the dream I was Odin's other eye, experiencing briefly with vitality and freshness what the waters of the unconscious could hold for me. But I was in the shallows, warning me of too-shallow an understanding. Let the animal head confront my eye and let me be afraid. I hear the rebuke Jung levies against intellectuals who "know neither themselves nor people as they really are" (1976b, p. 328) and who warns that "the helpful numina have fled from the woods, rivers, mountains, and animals, and the God-men have disappeared underground into the unconscious" (1976b, p. 261). To be back in the experience of the image as channeled through dream directs one away from the personal toward the numina (Otto, 1958, p. 236). What I dreamt was not "my" dream; it was the dream of Memory.

Mimir's well is Memory. I think it is the work of the artist to restore memory, to ensure that the remnants do indeed thrive. "Memory and its role in the human psyche is very deep and enigmatic," says Patricia Reis. "A great source for those of us who love to probe the mystery" (in Henderson, 2008, p. 257). We can find remnants of earlier wisdoms all around us, for surely "the blackbird is involved/ in what I know" (Stevens, 1972, p. 21). But do I know this? How can the poet as artist help us to intuit that what lies below the eye is yet a knowledge of most worth? The Norse myth of Odin's eye tells us of the staying power of bearing witness, on the one hand, and of the twilight atmosphere so necessary for dimming the literal vision, on the other hand. Odin's eye is also in water, which, Jung (1963) reminds us, is the very stream of life (p. 356). The image is mysterious and a little scary, as it should be. For the hidden knowings are not to be grasped by the right eye in lonely literalism. The murkiness of the setting under the root of the great tree that reaches toward the frost giants' waiting: this is the mystery caught in the setting. Stranger still, though doom is certain so is renewal. "The life of the centuries lives on," declares Jung (1976b) "and things are continually happening that have accompanied human life from time immemorial: premonitions, foreknowledge, second sight, hauntings, ghosts, return of the dead, bewitchings, sorcery, magic, spells, etc." (p. 328). This doubleness of the moment, both back and fore from the single seeing eye, suggests that we are not yet seeing with the left eye. The function of memory is to link us up with that which has faded out of consciousness (Jung, 1976b, p. 22).

As I consider a final commentary on seeing from below, I focus on the eye at the root. Memory, Marla Morris (2009) reminds us, is the root of dreams (p. 139).

The psychic root. Freud would term this root the id, which Morris describes as being in a liquid flow. "Id-ing is dreaming while contained.... Here is dream space" (p. 93). The root of the Yggdrasil tree is a metaphor, I believe, of the deeper stratum of the collective unconscious, the primeval psyche, difficult to access. The frost giants who lie just east of the root are first inhabitants, living in prehistory. This is a foreign realm, to be sure, made more foreign by the largeness of the inhabitants as well as by the murkiness of the atmosphere. The frost giants live on the other side of boundaries, in the water that is also the abode of the Midgard serpent out in the deep sea (Lindow, 2001, p. 291). Close to the giants are the dwarfs who dwell in rocks or mountains and who hoard treasure. The treasure is the hidden secret that "fills life with something impersonal, a *numinosum*. A man who has never experienced that has missed something important. He must sense that he lives in a world which in some respects is mysterious" (Jung, 1963, p. 356). This underworld of the Norse, at the root base of the great ash tree, is just such a mysterious world, frightening and wondrous. There, the mythic tree in all its parts– trunk, branches, and roots– provides the metaphor for Jung's (1963) idea of the psyche: "Among other things the psyche appears as a dynamic process which rests on a foundation of antithesis, on a flow of energy between two poles" (p. 350). All descriptors of this place, he continues, must be paradoxical and out of the reach of sense perception.

The frost giants are themselves out of reach, remnants from the distant past before the creation of the Norse universe. "At that time there was only Ginnunga gap, the vast void of potency and potential, and... the mysterious waters from which life was to emerge" (Lindow, 2001, p. 40). Life emerged in the form of the first being, a giant named Ymir, from whose feet came the race of giants. Eventually, the giants survived a flood and floated away to Jotunheim, the eastern-most root of Yggdrasil (Colum, 2005, pp. 168–169). The giants are not frozen in absolute stillness: they wait, at the ready, to arise. This incipient threat to upheave all that is in place is the constant reminder that the great tree shimmers with life. Like the wolf gnawing at the root, what seems to be set in place is not fixed. Hidden stirrings soon will loom.

Carl Jung came into his understandings late in life. He perceived the "processes going on in the background" (1963, p. 355), an ability to see and to think without seeing or thinking, one could say. The eye in Mimir's well lies there still, stirring still in the paintings of Meredith and Elise. The paintings of the most famous tree in world myth give testament to this particular tree's significance. Not all eyes can see the stream of life it contains within itself nor the timelessness of its wisdom. Some of us may forever be blinded in "the last lights from the black West" unable or unwilling to see the morning that springs "at the brown brink eastward" (Hopkins, 1921, p. 355). But in the classroom with artists, I am privileged to share my dreams as they share their paintings, as our left eyes contemplate myth.

CHAPTER 3

THE LIVING STONE

PRELUDE: THREE STONE HINGES

Last Night's Dream: I am in an empty room with several long floor-to-ceiling windows. I am lying down on a wooden floor on the second storey. It is afternoon. Outside two boys are walking in a path. Shortly, a stone is hurled through a very small opening in the window in front of where I lie. The stone lands beside me. Shortly after, another stone is hurled, also through the very small opening; it too lands beside me. The stones do not hit me, but they find me, where I am lying. Then more stones. I move but every time I move, the hurled stone finds me and lands beside me. The dream sequence changes. I see the two boys, one of whom eyes me knowingly. I put a broken watch on the ledge, a watch I am fond of. Scene shift again. I return to the ledge and the watch is gone. I suspect the boy of whom I am afraid because his throwing is so very accurate. How could the stone find its way through exactly *that* small opening? Why did he steal my watch?

Chicken Little: This children's story is supposed to teach courage because "the sky is not falling." According to whom? The story is actually frightening. Chicken Little is walking in the woods when an acorn hits her head. She thinks the sky is falling. So she tells all the little creatures that they must report this to the lion (in other version, the king). When the procession—Chicken Little, Henny Penny, Lucky Ducky, and Foxey Loxey—reach the lion, they go onto his den never to be seen again.

Meteorites: From time to time something falling from the sky is reported. The something is not an acorn; it is a rock, a bit of the solar system. According to a website, the meteorites "may appear to be just boring rocks," but they are of great interest to scientists because they are "our only material evidence of the universe beyond Earth" (nineplanets). The same website quotes President Bill Clinton, at the time: "Today, rock 84001 speaks to us across all those billions of years and millions of miles.... We will continue to listen closely to what it has to say."

POSTLUDE TO PRELUDE

The dream came to me the night before I began this chapter, a chapter I had been dreading to write so I delayed in writing it. At first I thought the dream was unrelated to my work. But as I turned the circles in my morning walk I thought: No! This is a little piece of the universe knocking. The rock coming through the small aperture, a cleft, could only be deliberate; the rock, though hurled, did not hurt me but was seeking me out. The small boy may be my *puer* child-self, closer to "the path," who is catapulting me into another look at the dream fragments, stealing my broken

15

watch, my logical, chronological tendencies—still with me in the autumn of my life. The real clue to the dream's wisdom is the sense of invasion from the outside into my vast, empty, interior self. Like the rocks I will be discussing in this chapter, rocks have been thought of as having their own, foreign interior "life"—utterly defying the materialistic logic that separates inside from outside.

Studying for this chapter I absolutely could not get my mind around the idea of the interior of the stone. I wasn't able to access the idea, so prevalent in myth, that "mind" does not pertain to the human realm only but also is the very nature of nature. And then this dream. So if the rock has a mind of its own, then the intentionality of the dream rock is to insist that I honor it. And if the rock is like the foreign interior of ourselves known as the unconscious, as depth psychologists and alchemists say, then I had better pay attention to its bidding as well. The mystical IT is calling me. The stone's speed and physicality was as much as saying that it is I whose interior is empty.

There is something to be said for wary fearfulness in the company of the rock that demands our listening. So too the Chicken Little story, so too the rocks falling from outer space. All have implications, a word that means to fold, to twist, to intertwine, interlace.

Now the stone hinges are also preludes to Stonehenge, which I saw years ago, a touchstone of my memory and the memory of Neolithic time, when the massive stones became a place to watch the sun rise, especially during the summer solstice. Stones are vast; stones are invisible; stones, as myth insists, are living: they grow, talk in a language only the Spider Inktomi understands, have gender, can engender, and express emotion ("He has a stony face," we say). Stones "people" the pagan landscape, since "pagan" means rocky hill (Flannery, 2008). Stones resist our acquisition. I can put a stone in my pocket but I cannot own it. It is no wonder that their stony silence holds but withholds layers and layers of ancient knowings. They implicate. Yes, stones have been around longer than we have, longer than trees, longer than crocodiles; they are the living presence of times long ago occupying our here and now; "all history is taken in by stones" (Griffin, 1992, p. 6). Who trod on their surface, sat in their indentations? They will never tell us. The pit inside my peach: it is the stone, the nucleus, the nut, "the precious kernel inside the shell" (Griffin, p. 113). And it is old:

> Being in a Greek temple or seeing the pyramids or seeing the graffiti on the walls of a cave in Spain evokes the eternal, essential images of the soul. It does not have to be the actual pyramid that I am seeing; that is the literalism of it. You are seeing the ancient images, the archetypal images, not merely the pyramids themselves. (Hillman, 1983, p. 115)

With Hillman, I would say that seeing the stone is not merely the stone itself. It is the "essential image of the soul." So sometimes the stone's stolidness takes flight, falls from the sky, or hurls itself through windows. Then the seeing eye must be trained to be an old eye, "the call of the old" (Hillman, 1983, p. 115), just as the hearing ear must acquire an older hearing.

The marvel with the stone, like new science, is that every question about its essential nature leads to other questions. That is its mystery and its lure. We are spectator and part, just as "mind, or awareness, or consciousness has a wavelike, space-pervading aspect" (Hayward, 1999, p. 74). We are not the only minds, and mind is not only human. We are stone and blood. These are oxymorons, paradoxes, truths discovered in opposite tensions. No wonder that stone qualities have long inspired myth, meditation, and metaphor. My discussion will revolve around those three.

"It was inevitable that meteorites should inspire awe," writes Mircea Eliade (1971, p. 19). Things falling from the sky could only represent a heavenly message, a gift from the gods, even the gods themselves. President Clinton must have had this intuition when he endowed a speaking sense to the fallen rock, mentioned above. I like to think of his comment about "listening" to the rock as issuing from a post-premodern awareness that dare not dismiss cosmic activity. Examples of meteorites inspiring myths and object worship—even today—are numerous and mostly associated with goddesses. Think of the Phrygian meteorite worshipped as the black goddess Cybele, later known as Magna Mater, still recognized in the Western world (Hathaway, 2002, p. 78). Think of the sacred Kaaba stone in Mecca, dedicated to the pre-Islamic Triple Goddess and bearing the emblem of the yoni, "like the Black Stone worshipped as Artemis" (Walker, 1983, p. 487). Still today pilgrims of a patriarchal religion journey to this stone in Mecca. Think too of the huge rock called Erathipa, of the tribes of central Australia, believed to have the power to make sterile women fertile because of the spirit of the ancestors dwelling in it (Leeming, 1990, pp. 339–340). Then there is the myth of the Agdos rock which assumed the shape of the Great Mother. Zeus, the story goes, fell asleep on it and spilled his semen, whereupon in time the rock gave birth to Agdistis (Henderson and Oakes, 1990, pp. 116–117). I had no intention (nor ability) to become pregnant when I had a stone massage recently, a therapy of the ancient science of Ayurveda (a Sanskrit word meaning "science of long life"). Since stones belong to the earth element, the application of heated stones helps to reconnect with the earth's grounding (Chabot, 2003). The healing powers of the polished stones, placed strategically along my body, "drew" energies from out there to in here and caused me the sense of reawakened freshness, a rebirth of sorts.

Lithic mythology concerns birth from stone, belief that stone is the source of life and fertility, and that stone itself is born from the Earth womb. Recall the early Greek myth of the survivors of the flood who threw stones over their shoulders so as to repopulate the Earth. Even certain Old European Christmas carols speak of "the Christ who is born from stone" (Eliade, 1971, p. 44). The stone is thus an archetypal image "expressing absolute reality," as shown by the myths of stone births. Eliade says, "their meaning is clear: force, reality, fecundity, holiness are incarnate in everything around man which appears as *real* and *existing*. Invulnerable and irreducible, the stone became the image and symbol of being" (p. 44). The rock is that out of which Arthur pulls his sword, the rock a womb for the sacred phallic sword. The rock hides the sword and sandals that Theseus needs to claim as his birthright. The rock is Jesus' tomb; it is the altar on which Isaac was nearly sacrificed; it is Mithra's birth cave (Leeming, 1990, p. 315).

Stone birthing of a similar sort is found in a strange little Sioux legend called "Stone Boy." It tells of a maiden and her five brothers who set up house at the bottom of a canyon, where the brothers one by one go out hunting. And one by one they disappear. When the last brother, like the others, goes out and never returns, the maiden leaves the canyon and climbs to the top of the hill. There, seeing a round pebble lying on the ground, she picks it up and swallows it. Lo and behold, she becomes pregnant and gives birth months later to a wondrous Stone Boy, who grows ten times faster than ordinary infants. After a journey to a far place, he finds an old evil woman who harbors five big bundles. The boy's magical energies are such that he performs several rituals involving an enclosure, red hot rocks, water, steam and song—and he brings the five dead brothers back to life. This non-European version of the living rock is charmingly simple, different from the Greek and Phrygian accounts, but similar; similar even to the Hindu Krishna boy stories. The Sioux legend relates the following wisdom of the mother:

> The mother knew that her baby had great powers. One day when he was playing outside the tipi, he made a bow and arrows, all on his own. Looking at his flint arrowhead, the mother wondered how he had done it. 'Maybe he knows that he was a stone and I swallowed him,' she thought. 'He must have a rock nature.' (in Erdoes and Ortiz, 1984, pp. 15–19)

What is it to have a rock nature? This question puts our mind in a petromorphic state. While myths anthropomorphize animals, trees, and stones, endowing the non-human world with human capacities to speak, suffer, and make love, I do not think this is a move of absolute anthropocentrism, any more than Jesus' parables are. The speakings of the natural world in myth, legend, and parable convey a sympathy among all living things. The speakings are metaphors, other ways of sharing knowing. Our distance from an animate world is such that we no longer "believe" in the living quality of non-humanity. Cambridge University physicist Jeremy Hayward (1999) sees this as the false doctrine of materialism: "All things from rocks to plants to animals to humans, to the gods, have some quality of awareness or inwardness," he writes …. "We need to rediscover our own traditions of how to connect our mundane world with that inner world of gods and nature spirits, dralas, and muses" (pp. 75, 76).

To acquire a petromorphic imagination asks us, in all our "sophistication," to become more childlike, which my dream urges as sensible but as developmental psychologist Jean Piaget disdains as non-logical. The animate world that surrounds us is charged with informing energy. Myths are prescient, as are dreams, in that they penetrate into, below, and under surfaces, where the informing energy lives. Myths are also pre-science, a word that comes from the Latin root *sci*, meaning to know. "Prescience: knowledge of things before they exist or happen; foreknowledge; foresight" (Webster). Having prescience is a divine attribute. No wonder myths contain gods, because myths were religion before religion was, and myths were science before science came to be.

Alchemy was also science before science. We must remember that Carl Jung's most mature writings on the nature of the human soul were derived from years of studying the arcane writings of medieval scientists' meditations on the Philosopher's Stone. Theirs was a theology of nature that understood the stone symbolically as containing spirit. It was not literal; the Philosopher's Stone of the alchemists continued mythic thinking that stones were the dwelling places of the gods (spirit). Stones were venerated as sacred objects, just as later the Celtic severed head was thought to contain the living soul and the Christian cross to represent the suffering Christ. Placing the Philosopher's Stone at the heart of Jung's psychology "suggests a petromorphizing of his psychological intuitions," writes Jungian analyst Michael Whan (2006b). He goes on to offer these Zen-like comments, "As a stone reveals itself by its very virtue of being a stone, it withdraws into itself. A stone gives and withholds itself" (p. 27).

What I hear in these conundrums is a new/old appreciation of objects over against subjects. If we are to adapt a petromorphic imagination, we must cease to think of subjects as the only ones with interior lives. The stone thus becomes the absolute Other. For depth psychology, following Jung, this means that the psyche itself is stone, absolutely other in the depths of our interior. Instead of endowing stones with human qualities, humans must think of the psyche with stone qualities: dark, hidden, its own own-ness. I think this otherness expresses the understanding of alchemical meditative work as "against nature": *opus contra naturam*. If nature intends growth, light, and development, a work against nature goes in the opposite direction toward what Beckett calls the Unnamable.

Jung's autobiography (1963) relates how, at the age of between seven and nine years, he had an imaginary game with a stone. The game was a dialogue: "I am sitting on top of this stone and it is underneath" he remembers. "But the stone also could say 'I' and think: 'I am lying here on this slope and he is sitting on top of me.'" Jung said the little game was perplexing: "I would stand up, wondering who was what now" (1963, p. 20). This section of Jung's autobiography surely accounts for his later interest in alchemy. It is fascinating for several reasons. Note the age, seven to nine years. This is the period that developmental psychologist Jean Piaget would say is the beginning of the dawn of reason in a child. Reason, for developmental psychology, is seeing duality: self from matter, self unlike nature. So was Jung backwards? I would say so. Early on he was an *opus contra naturam*, going against the upward bound of reason, intuiting presciently that nature has interiorization. Not only does this completely overturn the way the West has viewed nature, but it also forms the cornerstone of depth psychology, "whose object" writes Jung, "is the inside subject" (qtd. in Whan, 2006b, p. 31). The essential foreignness of the stone, like the psyche, is an unsettling thought if one assumes that the human mind is capable of all understanding. But Jung, in his autobiography, was comfortable, even as a child, with the idea of unresolvable oppositions which can elicit sym-pathy:

> 'The stone has no uncertainties, no urge to communicate, and is eternally the same for thousands of years,' I would think, 'while I am only a passing phenomenon which bursts into all kinds of emotions, like a flame that flares up quickly and then goes out.' I was but the sum of my emotions, and the Other in me was the timeless, imperishable stone. (1963, p. 42)

I see in this early game with the stone the formation of Jung's theory of the archetypes, which are ageless structures of the psyche that reside both out there and in here and resist appropriation.

Jung shared with Goethe this passion for stones, which, in Goethe's case was a passion for rocks. With both men, it was intuition that drew them magnetically it would seem to a contemplation of stone or rock as representative of both outer cosmos and inner being. It was said that Goethe wrote that rocks contain "power" such that the soul can be "uplifted." Granite, in particular, represents what is "deepest and highest" (in Bachelard, 2002, p. 156). For Gaston Bachelard, imaginer of Earth's elements, the "dream" of granite gives rise to an enduring quality of all things hard, endurable, and permanent:

> The very texture of granite gives expression to the permanence of its being. It defies penetration, resists scratching, and stands up to wear. It gives birth to an entire class of reveries which play a large role in education of the human will. To dream of granite, as Goethe does, is not just to establish oneself as an unshakable being but to promise oneself to remain inwardly unaffected by insults and blows. (p. 157)

To take the metaphor of the stone into postmodern parlance, we could say that the stone is Derrida's "différance." This means that opposition is necessary but not in the modern sense. Modernity has pitted things against each other, notably dark from light, birth from death, man from woman, and nature from human, active from passive, presence from absence. That is opposition in a simple sense, which must be "deferred." For Derrida "différance" is a "play" of differences that takes place in the gap or space between two terms of opposition, which he signals by the 'a' in his neologism "difference." But taken a step farther, or deeper, is to appreciate opposition, to see the other term appreciatively without attempting to interpret it to death. This holds the opposites together, while keeping them apart. Derrida (1981), refusing to attribute absolute meaning to any of his key words like "differance," which can slip into other key words of his like "trace" or "pharmacy," writes

> The *pharmakon* is the movement, the locus, and the play: (the production of) difference. It is the différance of difference. It holds in reserve, in its undecided shadow and vigil, the opposites and the differends that the process of discrimination will come to carve out. Contradictions and pairs of opposites are lifted from the bottom of this diacritical, differing, deferring reserve... We will watch it infinitely promise itself and endlessly vanish through concealed doorways that shine like mirrors and open onto a labyrinth. It is also this store of deep background that we are calling the *pharmacy*. (pp. 128, 129)

What slips out of our grasp may be maddening to what the discriminating mind seeks to "carve out," but just that endless vanishing (of meaning) is what the "stone" that is not a stone represents. A literal stone gives rise to the metaphorical stone, however, since both, in a Derridean sense, become "ungraspable"... "an infinite reference from one to the other, but no longer a source, a spring. There is no longer a simple origin" (1981, p. 36) and they "cannot be reduced to the form of presence" (1976, p. 57). This playful use of language (in translation) is Derrida's theater, where what is satirized is the realist's need to kill the many etymologies, mythologies, uses, and contradictions that words, necessarily, convey as their secret "trace."

Between speaking and writing a gap occurs: one cannot absolutely "get" at what one means, since saying is always unsayable.

Deferring one-sided meaning, in the face of such swirling livingness that is our experience in the world, is the intention of archetypal psychology and, when playfully understood, of language itself. And metaphor is the poet's province that brings two things together with what David L. Miller (1989) calls "simultaneous difference" (p. 116). He explains: "The mood of differentiating... consists in letting things be... bracketing the question of "meaning" or "meaninglessness" (p. 117).

I will end this discussion of stone as metaphor with a well-known hymn "The Rock of Ages" (not to be confused with the Broadway musical of the same name celebrating the rock scene of the 80s). The tune is deceptively simple while the words and rhyme scheme are Eighteenth Century, in other words, containing "traces." The first two lines, repeated as the last two lines, are "Rock of Ages, cleft for me,/ Let me hide myself in Thee." I confess, when I read those lines I had no idea what "cleft" meant and could not figure out the meaning. (Had I forgotten the cleft on Cary Grant's face?). I had to look up the word: "cleft: fissure, crack or rift; break, split, divided" (Webster). The literal image in the song is of a solid rock which nevertheless contains a crack or rift (a hole, a vagina, a womb) *into which* the singer seeks spiritual rebirth. But metaphorically, the Rock of Ages is the savior figure Christ who was cleft or broken for humankind. His *wound* is where the singer seeks refuge. Both meanings intrigue, for on the one hand the rock's crack will birth new life; on the other hand, the wound in the side of the Stone Christ will offer life after death and sympathy with suffering. While two meanings differ, they play back and forth to suggest that the Rock is both literal and metaphorical and, because it is "of Ages," belongs to originary time.

The hymn's Rock is thus a carry-over from the Philosopher's Stone but with different metaphorical meaning. From ancient times the unknowable Stone beckons by its uncannily postmodern perspective of différance While the singer of the hymn cannot hope to be Christ like, cannot identify with Christ, there is the fascination of absolute difference between the suffering Christ, Rock of Ages, and the petitioner-singer. Negativity is what attracts. The wound is what separates, resisting "mental penetration" (Hillman, in Whan, 2006b, p. 37). This is metaphor's magic: holding two terms together that cannot be clearly grasped or "held" and so must present itself in silence, as mystery. Michael Whan (2006b) explains further:

> When alchemy speaks of nature, it speaks of what it cannot say, of what cannot be told. A double negation or "not" haunts its *theoria* in the sense that it does not fall into a straightforward silence, but the silence of indirect language. (p. 34)

Such cryptic sayings! Cryptic: see crypt. "Crypt: a subterranean chamber or vault, esp. one beneath the main floor of a church, used as a burial place, a location for secret meetings, etc." (Webster). Stones are everywhere, in churches, in tombs, in hidden secret places. Jesus in the Thomas Gospel says "lift up the stone and you will find me" (in Pagels, 2004, p. 53). These ideas, like the metaphoric stone, disrupt and interrupt the forward way of thinking, rupturing surface understanding (so clear you can tick it in a box). In the cleft is the language of contradiction, and a gap opens out. The gap is the space of not-knowing, essential for real knowing of the "real-nothing" or "imaginal something" (Adams, 2001, p. 396). We are in the territory of ruins. The call, as Bill Readings (1999) put it, is for dissensus: "the community of dissensus… presupposes nothing in common [and] would seek to make its hetero-nomy, its differences, more complex" (p. 190). Teaching in the gap is admittedly risky business, especially in the information age where answers can be found in bytes. If anything is clear, it is that we should enter a new deconstructive phase in our teaching, where difficult texts might be approached as crypts. Then perhaps we could stand up, as Jung did from his stone, and wonder who was what now.

THE MONSTER AS OTHER, AS SELF

To look at Jeffrey Dahmer I could not tell he was a monster. His finely chiseled chin, neat hair, and quiet demeanor belied the hatred he had for himself. As the son of a fundamentalist, it is believed that Jeffrey repressed his homosexuality, and so this hatred turned inward to self-loathing projected onto those who were openly homosexual. True, most of the photos I saw and the clips on television when I watched the trial showed him with downward turned face: I could not see the eyes to his soul. So I remember being shocked at the horrors that Dahmer committed: not just murdering dozens of young men, but dismembering them, experimenting on their skulls, and eating parts of their bodies. Together with horror was a tinge of fascination, something akin to what Jay Scott Morgan (n.d.) wrote about Goya's painting of Saturn eating his daughter: "I look upon him, and I am implicated in the crime" (www.nereview).

My students seem unfazed by the cannibalism in the storyline of Greek myth. Incest is another given in myth world, none of which seems to overtly bother undergraduates. Is this because myth is thought of as "extreme," "ridiculously interesting," "back then"? I introduce Goya's painting of Saturn devouring his children. Then the grit of the story takes hold. Saturn is drawn in all his cannibalistic madness: wild grey hair, fiercely gripping fingers, gaping mouth: these details are almost caricatures of monstrosity were it not for the enlarged pupils and bulging eyes of craziness looking out at a viewer. In the artist's imagination Saturn's offspring are fully grown, not children as Hesiod writes. Somehow the adult-mangled body dangling before the devouring maw is almost comic, since the body is so out of proportion. To add to the bizarre quality of the piece, we are told that during his "black painting" period Goya placed this and other scenes of cannibalism around the walls of his own dining room (Morgan, n.d., nereview).

Killings of children by fathers is old myth, engrained in the Western imagination from Saturn to Abraham to God. But cannibalism? What is the taste for literal flesh, this perverse act of communion? Certainly inadequate sexuality is part of the answer; the monster is a bad seed, which wills its way in terrible urgings. But as James Hillman (1996) insists, "Demonism arises, not because of supposed or actual sexual dysfunction, but because of the dysfunctional relation with the daimon" (p. 240). The daimon, according to Hillman, is the very essence of Greek thought in that it is the fate one is called to, and fate for myth "acts as a personal daimon, an accompanying guide who remembers your calling" (p. 39).

The monster, accordingly, looms as a great awakener, calling to that which lies within the human soul as possibility for genius or madness. The monster is at the edges of our inner selves. Sometimes, however, the monster is so ordinary looking, as in the case of Jeffrey Dahmer, that we can forget how insidious he really is.

In a cynical lack of imagination and historical awareness, America's favorite family friendly eating establishment, McDonald's, chose a figurine of Custer, slaughterer of the Lakota, Cheyenne, and Arapaho Indians, to tuck into their Happy Meal boxes. Here is an innocuous-seeming corporation actually toying with a monster. To Native Americans, Lt. Colonel George Armstrong Custer was the Hitler of the Plains, whose troops made saddle horns out of Indian vaginas and coin purses from Indian scrotums. But the company spokesperson (whose last name is Proud) used this bland "explanation" when faced with outrage by the Indian community: "At McDonald's we value and respect people of all ethnicities, as well as their cultural history....Our goal is to provide families a positive experience that can be shared by all" (in Giago, 2009, p. 9A).

Too much positivity, too much sun, will push the monster farther into his saturnine depths. So, in the spirit of befriending the monster and letting it show us its soul, I will try to imagine with the images it presents in myth. But first, the word. "Monster: 1. a fabled animal combining features of animal and human form or having the forms of various animals in combination, as a centaur, griffin, or sphinx. 2. any creature so ugly or monstrous as to frighten people. 3. any animal or human grotesquely devia-ting from the normal shape, behavior, or character." Webster tells us, further, that "monster" comes from the Latin "monstrum," originally a divine portent, equivalent to "monere"=to warn. Interestingly, a "monstrance" is the receptacle used by the Catholic Church, in which the consecrated Host is exposed for adoration. So what we have here is a synergy of feelings and a synthesis of meanings, some quite opposite, as in Catholic adoration versus mythic monstrosity. When we are in the presence of the monster, we are fearful. But we also sense it as More. The monster is awe-full. It puts us in touch with primal feelings, like those of children dreaming of monsters (Doll, 1995).

The oldest recorded mythic monster is the bull of heaven in the Gilgamesh epic from Sumer. It is an earth-shaking bull with a savage mouth, unleashed upon Gilgamesh, as punishment for his insults to Ishtar:

Anu set loose a bull from out of the sky and,

At the bull's proclamation, there cracks the

Earth to swallow up nine dozen citizens of Uruk!

An earthquake fixed a grave for nine dozen of

Citizens of Uruk. (in Jackson, 1992, lines 130–134)

When Enkidu and Gilgamesh pride themselves on killing Heaven's beast, they do not reckon its power to ungorge three earthquakes. Worse, Gilgamesh treats the bull as his personal trophy, not the divine creature that it really is. He summons his artisans to adorn his throne with the bull's horns as evidence that he, Gilgamesh, is now "the finest, firmest, and most fair" ... "man above men" (lines 200–201). By wishing to use the bull's horns for personal aggrandizement, Gilgamesh misuses the sacred horns of the bull. As archeological digs in the Mesopotamian region attest, bull horns and eggs were once used as symbols on vases for the goddess' power of regeneration. In these early pot paintings, it was clear that the symbol of the bull, particularly its horns, was not to suggest strength and masculinity but becoming and femininity, since the female reproductive organs resemble the horns of a bull (Gimbutas, 1989, p. 266). Gilgamesh fails to honor the bull for its sacred powers, wishing to take those powers for himself.

It is certain that Gilgamesh, with all his hubris, will get his come-uppance. Not only is he guilty, without acknowledgment, of insulting the queen Ishtar, but he is also guilty of toying with the monster, seeing it only for its literal threat, not its metaphoric awe; seeing it only as opportunity to proclaim his own physical strength. To so miss the significance of the divine creature, no matter how disguised, is to warrant punishment.

Myth reminds us of this message time and again. In the Chinese flood myth, the unnamed father fails to recognize the Thunder God for who he is. When the god appears on earth to warn the family of the flood, the father, unlike Wainkaura in the Brazilian flood myth, simply sees him as dinner. He instructs his children to place the god in an iron cage while he goes out to find herbs to spice up his prisoner for better eating. The father's opportunistic approach to the intruder is a curious but telling detail. In all instances of non-recognition, humans in these stories suffer from lack of cognition, knowing: knowing their place in the cosmic scheme. If they were to re-cognize, they would know that the creature they behold is the god in disguise. The error is one of literalism.

Gilgamesh, too, is a literalist. A second part of the Gilgamesh story is his quest for immortality upon the untimely death of his soul-mate Enkidu. Again, Gilgamesh fails to acknowledge his place in the cosmos, seeking immortality for himself by attaining the green plant at the bottom of the sea. Perhaps one origin of the snake as symbol of immortality is to be found in this early myth, since it is the snake, not the man, who snatches the green plant; its literal skin-shedding suggests the overthrowing of death. Gilgamesh fails in his quest but records his life story on stone so as to receive immortality through writing. This commitment of story to stone is perhaps the earliest use of literacy to rival the goddess' power (Shlain, 1999).

I used to teach this early myth simply as a hero tale, with emphasis on the arche-typal quest pattern: departure, encounter, return. I used to think of Gilgamesh in the manner of this conclusion: "[Gilgamesh] was wise, he saw mysteries and knew secret things, he brought us a tale of the days before the flood. He went on a long journey, was weary, worn out with labor, and returning engraved on a stone the whole story" (Segal, 2000, p. 183). Simple, straightforward, period. But now I think there is more that lies beneath the carvings in cuneiform; namely, a hubris that accompanies any quester who seeks personal fame over transpersonal wisdom and who fails to re-cognize the monster.

It should come as no surprise, then, that monster and misogyny are thought of synonymously, especially in the Middle East. The myth of Marduk and Tiamat, written on *The Seven Tablets of Creation* in 170 lines, is one of the earliest recorded creation stories; it is also one of the most violent in its depiction of the slaying of the Great Goddess Tiamat. Here begins the association of female with snake, since Tiamat was a salt water goddess manifested either in human form or as a serpent. Her consort was Apsu, of the fresh waters. The swirling of the waters, salt with fresh, brought about generations of offspring who eventually fell into hostility among themselves in a major show of sibling rivalry. But the offspring were also Tiamat's children and grandchildren, which she vowed to protect with her own substantial powers–so substantial, that when Marduk was full grown he elected to challenge the serpent goddess for supremacy over all. The battle is described in gory detail, which begins when Marduk spins his favorite toy, the winds, into Tiamat's open mouth and then splits her body in two with an arrow.

That Tiamat is viewed as one huge devouring mouth in need of destroying is, at base, one way of misreading the progenerative powers of the goddess' vagina. Like any hatred, misogyny arises from fear. If the goddess can be desecrated, so too can her powers, the reasoning goes, which can then be allotted to the victor.

My students are astonished at the details of this creation myth, unlike the rather graceful dismemberment stories of other cultures. Tiamat's body becomes the bone and blood of the cosmos, a familiar cosmogonic motif. But Marduk is not content merely to create anew. He must mutilate. He must crush the mother's skull by a swing of his mace, pierce her eyes with his spear, prick her breasts in many places, and thrust "the Great Mother's pubic mound [up]to support the sky" (Shlain, 1999, p. 50). The verbs are all phallic actions to decimate the body of the Mother. And what is even more surprising in this account are two features: one, the sons rise up against the mother (in a twist on the Freudian father-son hostility); and two, this is an allegory of death, not a metaphor of birth.

The mother as monster! The birth place as monstrous! The Babylonian creation story is all violence and misogyny; and, to the point, female is monster. The female's uterus in these stories represents a challenge to the penis. We see this idea visually in the Greek story of Medusa, whose monstrous head is covered with snakes, like wagging penises, and whose gaze can turn men into stone. The Medusa head is like a vagina covered with hair that can swallow or bite the inserted penis; the snakes are the castrated penises. Such an image of horror for males is Freud's explanation for the "castration complex" or the fear of the Vagina Dentata. French post structuralist writer Hélène Cixous (1976), however, explains the image differently. She context-ualizes the penis as the dominant metaphor of authority in Western culture, just as the pen is the tool for authoring that authority. If, she argues, the penis is castrated, then Medusa has the last laugh (Cixous). Female authority does not come by the pen or the alphabet but in and through the image. De-literalizing the word opens meaning out into the depths beneath the word, into the dark terra-tory of the goddess.

As Ovid recounts the myth, Medusa-snake-stone are intermingled with the story of Perseus, slayer of the Medusa monster. I see the poet Ovid doing what Cixous centuries later urges, using metaphor to keep the goddess beneath the story hidden in plain sight. The first reference to stone is with Atlas, whose wealth is measured by the golden apples guarded by a dragon. Atlas and Perseus have a disagreement over this cache, whereupon Perseus, "lifted with his left hand Medusa's head/ at which the giant turned into a mountain" (in Gregory, 2001, p. 131). The second reference to stone and snake is with Andromeda, chained to a rock below which a dragon floated. To save the girl, Perseus fights the dragon, "thrusting, hilt-deep, the sword into its shoulder." Again, Perseus' left hand is mentioned: "With left hand grasping on a ledge of cliff/ He struck his sword three times and then again" (in Gregory, p. 133). Finally, Perseus recounts his slaying of Medusa to the men back at the palace, stone and snake coiled into this coda of Ovid's telling: three stones, three snakes surrounding this tale of female monstrosity.

Threes are the numbers of the goddess, whose regenerative powers simmer within the delta of her body; the Perseus tale is no exception with its whorls of three and its insistence on snake imagery. But one must look past, into the far past of the hero tale, to see the origins of the monster Medusa. Several peelings back from the patriarchal Greek period lies the original Medusa, once wise like Metis, the mother of Athena. Her wisdom is connected with the snake, which sheds its skin literally to cast off death metaphorically. Only in the patriarchal period does the head of Medusa become the icon on Athena's shield, and only then does Athena don her helmet to become Zeus' girl. But once, much much earlier, Athena, like Medusa, was a pre-Hellenic goddess. She was the other, light side of dark Medusa, serpent goddess of the Amazons whose blood birthed Chrysaor and Pegasus. Medusa's blood, in fact, was called "wise blood" (Walker, 1983, p. 629). Athena, back then, was not the virgin of classical Greece but an original triple goddess—Athena, Metis, Medusa– intimately connected (by blood!) to the wisdom of the snake. That she became the patroness of Athens, enshrined in the Parthenon, celebrated for virginity and martial prudence, is what happens when one culture devoted to the goddess gets overrun by another culture devoted to the hero.

Medusa, clearly, was a powerful figure of regeneration before she was turned into a monster. We see this in the names given to her and her Gorgon sisters: Medusa meant "Wisdom," Stheino meant "Strength," and Auryale meant "Universality." Their names indicate that these three were originally the three phases of the Moon Mother, which also correspond to the three phases of the life cycle: past, present, future (Walker, 1983, pp. 349, 649). This notion of the three in one and one in three is the venerated basis of the mythic trinity, and later the Christian Trinity. But in the patriarchal period, Wisdom, Strength, and Universality become hag-monsters.

Reading Ovid imagistically thus gives hints of the mother roots of the monster Medusa. No wonder I had to draw attention to Ovid's left hand symbolism in previous paragraphs with regard to Perseus. Recall, he holds the Medusa head by the left hand both times he uses it as a tool, first turning Atlas to stone and second conquering the snake beneath Andromeda. This is the hand that the right brain of compassion controls. This would seem to be Ovid's way of crediting the female prehistory of Medusa, before the hero comes crashing in with slashing sword. Within the images, the roots of meaning lie. Nevertheless, the surface plotline of the story concerns the action hero—and also his odd inactions. Note his indirection when facing the monster. Perseus does not directly look at the head of the snake-covered Gorgoness, meaning he cannot incorporate the image into his consciousness. Further, by stuffing the decapitated head into his magic bag he represses any feeling (Hathaway, 2002, p. 286). Perseus fails to see the monster as an opportunity to explore his own ravaged places, to see in IT a mirror of himself.

The monster of myth contains intrinsic doubleness, requiring the second look. It inspires terror, it inspires fascination. It is a warning, monere, to those who look on it to look deeper. The monster, we could say, is another manifestation of the divine, a monstrance, held up for our awe if not our adoration.

Something of this ambiguity "holds" us as we read of another famous Greek hero, Theseus. Theseus must slay the Minotaur, the part bull, part human monster in the labyrinth of King Minos. Why the labyrinth? Right there we see an image: the winding paths of the labyrinth, so like our own winding brain paths and intestine circles. We are connected in our bodies to the labyrinth; it is within us. The monster within the labyrinth is also metaphorically within us. If we slay the monster, we are pretending our inner monster does not exist, hoping to bag it, like Perseus, or kill it like Theseus. Like an action hero, we could go about our business, adjust our sword, fly off on our horse. But without looking at what lies in the shadows, we fail utterly in the quest to become human.

Once again the monster in the Theseus story is the bull, ancient symbol of... divinity! The bull with its body of charged energy and horns of uterine rebirth was a figure of reverence and ritual in ancient cultures, both of bull-gods and bull-goddesses. "Nearly every god of the ancient world was incarnate sooner or later in a bull," writes Barbara Walker (1983, p. 124). One can find associations between a bull and major god figures: Zeus, Osiris, Minos, Mithra, Dionysus, Shiva, and Yama. Joseph Campbell (1987) concurs:

> When the cult of the dead and resurrected bull-god... and of the bull and goddess... we have the earliest evidence yet discovered anywhere of the prodigiously influential mythology associated for us with the great names of Ishtar and Tammuz, Venus and Adonis, Isis and Osiris, Mary and Jesus.... and we celebrate the mystery of the mythological death and resurrection to this day. (p. 143)

It is not a large step from bull to pig to goat to lamb to see how the sacrificial animal became one and the same with the sacrificial god, whose death promised rebirth. This bull-god association is even seen in the Bible. Bull masks could cast spells on enemies (I Kings 22:11) and King Nebuchadnezzar "did eat grass as oxen" because his body "was wet with the dew of heaven" (Daniel 4:33). The divinity within the bull was like a sacred marriage of opposites. When ritual sacrifices were made to the bull or of the bull, it was as if the bull *was* divinity; the divinity's power could thereby be gained by the sacrificer. Campbell (1987) puts this succinctly: "The offered beast is a captured quantum of divine power, which, through its sacrifice, is integrated with the giver" (p. 450).

The Minotaur, of course, is only part bull; he is bull-man, the offspring of Pasiphae who mated with the bull given to her husband, King Minos, son of Zeus, who disguised himself as a bull in order to rape Europa, the mother of Minos. The bull forms a ring around this story, with the bull-man Minotaur caught inside the ring through no fault of his own. Pasiphae, too, is caught inside this ring, for her unnatural obsession was punishment not for her but for her husband Minos, who failed to offer sacrifice for a magnificent white bull sent him by the gods. The Minotaur is twice removed from fault, yet he is the tormented one who lives imprisoned and alone. "Monster in the labyrinth" is a major metaphor of hidden disgrace and monstrosity, which nineteen centuries or more later became transposed as "madwoman in the attic." While the monster is in the depths and the madwoman is in the attic, both are the alive hiddennesses of the soul.

I think it is this tragic human quality of the Minotaur that has drawn the attention of modern artists like Pablo Picasso and Michael Ayrton, together with so many of my myth students. Quite apart from the hero Theseus, it is the monster that interests. Picasso saw in the Minotaur his own sexual alter ego, as well as a symbol for the "dark powers of the labyrinthine unconscious" unleashed during the Spanish Civil War (in Nyenhuis, 2003, p. 62). Michael Ayrton's obsession with the Minotaur can be seen with his sketches and sculptures of the beast, covering its entire life cycle. He labels his ten etchings "As Embryo," "Consecrated," "As Calf," "As Yearling," "Rising," "Risen," "Full Grown," "Pent," "Revealed," and "Alone" (in Nyenhuis, pp. 182–183). Other sketches make their way into sculptures: "Minotaur Asleep," and "Waking Minotaur" (in Nyenhuis, pp. 184–185). So caught up was the artist with the image of the Minotaur that years before he executed his sketches and sculpture pieces he wrote a novel, using Daedalus, the labyrinth maze maker, as his persona:

> He was the colour of weathered bronze and ... I saw him as beautiful in his majestic absurdity. I saw him indomitable and ridiculous in all the grandeur and all the fragility of useless physical strength. Icarus, in his foolishness, had once believed himself half-brother to the Minotaur and believed me the father of both. In that moment I felt I could have been. (Ayrton, 1967, p. 197)

While other Minotaur pieces of Ayrton are catalogued (in Nyenhuis, 2003), none shows him with Theseus, the hero. Instead, Aryton sculpts the Minotaur seated, enraged, in jeopardy, restless, crouched, lowing, drunken or alarmed—not defeated. This may be the artist's deliberate intention to place Theseus very much in the background, if not eliminated altogether, seeking rather to extend and enrich the mythic message of the monster as a living embodiment of the preconscious psyche.

One critic has noted a possible reason for Ayrton's obsession with the Minotaur; namely, the artist's stiff spine and limited movement, a condition known as *ankylosing spondalitis* (in Nyenhuis, 2003, p. 184)). Seeing himself imprisoned within his own body would be an understandable reason to focus on the beast imprisoned within the labyrinth. It is as if the monster were a divine portent of Ayrton's own condition, so much so that he could acknowledge becoming "entangled in this particular myth" (Ayrton, 1962, p. 65), bonding himself with the monster he adored.

My mythologist students, too, have had their own compulsions in conjunction with the Minotaur, drawn in by his pathos, drawn in by his outpost humanity. Juan Sepulveda writes this:

> I have always had a direct fascination with the Minotaur. This abomination of mythology represents all that is wild and uncontrollable in the human mind. I am a Minotaur as are all humans in one sense or the other. This monster is my shadow and mask. In it I find shelter and relief from my human tendencies and in a way an excuse for my animal-like behavior that can be seen as savage. The Minotaur also encompasses an elegance that is found in its human body. It walks on two legs and moves in the fashion of man. The Minotaur has no

real evident power except its strength. Nevertheless, the Minotaur continues to engulf our imaginations. (Artist Statement)

Speaking as an artist, Juan, like Ayrton, takes exception to Theseus, writing, "The killing of the Minotaur symbolizes the conquest over the irrational and emotionless aspect of the human mind. This is just the human wanting to become perfect and godlike."

Another student created a bull mask for her final project, knowing, at the outset, that she was attracted to the beast. "I chose to do the Minotaur for its symbolic relevance to my psyche," she wrote:

> I found that as I was creating my mask I was getting into the mindset of the Minotaur. My project seemed to be consuming me, driving me to madness with the complexity of its understructure. Often I found my arms tangled in a conglomerate of yarn and mesh. Then I found further symbolism as I literally had to cover up this madness with layer after layer of the final piece. I covered the mesh with batting to smooth out the surface and give it a clean white form; then covered that with the 'skin' of the Minotaur and its facial features. This is exactly how we try to cover up our subconscious thoughts to be presentable in public.

To study myth for its imagistic wisdoms into our own deeper selves is an intention of my teaching. Art students, especially, appreciate the wondrous images that myth offers, enabling them to uncover meanings they did not know they knew.

I end this foray into the monster not with Lilith, the Sphinx, or the Centaur, all of whom have their own disguised wisdoms as monsters, but with an Olympian of exceptional rationality who might seem to be the very opposite of a monster. I choose Apollo, sun god of all that is light, the Shining One of Reason and Illumination, epitome of a left brained logical, sequential format. To look at his statuesque pose as Leochares portrays "The Belvedere Apollo" is to see composure itself, upon slaying the monster serpent Python. Of course, Frederick Turner (1995) (the poet) reminds us that the genius of the Olympians is contrariness, so there are "certain strange things" about Apollo (p. 83). The most known story of Apollo is his pursuit of Daphne, the lovely nymph, who wanted nothing to do with him—despite his beauty. The failure of the pursuit is, for Turner, the tragedy of reason. My students put it more stridently, citing not the Daphne story but the one involving the slaying of Marsyas. This is a lesser-known story of an unfortunate satyr whom Apollo challenges to a musical contest. When the Muses vote Marsyas the winner, Apollo skins the fellow alive. This story needs to be included in the decoding chapters of Apollo's character. One student writes,

> Reason and rationality, the process of cooling one's head and dispassionately viewing a situation from the outside so as to prevent emotion from ruling one's actions, is the province of Apollo. Yet Apollo is one of the least rational gods on Mt. Olympus—unless you consider a sociopath a rationalist. For one thing, he seems to have allowed his perfection to get to his head. Whenever anyone approaches or threatens those things which are his domain, he demands

a competition, brutally murdering him, as in the case of Marsyas; or chasing after to possess her, as in the case of Daphne. One could consider these flaws a warning to the rational man of the traps he can easily fall into.

Another student writes,

The rational abilities allow Apollo to be highly intelligent, but they also allow for an underdeveloped right-brained, emotional, social self. It is clear through Apollo's interactions with other beings that he has great difficulty addressing his reactions and desires in a controlled, objective manner. What occurs is an outburst of explosive magnitude that is frightening. We can see this clearly in his musical contest with Marsyas, in which Marsyas, a right-brained being, wins the contest because his music was more emotionally provocative. Unfortunately, as a god and an archetype, Apollo is fated to forever be the poster child of the young, unbalanced Rational.

If Apollo is the unbalanced Rational of myth, could Descartes be far behind, the monster of modernism? (Morris, 2009).

I think, too, of Ted Kaczynski, a recluse, a master of the mind, a monster. In his Unabomber Manifesto of 232 articles and 36 notes, he offers his rationale for waging war against the industrial system. This is thinking gone amuck. I think back to Jeffrey Dahmer, almost beautiful in his chiseled profile. Before we cast the stone too quickly, we might be cautioned to remember that the monster is a warning and a divinity: it warns against too self righteous judgment; it is divine as is the daimon, the acorn of the soul (Hillman, 1996). To say "thou art that" is to say with all humility that "any object, any stick, stone, plant, beast, or human being, can be placed in the center of a circle of mystery" (Campbell, 2001, p. 26).

PART II:
MYTH AS ECOLOGICAL PEDAGOGY

ARTWORK "FAUN AND NYMPH" BY JORDAN MORRIS, SCAD 2011.

THE BREATHING BARK

The force that through the green fuse drives the flower

Drives my green age; that blasts the roots of trees

Is my destroyer.

— Dylan Thomas

It is no wonder that fairytales frequently feature a forest as the place of initiation. Inside a dense dark wood the naïve venturer enters the realm of the metaphorical unconscious. Evil lurks, death happens, people get pushed into ovens. There are witches and hunters. Fairytale forests are fantasy places where demonic presences dwell, as they do in nightmare. Unlike the sheltering arm of domesticity—or the battering arm of domestic violence—fairytale forests give space for a child's imagination to take shape and to deal with "the existential predicament" (Bettelheim, 1989). While the characters in fairytales are stereotypically either good or bad, according to psychologist Bruno Bettelheim the very starkness of their presentation allows children to experience vicariously (he insists the word should be "consciously") the problematic nature of life so they may learn of danger and come to terms with the dilemmas of their inner lives. "Little Red Riding Hood," for instance, may have lost her innocence by meeting the wolf in the forest, but she has exchanged it for wisdom "that only the 'twice born' can possess: those who not only master their existential crisis, but also become conscious that it was their own nature which projected them into it" (p. 183).

While I admire the skillful interpretation of Bettelheim's fairytale readings, I think he credits the child with too facile a transfer from reading into knowing or from innocence into wisdom. And I seriously question if "wisdom" is the right word. The forest of fairytale holds an Other reality, but that this reality is understood by the child to the degree that Bettelheim suggests seems dubious. For him, the forest serves as backdrop to lesson-learning, thanks to the easy differentiation between the opposites in fairytale world. Actually, what I think Bettelheim proposes, coming out of ego psychology, is ego-strengthening. The child, by entering the forest in order to contrast good from evil, human from beast, domesticity from nature is actually being groomed into a Modernist mindset. The "green age" of the fairytale child will not see the green fuse of the flower, too intent will she be on overcoming the black force of Evil.

The trees that make up the forest in Classical Greek and Roman myths offer a very different approach to the forest. Myth never shies away from violence. As I have tried to argue in other chapters, myth is not, simply, pessimistic. Nor is fairytale, simply, optimistic (Bettelheim, p. 37). Bettelheim's too easy reach after dichotomy is precisely not the dizzying experience we have with myth. The trees of Greek myth introduce a far more subtle—sophisticated, even– understanding of human-nature interchanges that elucidate startlingly postmodern, new science ideas. These can be appreciated on both a literal and a metaphoric level, as the stories of Daphne, Myrrha, and the vegetation deities show.

Apollo, ever the rationalist, is the shining sun god in everything but love. His is the realm of reason that shines light into darkness and makes everything clear and simple. Everything, that is, but love. That Apollo is unlucky in love is such an interesting insight into reason's weakness: reason cannot use its force of logic when emotion gets in the way. Such is the tragedy of reason. Struck by the arrow of Eros, Apollo is overtaken with desire for the nymph Daphne, burning with love as he chases her through the "green deep forest" (Ovid, 2001, Bk, I, p. 44). Daphne calls out to her father, an old river god, to help her, since she had also been struck with an arrow, the arrow of lead that demands aloneness and virginity. Peneus, the father, reluctantly agrees to Daphne's pleas by changing her into a laurel tree at the moment of capture. As poet Frederick Turner (1995) puts it, "Our attempts to catch the Daphne of nature by means of reason" of course fail, but in the process a "great mystery" and a "wonderful transformation" takes place (p. 87).

I want to follow Turner's observation by way of Bernini's statue "Apollo and Daphne," since I find in that amazing Baroque artwork further evidence of reason's failure with "mystery" and "transformation." I show this famous statue to my art students in several close ups. We see first the entire statue: Daphne, both feet already rooted to the ground, halting movement; her arms upward outstretched suggest a forward thrust away from her pursuer; her mouth is open, head back, eyes back, wide. Apollo is close behind, his right arm outstretched as if to sweep her into him; his left foot is lifted in pursuit; his head and eyes focus with erotic intent. Then I show segments of the entire piece, such that we witness close up the moments of transfor-mation: her feet *becoming* the trunk, her fingers *becoming* leaves, her head "swaying in a cloud of leaves" (Ovid, Bk. I, p. 44). The statue in its fixed form conveys paradoxically the miracle of change within stasis.

Bernini affords us the privilege of witnessing what nature does, silently, beneath our eyes, the "coming into leaf" (Whan, 2006a, n.p.) of the process of transformation. Ovid describes this metamorphosis as follows: "A soaring drowsiness possessed her; growing/ In earth she stood, white thighs embraced by climbing/Bark, her white arms branches, her fair head swaying/In a cloud of leaves" (p. 44). The experience of seeing Bernini's statue gives my students and me a sense of theater about the little story, engaging us with the drama of Daphne's silent scream.

Several aspects of this mythic story seem to me to reflect amazing insight into what today is called the ecopsychological imperative. Carl Jung articulated the basic necessity of this imperative before the Green Movement when he wrote:

> The various lines of psychic development start from one common stock whose roots reach back into the most distant past. Theoretically it should be possible to peel the collective unconscious, layer by layer, until we come to the psychology of the worm, and even of the amoeba. (In Bradshaw & Watkins, 2006, p. 73)

Substitute "tree" for "worm," and "leaf" for "amoeba" and you have the idea Jung is expressing; namely, that a connection has always-already existed among all living forms, all species. It is up to humans to access the depths of consciousness "rooted" in this transpersonal intersection.

I am interested in how Bernini's white marble expresses the both-andness of such intersection with the interplay of solidity and fragility; strength and weakness; movement and stasis; desire and terror. The paradoxes, visually represented, are there for the viewing if we have eyes to see. Bernini captures within one entity the complex energy exchange suggested by myth. Rather than a dualistic, simple world of fairytale, myth expresses the dynamism that comes from a tensive interplay of opposites.

Bernini also captures the different emotions expressed by the actors: Daphne's terror, Apollo's intent. Daphne's silent scream speaks volumes. Here is the living tree crying out against possession and ownership, the very basis of arguments proffered by such naturalists as Rachel Carson, Terry Tempest Williams, Annie Dillard, Jane Goodall and countless others. Daphne's scream can be heard in the voices of such naturalists who seek to prevent ego concerns from deflowering the natural world. These naturalists argue for humans to develop a different set of capabilities, deeper listening for instance. All living species require from us the respect for their otherness: not ownership, not rape, and certainly not dominion. Rachel Carson was among the first to express this idea, and to express outrage at what human hubris was doing to plant species in the name of "development." Like Daphne's silent scream, Carson's *Silent Spring* (2002) exposes the horrors endured by plant and tree life because of the widespread use of synthetic chemicals, spraying, dusts, aerosols, utility rights-of-way, deforestation and so on. Refusing to stay silent, Carson spoke for species that can not speak: "Even large trees not directly sprayed were affected. The leaves of the oaks began to curl and turn brown... The new shoots began to be put forth and grew with abnormal rapidity, giving a weeping appearance to the trees" (p. 71).

Carson's anthropomorphism is not sentimental but rather insistent on the natural intelligence and sentience perceptible within all—yes, all!– of biology. As David Kidner (2006) puts it, "Non-human organisms, although lacking our cognitive equipment, are in many ways equally proficient. A tree 'knows' how best to distribute its roots" (p. 100). While it is easier to attribute feeling to animals (Jack London often describes dogs that "know), trees require more from our sensitivities. Daphne's silent scream is Bernini's splendid presentation of this fact.

A consideration of Apollo's role in this myth is important. Of all the gods he is the rationalist. Rationality demands distance and aloofness. Rationality separates and keeps things apart, human from plant. Hierarchical thinking requires dominion of humans over the nonhuman world. Rationality can not conceive of the possibility that thinking and feeling exist within nonhuman species. This is the egotism of the rationalist. But! Apollo *loses* his rationality in this myth, and he loses it because of Eros. Apollo is denied his desirous intention to possess Daphne.

What I see happening in this tiny mythic point is a caution for us today. Our human thinking needs to be warmed by the love of Other. If we can be caught by Eros, we can seek connection without ownership, intimacy without possession. This is movement of another kind, the sort that Eros instills, since his domain is that of creative stimulation (Guggenbuhl-Craig, 1980). I credit Apollo's loss to a mythic understanding that living forms require not just our respect for their implicit worth but love for their explicit Otherness. This is the essence of trans-species relationship, an idea that is old but in need of new understanding. Michael Conforti (1999) reminds us, "As cultures have revered the relationship between the individual and the trans-personal, we too need to find some way for including it again in our notions of consciousness" (p. 141).

Consciousness-raising depends on lowering our sights, listening deeper, thinking more poetically, with Eros. We are not the only structures with bone and blood, not the only species with feeling. My gods! what a luscious world we live in if we but extend our sym-pathies, our feeling-with. A larger force field embeds itself outside the human community, and this field includes plants as well as animals, and, yes, if we can stretch our minds a bit, amoeba.

Ovid's classic, masterful storytelling is postmodern in its disdain for narrative sequencing, certainly its disdain for logic, and most certainly its celebration of the waywardnesses of love. To that end, he allows even fringe characters to play important parts in any central story such that no "master" narrative prevails. I sense in Ovid a feminine cast of mind that shows an incredibly subtle understanding of feminine sensibilities. To that end, the minor characters in the Apollo-Daphne story have a behind-the-scenes major role to play, like a postmodern drama. Eros, as I have indicated, changes the intention of Apollo's lust when his hand feels Daphne's heart beat beneath the changing bark. And she, now tree, responds as lover to his touch:

Even now Phoebus embraced the lovely tree

Whose heart he felt still beating in its side;

He stroked its branches, kissed the sprouting bark,

And as the tree still seemed to sway, to shudder

At his touch, Apollo whispered.... (2001, Book I, p. 46)

These poetic lines foreshadow Jung's observation that life is "really a continuum... one tissue in which things live by and through each other." The individual is "cut out of the tissue of the collective unconscious" (in Evans, 2006, p. 137). If we can lose our human sense of privilege we might gain understanding of this ancient profundity.

Additionally, Peneus the old father river god is the ripple we feel throughout the storyline. The story's theme is not only about change; its poetic lines imitate change in the many gerunds that give flow to the static noun. That is the work of Peneus, the river god who, although unhappy that Daphne will not give him heirs, births instead the laurel that lives in nature and in art. Perhaps this is Ovid's sly way of suggesting that he, like a river god, will outlive the emperor Augustus, because he, like Eros and Peneus, is a minor player inside the Roman civic state.

Myth is fond of the logically impossible and the psychically shocking. These are the territories of Ovid, whom again I reference for his story of Myrrha-turned-into-a-tree. This time the tree harbors not an innocent nymph like Daphne but a daughter with an incestuous desire for her father. Freud would hardly blink at a daughter's desire to "marry" her father, since this early stage of sexual development is "natural" among many of us. Ovid, playing the devil's advocate, pretends that nature's way is known only among foreigners, not in the Rome that Virgil made famous. Such girls as Myrhha, Ovid writes coyly, can only be from "other lands" with "queer customs and disgusting habits" (Bk. X, 2001, p. 283). Myrrha's love-tormented mind "was like a tree... swaying from side to side" (p. 285) until she confessed to her nursemaid her secret. Since nursemaids are like old gossips, loving the ways of torrid romance, the nursemaid arranges for the consummation of Myrhha's desire while the mother is away attending a festival in honor of Ceres. When the father, after several nights of amorous delights, discovers that the nubile young thing he had been enjoying was his own daughter, he "went wild with horror" and Myrhha slipped away into the night. Improbably, she runs for nine moons until she prays to the gods, "'Make me a thing that neither lives nor dies'" (p. 288). Ovid, who in his invocation vows "To tell the shifting story of the world" (Bk. I, p. 31), writes in several lines the meta-morphosis of pregnant girl into tree:

Roots sprouted from her feet to hold her fast,

Her body upright while her bones grew strong;

Treelike, her arms became crooked heavy branches,

Rough bark encased her sides—she was all tree. (Bk. X, p. 288)

If becoming a tree was cosmic punishment for Myrrha's sin, think again. The story enfolds several other stories of miraculous birthings. Adonis, of course, is the child of Myrrha and Cinyras, her father; but he is also child of a tree: he is in a womb both human and vegetal. What is fascinating about this story, I think, are the circumstances of this birth as well as of his death, both of which point to a more-than-human aspect. We know from Greek myth, as well as from Ovid, that Adonis is extraordinarily beautiful, "lovelier than any man on earth" (Ovid, Bk. X, p. 289) and becomes the pet of both Aphrodite and Persephone. We know that these two goddesses must share him for part of each year; his return from the underworld where Persephone has reign coincides with the return of the crops. When he is gored by a wild boar, his side is pierced, and his blood turns into the anemone flower. So we know that Adonis is more vegetal than human, since both his birth and his death relate to the natural world.

What does it mean to be a vegetation deity? The archetype of a male young god with close association with the natural world can be seen with several other figures who share motifs such as early sacrificial death, piercing of skin, tree elements, and replication of seasonal rebirth. Odin, as explained earlier, hangs from a tree and through sacrifice learns the secrets of the cosmos. Orpheus, who returns alive from the realm of the dead, is connected with a veritable forest of different plant species: the poplar, oak, beechnut, laurel, hazel, ash, fir, maple, willow, lotus, boxwood, tamarisk, myrtle, viburnum, ivy, grapevine, elm, spruce, arbutus, palm, and pine! (Ovid, Bk. X, p. 276). Osiris, a major Egyptian god, resurrects from a tree: a miracle that gives him power of life over death, life in death. Also included in this archetype of the vegetal god is Hiawatha, from whose death rises corn, the mainstay of his people; as well as lesser male figures like Cyparissus, whose dying phallus provides the necessary seed for the growth of the Cypress tree. In fact, in the same Book Ten of *Metamorphoses*, Ovid clusters not only the Myrrha story but also that of Adonis, as well as of Cyparissus and Hyacinthus, the latter both lovers of Apollo and both vegetal figures. And let us not forget Dionysus, the ivy-crowned god of joy, who is torn from "limb" to "limb" and has mystical associations with the grape. The connection of Dionysus with Jesus has been noted by religious scholar Thomas Moore (2009), as a reviewer of Moore's book comments:

> A deepening mythology gathers around Jesus: the dark vegetative world of Dionysus, the rapture of inebriation, wine crushed, dismembered, altered so that the best of itself can be enjoyed in communal celebration. (Slattery, 2009, p. 225)

As Moore (2009) himself comments, "to live this intriguing way of the Dionysian Jesus is to say yes to life every step of the way, in spite of the possibility that you will be torn apart, judged and crucified" (p. 38).

Myth refuses to separate human from plant, from dirt, even foreshadowing the miraculous birth of the Christ child, whose sacrificial death on a tree brings promise of eternal life. As I tell my students, myth is the province of change, change, change. Death is the precondition for life. Not the other way around. Death composts the sprouting of new life, humanity from humus. Several motifs of the Adonis story in particular resonant with the Christian myth and offer profound insight into the mystery and miracle of natural transformation.

Recall that the name Adonis is derived from the Semitic *adon* or "lord," a word used to refer to the sovereignty of God, a word the Jewish Jesus would have known. Even smaller details suggest a connection between the one vegetal deity of myth and the other of religion. When Myrrha becomes a tree, the resin from it is known as myrrh, which has had spiritual significance since ancient times. Myrrha is from "Arabia of cinnamon and spice, /Sweet-smelling herbs and holy frankincense" (Ovid, Bk. X, p. 283), where the Three Wise Men "of Orient are, bearing gifts they traverse afar," as the song goes. The gifts of course were gold, frankincense and myrrh. Myrrh, used for embalming the bodies of Pharaohs in Egypt, was also used in perfumes and incense, giving off an earthy bitter odor ("Myrrh and frankincense"). This last gift of the Magi suggests an acknowledgment of Christ's death even at the time of his birth. As I commented with the Daphne story in Ovid, minor characters, those off-stage to the unfolding drama, often underscore a connection of the dying god with seasonal change. Recall that Myrrha's mother was away at the festival of Ceres, affording Myrrha the opportunity to gratify her lust. Ceres, the Roman name for Demeter, was the goddess of agriculture. Ceres/Demeter must suffer the temporary loss of her daughter Proserpina/Persephone to the realm of death; but the return of the daughter on a seasonal basis ensures that crops will forever grow again when the dead one returns. Demeter/Ceres thus makes her offstage appearance with the story of Adonis' mother Myrrha. And Persephone makes her appearance off stage after Adonis is born, since it is she who must share the beautiful, doomed, young Adonis with Aphrodite for a quarter of the seasonal year. Surrounding the drama of

Adonis' birth from a tree and death into a flower is the larger seasonal drama of winter (death) and spring (birth). Christ's birth in winter and death in spring mirrors this vegetation cycle.

Our myths and our religions are rooted in festivals of the seasons. This is not just to celebrate the return of warmth and light but also to offer opportunity to celebrate our deepest connection to the living earth. We wait for spring. As Marla Morris (2009) writes, "if one takes the time to take in psychologically the beautiful, the absurd and the grotesque, surprises *await*. But one must wait for such an experience.... Trees happen when they make an impression on the person who waits and watches." To feel oneself be the root of a chestnut tree, Morris continues, is a strange experience "if one allows it be become strange" (p. 151). Narratives like myths incarnate images, showing us the matter that matters.

And lest we forget, we are not only rooted in deeper forms, we too contain roots within our own bodies. A Chinese flood myth tells of the Thunder God who plucks a tooth from which a gourd tree grows. I thought this an interesting image at the time but puzzled aloud with my students what they (and I) thought the plucked tooth meant. It was my students who made the connection between the roots of our teeth and the roots of trees. Simple but profound; without our mutual musings I doubt I would have thought of this on my own. The imaginative wording of the myth in metaphoric language opens opportunities for the surprise, since metaphor, as Robert Romanyshyn (2008) says, "is always an allusion to something that remains elusive. As such, a metaphor is the opening of a possibility. It is a perspective that offers a vision" (p. 83). The stranger the vision, the stronger the message, if we but have the eyes to see and ears to hear.

This chapter has celebrated the tree, the lung of the world, as David Abram (1997) puts it. "How is it," he asks, that "we have become so deaf and so blind to the vital existence of other species, and to the animate landscapes they inhabit, that we now so casually bring about their destruction?" (pp. 27–28). Destruction of life forms for the sake of development was never the intention of the wisdom cultures. Quite the opposite. In early cultures the oak, for instance, was a "magical ancestor tree. Whatever was closely associated with the oak partook of its power.... And there were mother trees... giving birth to humans" (Hillman, 1996, p. 276). We have seen that, studied that. But have we seen that?! The sense of awe and gratitude for the mystery of the universe is that with which mythology is concerned, is that with which we must be concerned.

CHAPTER 6

READING THE TEXTURED WORLD

I surrendered myself to the beauties of the scene, I gazed at the trees, the fields, the sky, the birds, and I listened attentively to the sounds, faint and clear, borne to me on the air.

— Samuel Beckett (1958)

Since the past sixteen years or so, a growing concern about reading has emerged. The argument concerns a pitting of books against computers, of reading against digitalizing, of text against texting. Many teachers have experienced a problem in the reading classroom, when students assigned literary texts often lack the skills or patience to sit still with a book and absorb, then analyze what is on the printed page. The problem, in part, is a generation gap between those of us used to reading for sustained periods of time and those of them used to texting for short periods of time; those of them hopping from one site to another, gathering information, playing computer games. The latter is a zipzap enterprise rather than a surrender in forgetting one's self long enough to enter another slower world that unfolds in picture frames of one's imagination.

Sven Birkerts (2004) thinks part of the problem is Disney and the glib clichés that the Disney empire encourages. He laments the lure of studio-generated, high-powered special effects that encourages cookie-cutter responses to the world (p. 30). Nicolas Carr (2010) laments the loss of concentrated readership to the post-literary world of the juggler, more entranced with clicking and surfing than with solitary single-minded reading. Carr goes so far as to suggest that the brain itself is affected by the jagged actions required of internet surfing.

But is this attack on technology really such a stacked deck of loaded dualisms (Haraway, 1997, p. 68)? Does not the world of myth, for instance, relish, indeed (as Donna Haraway puts it) "promiscuously cohabit" with plot and pixels both, since both occupy the same material places? Haraway argues for teasing open the various threads that make up disparate disciplines. She writes, "The threads are alive; they transform into each other; they move away from our categorical gaze. The relations among the technical, mythic, economic, political, formal, textual, historical, and organic... matter.... [M]aybe we already live inside the well, where lines of force have become the sticky threads of our own bodies" (pp. 68–69). Myth the pre-literary meets the post-literary, has always met the pre-human, in the post-human, post-modern era!

I want to return to the Disney comment, however, because few if any sticky threads can be found in Disney. As my student Carson Nevada understands, the Walt Disney Corporation was his introduction to myth. But where was myth? Disney, Carson learned later, had turned a complex mythic character, Herakles, into a nice, loyal, father figure. This smoothing-over flattened not just the original story but Carson's expectations about the ancient world. By making mythic figures too-accessible, a child is robbed of exploring the depths not only of myth but of imagination itself. A child is encouraged to remain infantilized (but not polymorphously perverse).

So, what I try to introduce in all my myth classes is the strangeness of mythic metaphors and images. My intention is to draw the student's eye down into the little moments of a text, using a selected metaphor or image as starting point of wonder at precisely what had NOT been anticipated in the reading experience: otherness. When otherness becomes, via Disney, a way of making the strange merely cute, it can be put in one's pocket and forgotten. If, however, mythic metaphor is experienced as strangely other, it lingers, it gnaws, it pulls us in: it forms what Jane Yolen (2000) calls a "landscape." Inside this landscape one can gaze at trees, as Molloy in the above epigram does, and listen attentively. One can feel the texture of the world around one rather than exist in barren space. The thesis I am trying to promote here is that the text we can re-introduce to our students is texture itself. If we can no longer get our students to enjoy the long books we enjoyed, books with thick pages and fine binding, books that one could finger and smell, then we can show our students the wonder of the small and the strange. There is where the texture of a text can be felt – but not as language; or rather, as a different kind of language. There is where the warp and weft of myth beckons.

Disney is not strange.

Seeing may no longer awaken the strange.

Let us then see with the ear, see with the nose, see with the finger, see with the tongue, see with the third eye, see with the "eyes of the background" (Mogenson, 2006a). Let us reintroduce the texture of those senses that have atrophied due to too much visual stimulation. Myth offers a landscape for the seriously strange that can reintroduce us back to our thicker, primal selves.

Still, I am dismayed that some students could not disengage themselves from Disney-fying their approach to myth, emphasizing the "funny," "cute," or "pretty" aspects of mythic stories or figures. Their final projects, too-accessible, too real, lacked what I call texture. Rather than lamenting, I am at the same time intrigued by how many students used the word "texture" or created works with thickness for their final project. By getting away from the literal, visual re-presentations of myth, it seems to me that students were reading in a more textured way. Allow me to discuss a few of the more interesting projects.

Rebecca Adkins, for instance, created a necklace out of her reading of the garden landscape Gilgamesh enters during his search for immortality. This in itself is a move to interpretive, textured reading. Rebecca used as her inspiration this passage: "Emerging from the tunnel, he found a garden dripping with leaves of lapis lazuli and blossoms of hematite, agate, carnelian, and pearls. As he strolled through this paradise, Shamash called out, 'You will never find the life for which you are searching.' Gilgamesh was undeterred" (in Hathaway, 2001, p. 282). Rebecca commented that Gilgamesh, surrounded by beauty, was unable to see it for what it was, so focused was he on his quest for immortality; just so, humans surrounded by busy-ness too often neglect what is in front of their eyes. It is as if the eyes have grown stale. And so Rebecca created a necklace surrounded by chip stones, representative of the reality of everyday life. Hanging from the stones she placed several different gems—coral, lapis lazuli, turquoise, agate and pearls—which dangle from the chips to cover the neck of the wearer. Rebecca notes that the stones are felt reminders of earthly existence. If our quest is too future-oriented we miss the here and now. Perhaps the stone necklace can be thought of as an albatross in reverse: a heavy beauty hanging around the neck that gives weight to what our seeing eyes overlook.

I must insert here that the text Rebecca used differs from the translation of the Epic of Gilgamesh I have in my library. There is only slight reference in my translation to the paradise garden and no mention whatsoever of elaborate jewels. Recall, Gilgamesh is making his way through a dark tunnel, suggestive of a dark night of the soul, and emerges in a garden landscape. My passage reads:

And at your final dawn, / son of man, you will see only/ a heap of broken images in an ascending/light that gives you sight you may not want, / for you will then behold all precious goods/ and gardens sweet as home to you, as exile, / boughs of blue, oh unforgotten gem, / as true as any other memory from any other previous life. (Jackson, 1992, p. 59)

This highly symbolic passage suggests a lot of what Rebecca intuited: Gilgamesh does not wish to see the treasures that life can offer him since he is on a quest to obliterate death. The mention of the blue bough is a special gift which is "unforgotten" but which Gilgamesh "may not want." In one of Carl Jung's dream analyses, Jung (1976a) interpreted "blue flower" as a "numinous emanation from the unconscious, showing the dreamer... the historical place where he can meet friends and brothers of like mind, where he can find the seed that wants to sprout in him, too. But the dreamer knows nothing as yet" (p. 349). Although Jung never commented on the Gilgamesh legend (that I know of), his dream interpretation is uncannily similar to what I see as Gilgamesh's ego problem. Gilgamesh sees only broken images, not the blue bough, because he has lost the seed, his soul, his other half of like mind named Enkidu. The wisdom of the myth is that Gilgamesh ultimately fails in his quest for immortality. Instead, he finds his rightful home with his unconscious self. As with all great stories, myth suggests a paradox: failing is necessary, losing is finding.

Another student, Dixie Pizani, re-created the Chinese flood/creation story of NuGua and Fuxi with her Chinese ink animation. Her work captured a key moment in the myth, when Fuxi chops a flesh ball into tiny pieces that are carried by the wind to become the seeds of humankind. Dixie wanted to give the doubling sense of fluidity, felt by the wind and the waters, wherein the waters destroy but the wind creates. Her intention was to de-literalize the story, rather than copy it. In her artist statement she wrote, "Mythology, like Chinese brush painting, is an exploration of the unconscious. It is a way to draw from the elements of everyday life and make interesting stories and symbols that can speak to us in different ways." Her animated brush painting gives the very texture of the text's idea that we are all separate but inherently linked as one. The "all" here includes the natural aswell as social worlds. Again, paradox is key.

Two other students used their skill with fabric to convey a thick understanding of mythic ideas. I say this appreciatively. Thickening, like texture, is what the alchemists called coagulation (*coagula*), the seventh or final operation of transmutation

(Burkhardt, 1974). The *coagula* refers to earth, to grounding, to deepening. Psychologically, it refers to the release of the ego from its original infantile oneness, and so it represents a poetic basis of thinking. James Hillman (1981) in his writing on alchemy explains *poesis* as a process that can both see through the literal "as fantasy and coagulate fantasy into forms" (p. 40). The process, he says, illuminates the senses, "especially the ear" (p. 27). Now this is a fascinating move, eye to ear. For the students whose projects textured the text, I do think they selected an image that "spoke" to them. What the student-artists had to do was translate the speaking text into something else, some thing that would evoke feeling. This something else is what I call making the image thick. I see these selected art projects as intentional, turning the metaphoric word or the literary image on the printed page into another form of feeling. Literary art becomes reinterpreted, thickened, by an artist's imagination and becomes a showing-forth in a new light.

Andrina Calder interpreted the meaning of the Greek Moirae (Fates) as a woven piece that represents the life cycle. She created her piece from hand spun silk, cotton, and loose fibers made from lustrous synthetic material. She used the smoother silk yarn as the warp and the uneven, lumpy cotton as weft. The result combined a visual as well as tactile contrast: smooth with rough, up with down, big with small. By weaving opposites together literally (the unplanned pattern of lumpy cotton together with a smooth over-under pattern of silk), Andrina symbolized life's paradoxes: its ups and downs, smoothes and roughs, as well as momentous events next to ordinary, daily aspects. The greatest life paradox is that we live to die. As she wrote in her Artist Statement, "I created this piece as a representation of what I think the weavings of the Fates would look like. I chose the Fates not only because they are weavers like me but because this myth attempts to explain the complex questions of life, such as why our days contain opposites and such as why we must die." Giving the piece a lustrous sheen suggested what Andrina thought of as the stars' influence from which the Fates spun their threads of life. It is as if the stars are the perceivers of the Fates' action, not the other way around. This is similar to what Noel Cobb (2006), an archetypal psychologist, observed: "To see the stars as eyes we need to stop the habit of seeing as a subjective activity. It must give way to another kind of perception—no longer looking at a thing but being seen by it" (p. 124).

Priscilla Pena's art piece overturns a common (patriarchal) perception of Medusa as a monster. Hers was a head wrap inspired by Medusa's "fabulous locks." Priscilla represented the snakes around the Gorgon head with silky cords which she intertwined, some looping around one another to give the appearance of beautiful, organic, snake-like movement. She wrote, "My unique headband, Medusa's Tangles, is intended for evening wear and will make you feel not like a monster but like a beautiful, seductive princess." By using such words as "fabulous," "organic," and "beautiful," Priscilla gives a modern feminist twist to the female "monster" and she restores the snake to its proper realm with the goddess, giver of life and death.

Two final thick projects continue my exploration of student interpretations of their mythic meanderings. Geena Abbott became interested in the quiet goddess of the Greek pantheon, Hestia, simply because she was, well, unremarkable–without story. What Geena did was create a story for her, not an elaborate 200 page manuscript, but a simple story about an imaginary encounter with a potter whom Hestia visits frequently because she loves him and she loves his art that makes beauty from mud and fire. Reading the story to us was part of the charm of Geena's presentation, since she so obviously felt the story through her rendition. What impressed me, too, was the book she made: big, with heavy pages and ashy smell. She wrote, "I wished to give a little jolt to the imagination of the reader. People should touch and smell the book, wonder why it contains burnt splotches, engage it with the senses so that the imagination can set sail." Geena's invitation is what Eve Sedgwick (2003) means, I think, by the belonging-together of touching and feeling, which has less to do with what Sedgwick terms "close reading" or "thick description" than with a deeper pedagogy: an intimacy between textures and emotions (pp. 17, 21).

Ginette Paris (1991), a noted Jungian scholar, has written about Hestia's significance: "The name 'Hestia' did not only signify the central hearth containing the fires of the household or the city. It also designated the center of the earth, which, according to Greek beliefs, contained our planet's fire" (p. 174). Another scholar, Professor Stephanie Demetrakopoulos, (1979) wrote, "Hestia is the murky origins out of which we each issue and which always remain curiously unknown to us. She is the heat, the hearth, the center we live—and forget—in our daily rounds" (p. 73).What is so intriguing to me about students' interpretations is their intuiting the finer points of those stories with which they engage without necessarily reading the experts— simply staying with image and metaphor. I credit Geena's deep connection with Hestia as an understanding of the empowering of place, felt in hearth, fire, and home. But more: Geena realized that Hestia belongs to earth, not sky. Earth is home. Geena's book, made from fibers and twigs, brings back the feeling of earth in her tribute to Hestia. We must remember the preciousness of our planet home, its ashy material substance, suffering now from catastrophic oil and gas spills. Ecological disasters reflect what post-natural literatures fear: environmental apocalypse brought on by human waste, greed, and overpopulation. Chicksaw poet Linda Hogan's (1995) work is based on the grounded belief in an intertwining of homeplace and identity; when this belief is ignored, not only land but people, too, suffer.

Finally, Rodrigo Mitma turned his idea of a mythic project outside in, literally, as he presented his Box. Based on the myth of Theseus in the labyrinth, Rodrigo's Box was fitted with a dark cloth and six speakers. The Box was to be inserted over the head of a "victim," who would experience the labyrinth as perhaps Theseus did: alone and in the dark. Faced thus with only the imagination, a "victim" enters a dimension of his or her own mind. Seeing becomes de-literalized, since the Box forces the sense of sound emanating from the speakers to take precedence over the sense of sight. As Rodrigo wrote in his Artist Statement: "All of what Theseus "saw" and heard could have been solely in his head. His mind could have created the twists and turns of the maze and even of the Minotaur itself. Like the labyrinth, the human mind has twists and turns, is dark, and is not explored deeply enough. Furthermore, the beast, or human instinct, lies trapped within, but must be encountered if one is to be a hero (a full and complete human)." The students who volunteered to experience the Box were significantly disoriented, literally a-mazed. I am wondering if such is what the Misfit meant when, at the end of Flannery O'Connor's (1978)

"A Good Man is Hard to Find," he says, after killing the old grandmother, "She would of been a good woman if it had been somebody there to shoot her every minute of her life" (p. 133). The Box, like a gunshot to the head, blasts away the usual props of perception so as to usher edgy readiness in. Theseus, of course, was able to follow Ariadne's thread in order to escape the labyrinth; perhaps, one could argue, to escape finding his true labyrinthine self which resides together-with the part-man, part-bull Minotaur. This puts me in mind of Nietzsche's poem (1984):

Be wise, Ariadne!...

You have little ears, you have ears like mine:

Let some wisdom into them!—

Must we not first hate ourself if we are to love

Ourself?...

I am thy labyrinth. (p. 59)

The labyrinthine self hears what others do not, because sight is denied. The twists of the maze are necessary to break with everydayness, to hear differently, to experience what the alien world has to offer, its pre-human monsters. I credit my student with opening fellow students' ears to these possibilities.

Experimenting with other-sensory ways to appreciate the texts of the world has been the focus of my discussion of student works. Art students, usually eye-oriented, are able to manipulate their understanding of image and metaphor, taken from myth, to produce new textures from the text. Their work shows the fabric of their understandings, the texture of their ideas. This is an old sense, pre-Cartesian, of a world that entwines the boundaries of human with nonhuman, word with matter, metaphor with material form. "Art," writes novelist Amy Tan (2006) "despises placidity and smooth surfaces" (p. 44). Just so. And this artistic endeavor for my students involves the hand, just as we the audience (hearer) and spectator (viewer) are encouraged to leave our eyes and ears behind when we touch the art object, feel the thickening between text and texture. Gaston Bachelard (1971) writes that hands "dream." "Between the hand and the things, a whole psychology unfolds.... For things, as for souls, the mystery is inside" (p. 72). My students are in good company.

Writers and theorists today are increasingly engaged with the way living in the post-human, post-literary world offers challenges but also opportunities, both. How to read the world as text is the issue, and how to get beyond the limitations of sight is the challenge. Pulitzer Prize writer Paul Harding (2009) offers readers the strange opportunity to experience what an epileptic named Howard feels during seizure and what Howard's son George experiences days and hours before he dies. Without romanticizing illness, Harding's characters exist in a "between" state that opens them to energies not available to ordinary perception. Such disorientation of normalcy allows Howard, the epileptic, a sort of Nietzschean mad-wise in-sight. It is as if Howard becomes possessed of an astral spirit that turns all the senses inside out, snaps open the synapses of his brain, and allows visitation by the "star-gushing universe" which is usually obscured by "the curtains and doors of this world." In his frenzied state Howard "tasted the raw stuff of the cosmos" (p. 47) and smelled the "mineral smell of cold, raw green" (p. 60). In an instant, Howard acquired an eco-imaginal awareness of time, space, and matter. "My goodness," Howard thinks, "I am made from planets and wood, diamonds and orange peels, now and then, here and there; the iron in my blood was once the blade of a Roman plow.... and the only thing common to all of this is that I feel sorrow so deep, it must be love" (p. 136). Howard could be a modern day alchemist whose fantasy insights into earth's matter give him rare access to secret recesses of his own consciousness. He would also seem to be a literary representation of what Jungian analyst Jerome Bernstein (2005) termed "Borderland Personality," distinct from borderline personality, because of inhabiting a psychic space that interconnects human and environmental realms.

Harding's experiment with other nonrational ways of being in the world is both post-human and pre-scientific. Curriculum theorist John Weaver (2010) explains the post-human as an enhancement of natural capabilities as well as an extension of the physical body, including the mind. "When one enters into the ranks of the post-human their relationship to the world and themselves changes" (p. 13), he comments. Weaver could be providing a gloss on Harding's text when he writes about the radical transformation of aesthetic sensibilities felt by the post-human: "Aesthetically, the post-human condition is marked by the explosion of the frame and the digitalization or dematerialization of the image" (p. 14). Nor is the text left out of the equation of human with new media forms. "With the advent of biotechnology, biosciences, and digital imagery," Weaver asserts, "the craftsperson (now referred as the computer programmer or software developer) has been reunited with the artist (the graphic designer, bioinformatics reader, laboratory technician, medical doctor, digital artist and geneticist). Because of technology, poesis has returned" (pp. 30–31). These claims by a curriculum theorist counter the pessimism of literary formalists who read "text" narrowly. But by no means can curriculum theory be sanguine about reading texts if, as Weaver observes, the texts that matter, readerly texts, are being supplanted by textbooks. He writes, "The textbook is the valet parking of higher education" (p. 114). Too easy. Too tedious. Too linear. Too Vapid, Boring, Uninteresting, Stupid. A handing over of the keys to someone else, as Weaver puts it (p. 114).

Paul Harding gives the reader an entirely Other experience. He offers an accounting of the post-human condition sparked by epilepsy, a disorder that undoes the perceived order of things with a sort of x-ray vision into the interiority of the world. The explosion of the nervous system is like sparks that ignite fusion with the cosmos. If this sounds impossibly strange, so does the literature of alchemy. Earlier, I invoked this pre-science to offer a way to suggest what the student artist can do with myth. Those early scientists believed that metal, heated over long periods of time, would release its properties to reveal the Soul of the World. This World Soul was the language with which all things communicated (Coelho, 1998). Like the alchemists of early times, I like to think of my student artists working on a selected metaphor or image as prime matter, from which they will extract the gold. Through various operations (as the alchemists termed their process) the text-matter is manipulated, whirled, digitized into another form.

Such sym-pathy between object and imagination has a long history from Paracelsus, a sixteenth century Swiss alchemist, onward. Paracelsus wrote of the astral spirit, invisible to the naked eye but dwelling in nature, animals, and humans (in Mogenson, 2006a, p. 54). This indwelling of sparks or stars appeared to the alchemist's unconscious mind and worked on his imagination to reveal his mysterious participation between organic and inorganic form. The "work" was the process of analogy-making, which is Wordsworth's (1805/2008) "inward meaning," of rock, fruit, or flower to which the poet ascribed "feeling"; or Carl Jung's (1963) "ray of relation" with all things in a unified cosmos. Emerson (1836/2008), a nineteenth century Transcendentalist, explains:

> If the Reason be stimulated to a more earnest vision, outlines and surfaces become transparent, and are no longer seen; causes and spirits are seen through them. (p. 64)

I have used the words "texture," "thick," and "twist" together with the words "strange" and "other" to suggest a relation that exists between a very strange metaphor or image and its thickening of thought inside an artist's imagination. "Thought" has been described as a "spark." Reading the image involves more-than sight, since the pieces I have selected by students require touch, smell, and hearing. Indeed, I have been faulting sight. Sight is the tyranny that has prevented a thickening of artistic imagination: what is other and strange cannot be easily assimilated into a catalogue of familiar knowns. I have been suggesting that, like pre-scientists, student artists intuit that what one touches can introduce dimensions of feeling that imply interconnectedness among opposites in new, twisting ways. This is mythic through and through. Myth is the world of both/and. Myth twists logic. Myth and paradox are sisters. "How wonderful we have met with paradox," physicist Niels Bohr has said. "Now we have some hope of making progress" (in Kaku, 2008, p. 53).

And so, like dream, myth allows a synesthetic approach: we can hear metaphor and see ideas and smell words and touch feeling. My interest with small pieces of text is to encourage a dwelling in small spaces, like an alchemist's vessel, where the few words that make up the metaphor can be trammeled and pummeled until they coagulate. The artist then can release the product to our experience for our re-imagining. As James Hillman (1979) wittily puts it, "To restore our earth to a ground in creative imagination we must re-imagine the creation. To recover imagination we must first restore the preposterous sea-monsters and every winged fowl and every thing that creepeth" (p. 142).

Does this restoration process answer the problems of reading texts? Does the recovered imagination include the wires and pixels of new technology? The answer is a qualified Yes. Students are reading in new ways, concentrating on image rather than narration. This does not mean students are not reading; they are reading differently. They must halt, stop, make haste slowly (an alchemical slogan) if they are to attend to the otherness of the image. Of course, this is a different rhythm from what cyberspace demands. The cyberworld has not found sufficient depth beneath its glittering surface; whereas, the textured world requires reflection. The speed of the cyber world has made its junkies jumpy. But the two rhythms need not be oppositional. And if given sufficiently daring pieces with seriously strange images, students will/might/should see the texture in the text and listen to its voices.

ONCE BELOW A TIME[1]

Writers in the Mythic Mode

What is it to write "in the mythic mode"? Looking back over the chapter headings of this book, I suggest that some writers through time from all corners of the Earth have had the sense that trees breathe, the cosmos speaks, memory has both an ear and an eye; that small is smaller than imagined, and that birthings occur in wombs other than in human form. Certainly, too, myth abounds with shape changes. And perhaps that is a central understanding of myth: the ever-on-goingness of life forms, the constant occurrence of change. As we now understand from quantum physics, changes can be brought about on an object simply through the act of observation. One of the most mythic domains of size is that which cannot be seen, the picometers existent in the microworld (Smith, 2009) — even the cells within our human bodies. AND, these cells belong to the cosmos, science tells us, as myth already knew. We contain within our own flesh the remnants of hydrogen atoms that are fourteen billion years old! What this means, as Matthew Fox (2006) explains, is that our ancestors are "stars, atoms, galaxies and rocks; our ancestors are carbon, oxygen, hydrogen and helium; our ancestors are fishes and primates, sun and moon" (p. 71).

To read these sentences with disbelief is a good thing. Belief has always been the bug-a-boo of wisdom. To be disillusioned by these ideas is a good thing too. Illusion has been the prop of belief, and beliefs have caused us to put on our stalking boots. Writers in the mythic mode are the ones who embrace comedy with a capital C, writing stories that show us the aliveness of life, including death. Mythic writers write texts full of hardship, color, shape, dialogue, love in multiple as well as diverse forms. There is the sense that all things rise and fall, wind and circle back, always with verbal awareness, the –ing in motion. Writers in the mythic mode confuse students, which is why, precisely why, we should teach writers in the mythic mode so as to disillusion the next generation from their too-secure mooring in knowledges that are not wise or in faith that is mounted in stone. Flannery O'Connor (1980) once said, "The thought of everyone lolling about in an emotionally satisfying faith is repugnant to me" (p. 100). Exactly. We don't want our students to be jellyfish.

An early mythic writer, of course, was Ovid. How I love my Ovid. He is so subversive, writing always about love, tweaking the great emperor Augustus, who was trying to establish Christianity as the official belief system to a peoples long familiar with paganism. No wonder Ovid was banished from Italy. Not only did Ovid's *Metamorphoses* (8 CE) write against the heroic tradition of *The Aeneid* and *The Odyssey*, whose purpose was to glorify male dominance, but he also wrote in a surprisingly postmodern way. His stories intertwine with one another rather than narrate a nice sequence of action. His characters are not just emotional, like the pouting Achilles; they are not concerned with morality. Daughters fall in love with fathers, boys with boys, boys with animals. Trees bear beautiful, beautiful boys; women go mad; fathers fasten daughters to cliffs at the edge of the world. These are the motifs from Greek myths, of course. But Ovid wove these early tales in such a way that the stories become little nuggets of amazement that speak back and forth with one another. These stories exercise our fantasy and jolt our imagination.

Another postmodern trait of Ovid is his use of juxtaposition. Beautiful images re-act with the grotesque; mild stories are placed next to stories of torture. The world of normalcy is thrown out the window. Indeed, the window, long a symbol in modern literature as the place from which to glimpse an Other, becomes in Ovid the idea of the portal. Nature contains portals, humans contain portals, and the natural world offers portals to what lies buried beyond, below, or beside.

These "postmodern" moves of Ovid reflect a feminine sensibility. Much of mytho-logy, especially early pre-Olympian Greek mythology and the mythologies of the Celts and Native Americans, share a matriarchal mindset. This would be the sensibility that does not care much for morality or for opposition or for clarity. It is a sensibility that re-cognizes the vastness of human interiority, a wildness: a wildness that lies beyond the pale in the territory of the unknown. This would be a sensibility that appre-hends a livingness beneath surfaces, contained in such punning word combinations as Beckett's felicitous "*Stirrings Still.*" A gloss of that pun might be J.M. Coetzee's (1999) observation that because sense-images are fleeting, they stir what lies buried "more deeply in the soil of memory" (p. 22).

Unlike postmodern writers, the Modernist writers sought to counter the lack of a center in the fall-apart world after World War I by seeking unity through a return to classical myth. We could say that Joyce and Eliot and Shaw are writers in the classical mythic mode. D. H. Lawrence's primitivism, Yeats' mysticism, and "A.E's" religious vision all share, too, in Modernist mythic ideas such as the quest pattern, particularly. But I would argue that the classical mode is itself paternalistic, favoring clarity and linear progression, conquest and conclusion. What is mythic, but not classically so, can be felt in Ovid's opening invocation, which if kept alive in the inner ear can serve as a guide for reading writers in the mythic mode:

Now I shall tell of things that change, a new being

Out of old: since you, O Gods, created

Mutable arts and gifts, give me the voice

To tell the shifting story of the world

From its beginning to the present hour. (2001, p. 31)

I propose to discuss three writers whom I consider mythic but not necessarily post-modern. In my discussion I will move from texts that are accessible to those barely accessible in terms of the level of difficulty each writer presents. Myths, after all, are not meant for children, although with bright enough pictures and simplified story lines myths can be appealingly gory to naïve readers. What I see in the writers that I nominate is an interest in mystery. Their texts fascinate and resonate, as do myths. They cannot be analyzed easily and in some cases seek to elude analysis altogether, preferring to let the images do the work. Indeed, mystery and myth share important characteristics. Myth: "a story usually concerning some supernatural being or some alleged person or event, with or without a determinable basis of fact." Mystery: "anything kept secret or remains unexplained or unknown; any truth unknowable except by divine revelation" (Webster).

Flannery O'Connor, Eudora Welty, and Samuel Beckett might seem an odd threesome but are writers whom I will consider for introducing prose that, though written in English, seems to access other languages altogether, as if speaking from another older place: below the text. I select three, not four writers, not six or two writers, because of the power of three to suggest interplay and connection, as per Ovid's stories. I choose writers whose texts offer what I consider to be an interesting juxtaposition of themes, again in the manner of Ovid. And these writers are all committed to the mystery of life on Earth.

Flannery O'Connor wrote what I call serious comedy, as Dante's *Divine Comedy* is serious, taking us on a journey from *inferno*, into *purgatorio*, through to *paradisio*. Writing as a Catholic writer, she embraces the mystery of God's grace, which she says eludes formula (in Fitzgerald and Fitzgerald, 1981, p. 153). I see her writing against orthodox Christian Catholicism when she chooses as her typical protagonist the pious believer. O'Connor hated piety. She says the pious character has "reduced his conception of the supernatural to pious cliché and has become able to recognize nature in literature in only two forms, the sentimental and the obscene" (in Fitzgerald and Fitzgerald, 1981, p. 147). O'Connor goes on to argue that it is "the business of the serious writer to writer dangerous fiction for believers, while it is the business of the church to protect believers from dangerous fiction" (p. 149). Anyone who has read O'Connor knows where she is going with this distinction, since violence is so much a part of her plots. But like a blow to the blades during zazen ('kyosaku'), the act of violence or "breaking through" serves to awaken imaginations deadened by belief. Mystery, as she conceives it, is not kind and not simple. It is found, she goes so far to say "in territory held largely by the devil" (in Fitzgerald and Fitzgerald, 1981, p. 118).

O'Connor's themes borrow from St. Augustine. She recalls reading his notion of God's pouring forth the things of this world in a double way: "intellectually into the minds of the angels and physically into the world of things" (in Fitzgerald & Fitzgerald, 1981, p. 128). The visible world reflects for her the invisible mystery, which she calls God. Religion in its root meaning is *re-ligio*, linking back. The linking is between now and what was back then, a *then* that myth inhabits and mystery reveals.

Flannery O'Connor's comedy, besides being divine, is hilarious. Her people, pious churchgoers and Bible thumpers, are unrepentant bigots—drawn from the "Christ-haunted" rural South (in Fitzgerald and Fitzgerald, 1981, p. 44). Their focus is narrow. They read the Bible but do not understand Matthew's gospel: "And why beholdest thou the mote that is in thy brother's eye, but considerest not the beam that is in thine own eye?" (7:2–3). Her characters cast judgment on others in the hypocritical notion that they themselves lack fault. What I see her doing is addressing the problem of belief. Belief has hardened the heads and hearts of her protagonists.

When struck, literally, in the head, or pierced, literally, in the heart, the protagonist has a sudden epiphany, able to see differently; that is, to see through to that which before had been invisible. Fiction, she says, "leaves us, like Job, with a renewed sense of mystery" (in Fitzgerald and Fitzgerald, 1981, p. 184).

This idea is put to the test with a difficult little story called "A Good Man is Hard to Find." While this is a journey story, it is not a quest: it does not end in triumph in any usual understanding of that word, and it insists on a mingling of opposites. The characters are enclosed in a car, which serves as a kind of waiting room or purgatory for the protagonist grandmother who, unbeknownst to her, will have her entire belief system turned upside down. The literal becomes symbolical when the car does indeed turn upside down, landing in a gulch far, far away from civilization. There, the family meets an escaped convict called The Misfit. And there, the convict becomes the angel in disguise, delivering to the grandmother her sudden bliss. In the territory of the devil, so to speak, sudden understanding occurs.

What is typical about an O'Connor story is the manner of illumination. Always, there is violence, a shattering in the manner of apocalypse, which is an extraordinary event that breaks apart what before had been taken as one's entire world view. Eileen Gregory (1995) explains: "Apocalypse is an uncovering or unveiling of a mystery which is hidden or obscured in time.... It reveals to us, as John's vision does, the old and the new, the old which is being destroyed, the new coming into creation" (pp. 145, 146). Another O'Connor feature surrounding the illuminating moment is the deliverer of this new knowledge, the "angel," in an unrecognizable form. For O'Connor, the angel can be a convict, a con man, a wild animal, a hurled book, a fierce bird. It is important to feature the "angel" as an Other since he comes from an Other sphere of experience altogether and delivers a message unknown perhaps even to himself. The absolute foreignness of the angel's presence turns upside down the sense of an interpreted world. Following Augustine, O'Connor shows us what lies beneath the visible world of things is the invisible world of divine mystery. But to apperceive this other world requires that the chosen one (the protagonist) receive a blow to the head and a removal of the mote.

The eye as portal to new awareness changes for the protagonist in many O'Connor stories, symbolic of new seeing. In "Everything that Rises Must Converge" the mother's eye becomes "unmoored" (O'Connor, 1978, p. 382). In "The Enduring Chill," the "last film of illusion was torn as if by a whirlwind from [Asbury's] eyes" (O'Connor, 1978, p. 382). In "Good Man," O'Connor tells us The Misfit's eyes are "red-rimmed and pale" (1978, p. 132), as if he has suffered much, perhaps like the grandmother from the mote that is stuck in his eye. Their eyes reflect each other in obverse, just as his Christ-dominated sentences spin off her clichés about social standing. The grandmother sees The Misfit's face as like that of one of her own children. If this abomination of society is kin to her, with all her mannerisms of propriety and niceness, then what does this imply? The two are opposite sames. When the grandmother has a sudden re-cognition of The Misfit as like herself, she gains immediate insight into a secret chamber of his heart—and of hers. They are both children of Christ, but from two different directions; he is a much an outcast from society as she would seem to be its central player. Both are misfits in their capacity for grace in a commodified world: he as the unwitting angel of grace, she as the receptacle. Thus, protagonist and antagonist are symbolically connected, "joined," O'Connor tells us, "by ties of kinship which have their roots deep in the mystery she had been merely prattling about so far" (in Fitzgerald and Fitzgerald, 1981, p. 112).

This amazing revelation comes to O'Connor's protagonist-grandmother at the moment of her death: the Misfit without remorse shoots her on the spot three times. The horror of this act is immediately linked to a description of the dying grandmother as a reborn child whose vision once clouded by prejudgment and hauteur is erased: she "half sat and half lay in a puddle of blood with her legs crossed under her like a child's and her face smiling up at the cloudless sky" (O'Connor, 1978, p. 132). Open to the universe in a cloudless sky, the death is a beatific return to the innocence of childhood and the emptying out of ego. No clouds, no thoughts, no judgments, no false icons, no self: just the smile of a return to innocence and bliss. This is her state outside the "woods." Her outside position is what has separated her from her own son and his family, indicating that she, too, has become a misfit in a world of false pretensions. At the very end, she sheds her illusions; in her dis-illusionment she finds the mystery of the divine.

A familiar O'Connor motif is that of the Technicolored landscape, which I interpret as the natural world infused with divinity. In "Good Man" color dominates the imagery even in the smallest details: Bailey reads from the orange sports section of the paper; June Star has a yellow head; the grandmother has a blue hat with white violets and wears a spray of purple cloth violets; the vista out of the car window as the family makes its way to Florida (Flora-da) contains blue granite, red clay banks streaked with purple, green lace-work on the ground, and trees that sparkle with silver-white sunlight. The predominance of the color purple suggests the Christian color of passion, both of suffering and of deep feeling. When one suffers and feels deeply, one experiences divine love which surpatheth understanding. While she is a simple-minded woman who thinks only in black and white terms, the grandmother inhabits, unknowingly, a graced landscape. As O'Connor puts it, "As to natural grace, we have to take it the way it comes—through nature. In any case, it operates surrounded by evil" (in Ellsberg, 2003). Surrounded thus, the grandmother is the character whose outlook will change.

This surreal world of nature is the mythic aspect of O'Connor's work, in my view. Rather than mythic trees that birth forth babes, stones that speak, or stalks that grow into penises, the O'Connor natural world is infused with color to suggest, as myth does, that there is another reality surrounding the human realm with its own illuminations. If the deities in myth act in mysterious and violent ways, O'Connor's deity acts through the sun (pun intended) in an ethereal sky. In "The Temple of the Holy Ghost" the sun is "like an elevated Host drenched in blood" (O'Connor, 1978, p. 248). In "The Enduring Chill" it is "like some strange potentate from the east... rising beyond the black woods" (O'Connor, 1978, p. 357), and in "Greenleaf" the sun is "like a silver bullet ready to drop into [Mrs. May's] brain" (O'Connor, 1978, p. 325). The natural world takes an active part in awakening human consciousness, just as in myth, nature's shifts and metamorphoses express the natural world as pulsating and alive.

"Greenleaf" is my favorite story of O'Connor's probably because I see it as her most overtly mythic. In the act of writing it, she summarized the plot as about a woman "aged 63" who will be gored by a bull. "I am not convinced yet that this is purgation or whether I identify myself with her or the bull. In any case, it is going to take some doing to do it and it may be the risk that is making me happy" (in Fitzgerald and Fitzgerald, 1981, p. 129). The backstory to the goring is that a roaming bull has invaded Mrs. May's pasture and is so threatening to her that she wants her hired hand Mr. Greenleaf to shoot it with a bullet. But as we have seen, the bullet becomes the sun in the sky which, like the invader bull, singles her out for the killing. Eventually, the sun and the bull win, with the story ending in what can only be described as an ecstatic embrace of bull in the lap of woman.[2]

Clearly, this is no ordinary bull. He is described as being "silvered" and having a wreath on his horns (O'Connor, 1978, p. 311), as being "a patient god come down to woo her" (p. 311) and as containing an aura that emits a pink glow that fills Mrs. May's window (p. 311). His wooing takes place at dawn, just as a new day is awakening and as Mrs. May herself is in a state of waking consciousness. In her dream she hears "a steady rhythmic chewing as if something were eating one wall of the house" (p. 311). Here is penetration through the portal of the ear. Gradually, she arises and like a reluctant bride in her green rubber curlers and nightgown, she waits by the window.

The bull as manifestation of the divine is an idea familiar to myth. Celtic, Egyptian, Mesopotamian cultures all had divine bulls. The Indo-European Thunder God was a bull. The goddess cultures of Northern and Eastern Europe worshipped the bull, considered to be a power animal that contained the massive life force. Isis and Hathor of Egyptian culture were pictured having bull horn headdresses containing the solar disk, representing the womb cradled in the light of life. The bull was often sacrificed to honor the gods and show respect. Classic Greek myth contains the familiar story of Zeus taking the form of a bull in order to rape Europa. These powerful mythic images cannot be sentimentalized. The move from bull to lamb, with Christian iconography of Jesus the shepherd, Lamb of God who takes away the sins of the world, does sentimentalize the animal and turns the god into a scapegoat for human error. The Christian lamb is tame, not demanding. But gods, far from being tame, know that their divine radiance casts unbearable light, since they are truly awe-full, full of awe.

According to one Purana of Hindu myth, the divine bull was born from the right side of Vishnu, the Hindu preserver god. The bull's name, Nandi, meaning "joyful," expressed joy in primal stages, especially sexuality. Vishnu, as preserver, is also destroyer of life on earth when one great age moves to the next, becoming morally corrupt. Then Vishnu shape- changes into the destroyer god Shiva-Rudra, whose destruction of life forms allows the cosmic slate to be wiped clean so that the world can be created anew. He will usher, in one night in the life of the world, a period lasting as long as the day. First he will enter the sun's rays and intensify them, and then the three worlds of heaven, earth, and the underworld will burn up from the intense heat (Rosenberg, 1994, p. 329). This apocalyptic scenario is myth's way of rebirthing the earth, of revolutionizing human consciousness, and of providing opportunity to start over, anew.

The prevalence of the sun's intensities in "Greenleaf," as well as the long night of the bull's chewing, might be O'Connor's rewriting of the Hindu myth. The sense of apocalypse in both stories provides a mythic and religious basis for the necessary destruction of false beliefs. That a new epoch is about to come is imaged in many O'Connor stories by a treeline or a line of dark woods that, in my view, serves to separate the two Augustinian worlds of ordinary time from eternal time. That both worlds are present but not perceived is the point of the stories: human eye-ear-heart portals need to be forced open if the whole universe is to be seen without division. The opening of the portals is the emptying out of the ego, necessary "lest the habits of a lifetime reassert themselves and close in once more" (Batchelor, 1997, p. 80).

Flannery O'Connor's comedy is difficult, like her theme. As David Miller (1995) writes, "[Genuine comedy] is challenging assumptions, testing limits, crossing boundaries, disabusing any public of its most firmly held beliefs" (p. 71). O'Connor hits us over the head; Eudora Welty, on the other hand, soothes. O'Connor takes Christian belief by the horns and gores it; Eudora Welty surprises in her mix of myth and religion. The gracefulness of Welty's style together with her childlike characters awakens our own remembrances of things past, long forgotten. The differences between these two Southern writers are instructive, I think, for seeing how myth enriches storytelling.

Perhaps a most telling difference between Flannery O'Connor and Eudora Welty is their sense of mystery. O'Connor's emanates from an Augustinian understanding of a hidden divinity that reveals itself by physical force when bidden, smashing to bits all oppositions and separations. Welty's, like her entire style, is mythic in a subtler way in that it arises from within any given circumstance and is recognized by stillness. In Welty's stories, stillness is the center point around which the mystery circles. Too, Welty sees magic in the number three, which, like the childlike quality of her characters, reflects something of a fairytale three. Her characters often come in sets of two, but the third element offsets the dualism; three keeps the energy moving, quietly in the stillness.

"Livvie" is the story I prefer to teach, rather than the highly anthologized "The Worn Path." The latter, a journey story, arouses no curiosity or joy in my students, who imagine themselves superior to the text because they "get" the journey motif and they find Phoenix (whose mythic resemblance to the phoenix bird they also "get') childish in the extreme. My students rise above the text but they do not soar. I can outline the various hurdles in the old woman's journey—the thorny bush, the black dog and the hunter, the condescending city folk. Students get it. But what they don't "get" is the old woman's child-wonder side, as when she reaches up into an imaginary cloud and accepts an imaginary piece of marble cake. They are annoyed, frankly, that Phoenix stoops to steal a nickel, although they can "explain" it. But do they see the description Welty offers at the moment of the stealing, a still moment? "Her fingers slid down and along the ground under the piece of money with the grace and care they would have in lifting an egg from under a setting hen" (1979, p. 64).

"Livvie," on the other hand, can offer teachable moments, possibly because Livvie's age is closer to that of my students and because of the quieter mix of fairytale and mythic motifs. The story concerns a young black innocent who is selected by a very old black man named Solomon to be his wife/possession. He takes her off to a cabin in the depths of the Old Natchez Trace to possess her as his own, and there he keeps her very well (in his pumpkin shell). As with "Path," Welty plays with the opposites of old age and young age, in this case clearly signaled by the two main characters. But what is more nuanced is that Livvie, while naïve and in whose voice Welty writes, is a child of the Trace. As such, she, not Solomon, contains natural wisdom, which in Welty's view is the heartbeat of life. Livvie has the wisdom to know when to keep the stillness and when to allow the stillness to become quickened. Hovering over the story of this imprisoned "princess" is the lure of life beyond the doorframe. One day a third character appears, as if by magic. Upon his entrance into the house of the dying old man, the inside stillness takes on new life and all the imprisoned spirits are let free.

Welty describes the old man's house, using the vocabulary of the innocent bride, Livvie. The house is "nice" and contains objects that are "always" sitting there; outside in the yard is a bottle tree, groomed by Solomon himself against spirits coming into the house. Welty's understanding of folk culture is referenced by the bottle tree: "Livvie knew that there could be a spell put in trees, and she was familiar from the time she was born with the way bottle trees kept evil spirits from coming into the house" (1979, p. 157). What the old man, with his symbolic watch ever by his side, does not know is that the spirits cannot be kept away forever nor are they necessarily evil. Specifically, what cannot be kept away from his young obedient bridewife is her desire to love rather than to obey. But because she is a "nice" girl, Livvie honors the deathlike stillness that Solomon requires:

> She could keep from singing when she ironed, and to sit by a bed and fan away the flies, she could be so still she could not hear herself breathe. She could clean up the house and never drop a thing, and wash the dishes without a sound, and she would step outside to churn, for churning sounded too sad to her, like sobbing. (1979, p. 158)

This story reads like a variant on the fairytale motif of the imprisoned princess in a chamber. Like "Rumpelstiltskin," naming is significant, reflecting a folk belief in the interdependence of name and identity (Opie and Opie, 1980, p. 253). Livvie cannot come into her name, which sounds like "living," so long as she is watcher and preventer of death; so long as she maintains a deathlike stillness in the chamber of her house. The power of her name will only be released with the entrance of a magical third character, who will also release the spirits bottled up in the bottle tree.

Livvie moves in her mind with the seasons, so that when winter ends she feels "the stir of spring close to her" (Welty, 1979, p. 160). This will be the coming back to her of her real youthfulness. The "livvie"ness of life is expressed outside the house in the landscape of color, the noises of the field folk coming to till the earth, the sight of food prepared and still growing in the ground, the overflowing streams, children running, and birds rushing. Everything outside expresses the great still wheel of life:

> High above everything, the wheel of fields, house, and cabins, and the deep road surrounding like a moat to keep them in, was the turning sky.... And

sound asleep while all this went around him that was his, Solomon was like a little still spot in the middle. (1979, 160)

Welty shows us two conceptions of stillness. One is the stillness of Solomon, with his watch, his possessions, and his chronic oldness. His is the stillness of death in the middle of life that holds back the flow. The other stillness is of the silent wheel of the seasons, promising new life every seasonal change. Always. Death can either bottle up life in a cold stillness, or it can be the energy that powers life, still to this day. For Welty, the mystery of death *intertwined* with life is a central understanding. That is the mystery. Consider that many opposites that are a typical signifier of Welty's themes: inner and outer rooms, male and female, age and youth, winter and spring, wisdom and innocence, silly and serious, city and country; as long as these opposites remain static, no livingness can occur. Something, a medium for the activity, must break death's absolute stillness and the oppositions that hold firm. Welty has said, "Brutal or lovely, the mystery waits for people wherever they go, whatever extreme they run to" (1979, p. 10). Livvie, whose psychological depth and complexity of character far outweigh her seeming simpleness, feels the mystery of spring and allows it to free her from death's thrall.

The third character who breaks up the opposition of Livvie and Solomon is Cash, a field hand, who is more like an elf or harlequin figure of fairy or folk tale. Cash represents the wealth of exuberance. His appearance is at the right moment, supporting Welty's view that timing is everything in terms of what we can be open to in life. "It might be, if he had not appeared the way he did appear that day," Welty writes in "Livvie," "she would never have looked so closely at him, but the time people come makes a difference" (1979, p. 165). So there he arises, seemingly from out of nowhere, a vision: he has pointed shoes, peg-top pants, leaf-green coat, baby-pink satin shirt, round hat "the color or a plum," and feather, "emerald green, blowing in the spring winds" (p. 165). This unlikely character is made even more peculiar by his carrying a guinea pig in his pocket. He laughs, is insolent by kicking flowers and smashing bottles on the bottle tree; and he is impish, taking three jumps to be by Livvie's side.

Cash reminds me of Conrad's harlequin in *Heart of Darkness*, who also appears as out of nowhere. This time, in the jungle, the unnamed figure wears a multi-patched coat of colors, like a map of Europe, with patches of blue, red, yellow, orange, and purple. Conrad (1986) writes of the harlequin, "His very existence was improbable, inexplicable, and altogether bewildering. He was an insoluble problem ... and there he was gallantly, thoughtlessly alive, to all appearance indestructible solely by the virtue of his few years and of his unreflective audacity" (p. 91). In both cases, the mysterious stranger defies a death-filled backdrop. Indeed, Harlequin is an old world figure, an archetype of ambiguity and spiritual freedom (Willeford, 1969, p. 325). His silly appearance makes a carnival of life, reminding us that chaos is just around the corner when we least expect it, smashing to bits the shards of our comfort. Just so with Cash. He comes into the inner room from the larger, wider outside world, bringing spring into winter and life into death. Inside the stillness of the room, Cash and Livvie view the dying man, who could so easily be brought to his death quickly by the downward blow of the interloper. But that does not happen. Solomon's face is fragile and ancient and "illuminated." Dying ebbing into death is seen as an illumination, "like a small boat in the wake of a large one," as Welty (1979) expressed it elsewhere (p. 30).

The stillness enhances the room at that moment, becoming a "gathering-spot of all that has been felt, is about to be experienced," Welty (1979) writes (p. 7). As long as the old man holds tight to his thralldom, living as a dead man, the oppositions hold firm. The final scene in the inner room is particularly poignant, then, when the old man releases his death grip by dying. His illuminated face expresses the mystery of death as its own *kind* of enlivener. Then, paradoxically, the stillness of the illuminated face is the passing moment of death into a deeper life, an acceptance of this deeper life, and a release of the power of death to re-energize life. Then, the circle of life rewinds itself as the old man dies and the young couple quicken the silence by moving "around and around the room and into the brightness of the open door" (1979, p. 170).

It is easy to miss Eudora Welty's profound mythic awareness, I think, because her characters seem from another planet. Perhaps that is the point. Their outrageous attire and childlike simplicity are unlike the way characters are "supposed" to behave. But there are no "supposed to's" in Welty's world nor in the world of myth. She celebrates the exuberance that life offers in the characters that seem born from swamp wisdom. The Natchez Trace is the setting for many of her short stories, the "place" (Pinar, 1991) that lends itself to her vision: "It is through place," she writes, "that we put our roots, wherever birth, chance, fate, or our traveling selves set us down; but where those roots reach toward ... is the deep and running vein, eternal and consistent and everywhere purely itself—that feeds and is fed by the human understanding" (1979, p. 7).

The last story that summarizes what I hope to suggest about the mystery of Welty's stillness is aptly titled "A Still Moment." Unlike most of her other stories, this one focuses on murder. She had written before of murder, specifically recounting in her imagination the mind of the man who murdered Medgar Evans in the '60s. About him she wrote, "Whoever the murderer is, I know him: not his identity, but his coming about in this time and place" (1980, xi). What an amazing statement, emanating from a writer known primarily for the surprise and grace of her metaphors, such as the description cited earlier of Phoenix stealing a nickel as if "lifting an egg from under a setting hen" (1979, p. 64). What makes Eudora Welty great, in my view, is her long familiarity with the thoughts and feelings of those around her "in their many shadings and variations and contradictions" (1980, x). No one person, no single isolated incident, no still moment is simply one, single, isolated or still thing, person, or object. Her imagination fuses and intertwines. That, I suggest, is the mystery she reveals to us in her instances of stillness.

What keeps the moment shimmering, whether brutal or lovely, is the presence of the magic number three. In "A Still Moment," three characters, two of them drawn from history, share a moment. The three are an actual itinerant preacher, Lorenzo Dow; an outlaw, John Murrell; and an actual painter-ornithologist, John James Audubon. Some may be shocked to see the famous painter of such magnificent birds of North America portrayed as a murderer. But to Welty the very act of killing in order to create is the sort of oxymoron that interests her. It is, as well what interested Coleridge in his "Rime of the Ancient Mariner." When the Ancient Mariner shoots an albatross for no reason, the cosmos responds in kind. A gratuitous human act that kills is reciprocated by a gratuitous cosmic act that stills. The mariner's ship becomes in irons, "As idle as a painted ship/Upon a painted ocean" (Coleridge, 1964, lines 118–119). To keep the rhythm of the cosmos going, breathing out and breathing in, the mariner in penance must tell his story to one of every three people he meets, the number three being the mystery between the breaths.

So what if a human being attempts to *solve* life's mystery? Would that not be a kind of hoarding? Of absolute possession? Of murder? The still moment can raise a most troubling question about evil, not just about love. This other still moment is registered in her story about the three men who come together unbeknownst to one another and witness a heron at sunset, feeding. Each is fascinated by the heron's "luminous shell that drew in and held the eyesight" (1979, p. 93). Each is stopped by the simple beauty that greets their eyes. For five pages, Welty describes the heron in phrases that are both beautiful and Biblical in their grace. It seems as if the writer sees a Christian sacrifice about to occur, as did Coleridge with the shooting of the albatross. Welty writes,

Before them the heron rested in the grasses with the evening all around it, lighter and more serene than the evening, flight closed in its body, the circuit of its beauty closed, a bird seen and a bird still, its motion calm as if it were offered: Take my flight... (1979, p. 94)

Welty then offers her chastisement by writing that what joins the three strangers "was simply *all*" (1979, p. 95). The preacher wanted to save all souls; the convict wanted to destroy all men; the painter wanted to paint all birds. This is their common evil. The bird is to be the sacrifice for such literalism. Tellingly, it is the artist whom Welty singles out for most condemnation. Because he could not paint from memory he had to possess the bird, make it his object in death: "He had seen the bird most purely at the moment of its death" (1979, p. 97).

This still moment, like the one that occurs in "Livvie," offers a mystery, but of a different kind. I wonder if Welty's meditative piece, her most complex story, is in some way a comment on the artist's conundrum. To get likeness, one freezes time forever. Isn't that a kind of death? I wonder if Welty, who was a skilled photographer before she was a writer, worried that the act of clicking the shutter on a lens is comparable to pulling a trigger? I wonder if perfection, getting an image exactly right, could be thought of as stealing the life force of the subject, turning it into an object? There is a worrisome connection between camera and rifle, especially when considering that the scientist Etienne Jules Marey developed a camera in the form of a rifle (Cremin, 1990, p. 332). In commenting on photography, however, Welty takes the opposite view: the revelation of an image is forever ongoing, not imprisoned, she argues. "A snapshot is a moment's glimpse," she says, "into what never stops moving" (in Bishop, 2009).

Indeed, the word "still" contains a riddle. Stillness is both motion-less and motion-full. Consider: "Still: remaining in place at rest; motionless; stationary. *Photog*: pertaining to or using a photograph of a stationary subject or one instantaneous photograph of a moving subject. *Archaic:* steadily; constantly; always" (Webster). The joining together of opposites within a single word is the pun. It is the height of language facility, which both writers Welty and Beckett display, albeit from very different intentions and very different modes of myth.

Samuel Beckett's (1988) *Stirrings Still* was written in fragments and over a period of three years. When completed, a year before Beckett's death, he dedicated it to his long-time publishing friend at Grove Press, Barney Rosset, who, I am honored to say, inscribed my copy in 1991. The text is unnumbered and is spaced on the page exactly two and a half inches from the top and three and seven-eighths inches from the bottom (with one exception) forming two inch blocks of writing (with the same one exception). Most "sentences" do not complete a block of writing on any one given page but rather follow over to the next page. Most "sentences" are not real sentences since they lack verbal connection. Intermittently spaced between the blocks of text are sketches by Louis Le Brocquy that look like Rorschach ink blots, usually centered on an otherwise blank recto page and followed by a blank verso page. The entire piece is seventeen two-inch blocks of writing (plus one one-and-one-quarter inch of writing) on eighteen pages, seven drawings, and seven black verso pages, for a total of thirty-one pages of blocks, blots, and blanks. The arrangement offers a visual approach to what I see Beckett accomplishing: a meditation on silence that is precise but fluid.

The piece is in three sections. The first section contains nine blocks, five of them broken in two uneven sections, four drawings and four blank verso pages. The last block of section one is shorter than all the others, being only one-and-one-quarter inches instead of the regular two. The second section contains six blocks, two drawings and two blank verso pages. The third section contains three blocks, one drawing and one blank verso page. A little more than half of the total pages contain Beckett's writing, measuring less than one yard of text.

Normally, I do not apply ruler to writing. But Beckett is so deliberate in the precisions of all his work, including the precisely right word for the right ring, that I think it is interesting and important to point out the unusual formatting of this, his last major published work. His minimalist text and "plot" belie the huge ramifications therein. What I will focus on is Beckett's accomplishment of compacting much in little, the more of less that has been a hallmark of his entire oeuvre. I consider this work a masterpiece of exploring the rings we can hear in *Stirrings Still* that resonate, as well, with the previous commentary on Eudora Welty. Sound, more than sight, will be the shift I see Beckett making at the end of his own life, for it is in stillness that the rings of sound can be heard.

Mythopoetic writing writes in the between of the senses, allowing us to experience the world in a more fluid way. In phrases that sound Beckettian, Jamaica Kincaid (1992) describes the nature of apprehending the world when silence is most dense:

> I hear the silent voice; it stands opposite the blackness and yet it does not oppose the blackness, for conflict is not a part of its nature… Within the silent voice, no mysterious depths separate me; no vision is so distant that longing is stirred up in me. I hear the silent voice—how softly now it falls, and all of existence is caught up in it. Living in the silent voice, I am no longer "I." Living

in the silent voice, I am at last at peace. Living in the silent voice, I am at last erased. (p. 52)

Kincaid's impetus is in the opposite direction from most "I" characters, as is Beckett's: an impetus of de-evolution, going downward. In the darkness of the downward spiral, sounds are experienced differently, with much more awareness of the mystery of silence, since silence is, to borrow from Welty, an illumination: "still" in both senses of the word. Understanding, if such can be achieved, comes from a replication of images, echoing-back, deepening, thickening (Doll, 1988, p. 6).

What I hear Beckett doing in this final meditation is using language that refuses to "make" sense because it invites sensing. His unusual use of nouns and prepositions thrusts the listener into ever deeper listening. Without helper verbs or linked conjunctions we are on our own; we can only sense the text; we can only hear the stirrings, and wonder. *Stirrings Still* is a final meditation on silence and darkness in words that express a language long forgotten. In this way, according to my thesis, Beckett returns us to a very simple, very old world, as it was in a mythic beginning when creation came out of chaos.

The first section focuses on a room, a male character, a high window, a stool, a table, and a phantom second self who leaves and comes back again. The shifting phantom self blends with personal characters from Beckett's past, dead figures whom he resurrects fleetingly or dead poets, possibly Verlaine or Walter von der Vogelwide (Knowlson, 1996, p. 613). The figures he sees are reminiscent of the tramps of Beckett's earlier writings with hat and coat traipsing along back roads. All are faceless, "Seen always from behind withersoever he went" (n.p.). The sounds that enter into the phantom scenes are from a clock, its strokes, and from cries. The words "perhaps" and "again" mark the scenic mystery as ongoing but vague: "Till so many strokes and cries since he was last seen that perhaps he would not be seen again" (n.p.). The character cannot be seen unless the sounds re-occur; the character's essence is thus defined by sound. He seems bodiless, as if already dead, looking at the ghost of himself: "Lift his past head a moment to see his past hands" (n.p.).

The second section takes the speaker outside his confinement, wandering, perhaps in his other mind, since he wonders if he was in his "right" mind. The character doubts his own rationality, appropriately enough, since so much of mythic mystery has to do with nonrational experience. This middle section is the longest of the three, all six blocks absolutely even in precise measurements, a counter-measure to the vagueness of the speaker's memory: "Bringing to bear on all this his remains of reason he sought help in the thought that his memory of indoors was perhaps at fault and found it of none" (n.p.). That "sentence" with its unusual syntax shows the attempt by a not "right" mind to try to express meaning. The next "sentence" further suggests the difficulty of speech, since the speaker with his "soundless tread" seems really a ghost. Would these utterances be how a ghost would speak? Certain archaicisms, as in "whithersoever," "hoar," "bourne," and "whencesoever," suggest the ghost-speaker's attempt either to dignify his confounded memory or to use language that emanates from an ancient past. This second section ends with the speaker drifting in a horizonless landscape, alone except for the strokes and cries "now faint now clear" (n.p.).

The third section dispenses with any attempt at "sentencing." What comes between the capital letters and the periods are extended phrases, missing words, and an expression of longing. The desire "to end," however, is foiled by the repetition of the phrase "so on." This echoes the ending of *Waiting for Godot* (1954*)*, written some thirty years earlier, when the tramps agree to go but do not move.

Beckett's themes throughout his life thus come full circle with *Stirrings Still:* questing but not finding; movement in stasis; knowing the dark, seeing the shadow; seeing into the night, feeling the universe; unabated longing. All is extraordinary, all is extra-audenary, to cite Beckett's pun (1938) in an early writing (p. 293). The blocks of text contain haunting images, graced by a strange use of language that manages nevertheless to "strike sparks of life" (Knowlson, 1996, p. 613). It is this mystery of the power of the unnamable, I think, that separates Beckett from other writers in the mythic mode: the ability to use language differently, always bringing together the contradictions that words themselves contain. Finally, the three writers I have cited—Flannery O'Connor, Eudora Welty, Samuel Beckett–all suggest stillness as mystery. When the "left" mind abandons itself to what is "right," it would seem we are in the midst of the mythic mode.

NOTES

[1] Part of my title I owe to Eynel Wardi, as listed in my references.

[2] The embrace of woman in the lap of her dying lover echoes a variant of the Christian Pietà, mother cradling her dying son in her lap, or the Egyptian Osiris being brought back to life by his sister-wife Isis. I think, too, of Bernini's statue of the rapture of St. Teresa, who wrote of her epiphany about Jesus, "He appeared to me to be thrusting [the spear] at times into my heart" (2002, Chapter xxix, 13)—words echoed in O'Connor's text. These are transforming moments, the meeting of human and the divine—love cradling death, love transforming life.

ECO-WISDOM, OR, MIND THE DOG

Natural Roots to Unconscious Knowing

What do you know of the world beneath its bubbling surface?
What can you know of the bubbles unless you comprehend the forces at work
in the depths of the cauldron?

— Jack London (in Labor, 1994)

For indeed our consciousness does not create itself—it wells up from unknown
depths.

— C.G. Jung (1963)

The condition we face today in the eleventh hour of ecological recklessness requires
more than changes in what we are doing (using fossil fuels, wasting resources,
throwing away food, overpopulating, accumulating plastic, despoiling the planet). The
condition requires a fundamental change in thinking about our place in the cosmos.
To help us make this shift, I turn to the wisdoms I most honor in my fields of study:
writers, mythmakers, and a psychology based on archetypal knowing, such as that
propounded by Carl Jung. My focus in this chapter is on a writer most of us encountered in eighth grade and have not returned to since: Jack London. Who would
know that the respect London had for unconscious knowing reflected his long-felt
admiration for the writings of Carl Jung, as evidenced by the two epigrams above.
But the Jung-London connection is not odd considering London's love of the wilderness and disdain for the overly-civilized human. Somewhat like Buck in *The Call
of the Wild*, London wrote in 1906 that he did not like to live "on the parlor floor of
society" or "in the bone-head world," preferring instead adventure, aliveness, and
pulse (in Labor, 1994, p. 481). Perhaps it was synchronistic, to use Jung's term, that
just months before his death in 1916, London read Jung's recently published *The
Psychology of the Unconscious*, which, according to London's wife, became "the
most heavily annotated book in his vast collection (in Labor and Reesman, 1994,
p. 107). Yet London had always been open to the bubbling forces below, his first and
most famous novel almost writing itself, the mythical powers of Buck seeming
to emerge as if "a message from London's unconscious" (Tavernier-Courbin, 1994,
p. 77). Indeed, the world of dream, myth, and primal knowing had long been a
fascination for London. "To Build a Fire" is no exception. The short story shows
precisely the error that comes to modernist thinking when humans avoid bowing
to other bases of consciousness found, in "Build," with the archetypal figures of

the old timer, the animal, and the wilderness. The human in question for this story is the unnamed protagonist, whom I call the Mechanical Man.

Key descriptions London employs about the Man are words of instrumentation. He relies on his watch rather than his senses; he times his lunch break down to the minute; he ignores the tobacco stains that make a crystal muzzle of his beard; and his heart becomes a pump that no longer connects with the rest of his body. Recall: the story takes place in the frozen tundra of the Arctic, in forty-below weather. The formidable landscape puts the Man to the test, which he fails. Relying on his instruments rather than the three archetypal figures that surround him—the old timer, the animal, and the wilderness—means that the Man is clueless as to survival skills. Slowly, the Man's organism disconnects from its heart source, "The wires were pretty well down between him and his finger end," London writes (in Labor, 1994, p. 143). Unable and unwilling to see, feel, touch, or imagine himself in conjunction with the world surrounding him, he is doomed. Reduced to a system of wires—some receivers, some transmitters—the Mechanical Man becomes merely an embodiment of his mind. But because his mind is not connected to the natural elements, his organs body forth the way his mind thinks: all wires down.

The Mechanical Man reveals his disconnection from self and world in other ways as well. He is prideful, arrogant, careless. He is cock-sure. He makes what he calls "mistakes," "chuckles" at his "forgetfulness" and is pleased with "outwitting" "the cold of space." Thinking himself superior to the more-knowing forces around him, he dismisses their transmissions as "weird." London writes, "But all this—the mysterious, far-reaching hairline trail, the absence of sun from the sky, the tremendous cold, and the strangeness and weirdness of it all—made no impression on the man" (in Labor, 1994, p. 137). So encased is the Mechanical Man in his instrumental way of going about things that he cannot even muster an interesting way to think about his predicament. "It certainly was cold," he says six times. Unable to generate images, to develop an image-sense about the way the world was presenting itself to him, he is reduced to being a mere receiver of automatic transmissions from his mechanical brain. If, as many dream analysts suggest, the protagonist in a dream is the dreamer's ego, then the other characters serve a function of advising, correcting, compensating, or balancing the one-sided approach of ego. If we read the story as we might a dream, it is to the fringe actors we must look for understanding the power of the unconscious welling up from the depths.

Of the Mechanical Man's three compensatory, fringe characters (the old timer, the animal, and the wilderness), the old timer is an ancestor figure, in the text as a kind of memory trace. London presents him only through the Man's recollection of his words of warning. Seven times the old timer appears inside the Mechanical Man's thoughts, like a figment of the imagination. To the Mechanical Man, however, the old timer's words are not just foolish, they are unmanly:

> He remembered the advice of the old timer on Sulphur Creek, and smiled. The old timer had been very serious in laying down the law that no man must travel alone in the Klondike after fifty below. Well, here he was: he had had the accident; he was alone; and he had saved himself. Those old timers were rather womanish, some of them, he thought. (in Labor, p. 143)

Amazingly, even after the first brush with death, the Mechanical Man's frozen ego cannot shift off its center position. He considers himself The Man; the old timer is "womanish."

The old timer can be thought of in the manner of what hunter cultures of pre-modern times teach, even today. The hunter has a special relation with animals and nature. Like a wise one, the hunter knows not to presume; therefore he must pay special attention when out in the wild so as to avoid inattentiveness to forces beyond control. The hunter lives life as "complete alertness... from within his environment" (Ortega y Gasset, 1986, p. 46). This prepositional awareness, attending to that which is "from within" is an attitude that prepares itself differently from when near the warmth of the hearth. Out in the white cold one must be reverential, humble, apologetic. The act of hunting brings the hunter "into direct contact with the reality of life and death [and] with the reality of how our lives are dependent on animals" (Lacourt, 2010, p. 87). The old ways of doing, which are also ways of being, are part and parcel of what the hunter is: a simple, no-nonsense, working model of "a just exchange between the human being and the powers that rule his universe (Vanderburg, 1980, p. 20). None of this is seen with the Mechanical Man, even after his first accident. He would be better off thinking of the womanish advice of the old time as his *anima* or soul trying to warn him of overstepping his bounds.

As if one anima figure were not enough to prompt the Mechanical Man to change his ways, the dog provides another prompt. Jung (1963) writes that the primal mind understands an unconscious identity with animals (p. 101). Elsewhere (1976b) he elaborates:

> The archetype of spirit in the shape of man, hobgoblin, or animal always appears in a situation where insight, understanding, good advice, determination, planning, etc. are needed but cannot be mustered on one's own resources. (p. 216)

But if the Mechanical Man is not listening to the words of a fellow human, he certainly won't heed the dog's actions. What does a dog know!

For Jung, animals generally signify the instinctive forces of the unconscious, which London has shown in this and other works. In *Call of the Wild*, for instance, London's focus on the instinctual power of the dog Buck is instructive. So long as Buck was a hearth dog, he was mastered by domesticity. Once out in the wild, however, he is "called." Instinctively, the dog hears "the ancient song" of his ancestors:

> And when, on the still cold nights, he pointed his nose at a star and howled, long and wolflike, it was his ancestors, dead and dust, pointing... and howling down the centuries and through him. (in Labor, p. 364)

Buck is literally animated by ancestral urges; the *anima* comes alive inside the animal, allowing him to become a composite of self and other, more primal. Buck's whole being exudes a deeper joy and a spirit-kinship with the cosmos. Buck's howl "was an old song, old as the breed itself.... that harked back through the ages of fire and roof to the raw beginning of life in the howling ages" (in Labor, p. 371). In describing Buck's actions with gerunds (nouns taking on verb functions), London symbolizes the transformation of dog-tamed into dog-wildened by Buck's surging, sounding, running, and yelping. Even the cosmos comes alive to the sounds of the dog, to the point of "stars leaping in the frost dance" (in Labor, p. 371).

For all the unconscious emergence of the wolf call, the dog also "knows." London uses mind language deliberately to insist that the animal acts consciously from within a very deep place. Buck knew, remembered, heard, and saw. "He had made up his mind"; "he became more and more conscious"; "Buck knew [the sounds] as things heard in that other world which persisted in his memory. He walked to the centre of the open space and listened" (in Labor, pp. 372ff; p. 415). In "To Build a Fire" the dog "knew it was no time for traveling"; "it knew that it was not good to walk abroad in such fearful cold"; "it merely obeyed the mysterious prompting that arose from the deepest crypts of its being" (in Labor, pp. 138 ff). As neo-Jungian James Hillman (1979) writes, "Only the animal can answer Descartes" (p. 142). Thinking is not just a mind function; it is also a sense function, like the old dictum: nothing in the mind that is not first in the senses. Knowing is mindful and sensual. This, the dog knows.

Now, the dog has always "known" in myth but we have to look under surfaces to "under"stand the dog's mythic purpose. How very interesting, for instance, that mythic dogs are associated with the under world (London's "deepest crypts"). Cerberus, the three-headed dog, guards Hades. Virgil describes Cerberus as monstrous, with three heads and snakes entwining his necks. The number three and the snake both are goddess symbols. The dog Garm guards the gates of the Norse underworld Niflheim, where the goddess Hel reigns. Both guard dogs of the land below the land serve the function of keeping the living out and the dead in. The Mesoamerican underworld, called Mictlan, contained a yellow dog, whose purpose was to guide the souls through obstacles and levels. Yellow may be the dog's association with the newly dead soul still containing the gold of daylight which becomes darker during the descent into the night world. Of the many canine gods, the Egyptian Anubis was originally called "Opener of the Way" and was also known as "He of the Mother." Coptic Christians later identified Anubis with Gabriel, judge of the dead (Walker, 1983, p. 241). These associations of dog with death suggest a particular *kind* of knowledge that the dog "knows." This would be the mystery of the cycle of death and life, closely connected with early goddess cultures. And as with any mystery religion or myth, rituals of necessary sacrifice would ensure that the cycle could continue—especially if the knowing dog were present. Jack London's deliberate use of mind language in his fiction suggests that it is animals, not humans, who understand better the ways of the natural world: how to survive in it, how to reclaim a connection to it, and how to avoid its dangers.

The third compensatory figure to the ego-driven Mechanical Man in "To Build a Fire" is the wilderness itself, the white Arctic landscape against which the story unfolds. On the literal level, the wilderness acts as antagonist to the protagonist's intentions, foiling his every move. On a cultural level the wilderness represents whiteness, like John Locke's *tabula rasa*, the blank slate of the white "civilized" man who knows nothing of the cosmos or of other cultures red, black, or yellow. Whiteness is the privilege handed to the white man, onto whose blank slate nothing has been written. On the psychological level, the surrounding white landscape implies a frozen field of consciousness. The surface is hard, like the Mechanical Man's reified ego which holds a "fantasy of omniscience" and a "denial of the unconscious" (Phillips, 1993, xiii).

And so to be seventy-five degrees below zero and not to "imagine" what lies beneath the frozen tundra is to court a meaningless death. On the one hand the Mechanical Man understands that the "springs that bubbled out from the hillsides" were traps: "they hid pools of water" (in Labor, p. 139). He knows this, but he presses on. Water, long associated with the soul, is the force of creativity and imagination, "the wild creative force [that] flows into whatever beds we have" (Estés, 1992, p. 299). The Mechanical Man, however, fails to read the land. He has never passed the curriculum of the self, *currere* meaning "the running of a course" (Pinar and Grumet, 1976); a coursing; that which courses within; "a flow from who one is" (Aoki, 1988, p. 8); that which courses through time, memory, and dream. He fails, because he lacks the flow to see that the tree that offered him twigs for burning were not just tools for his purpose. He fails to understand the microcosmic connections of snow on bough on tree that would eventually collapse when perturbed with a slight agitation—"an imperceptible agitation, so far as he was concerned," writes London—foretelling the basis of Chaos Theory–"but an agitation sufficient to bring about disaster" (in Labor, p. 144). He thinks of nature as only inert matter, there to serve his immediate needs.

What the Mechanical Man sees is an inheritance not from traditional wisdom but from an evolutionary principle that views all things by the "very high regard the dominant world has of itself" (Highwater, 1982, p. 19). Is it any wonder, then, that London ends this story of the death of the Mechanical Man with a wide angle lens that takes its view from the frozen body, back to the animal, and finally out into the cold sky where the stars "leaped and danced and shone brightly" (in Labor, p. 150)? The cosmos swirls and dances, as it always has, no matter one man's death. The final sentence offers a comment on London's disgust for human disregard of the cosmos. That which is very far away, the sky, becomes a new center of action. The reader is no longer on the Artic playing field with the Man. It is with the stars that London ends his story. The protagonist has died, the dog slinks away. London leaves the reader with the dancing stars as if the man's death animates a cosmic response of glee. By ending his story with such a telescopic vision, Jack London reminds us of our small place in the vast cosmos. We must remember that we are part of a larger system than that which is perceived only by the human mind. As the dog hears the ancestral song and the stars leap and dance, this cosmos we are privileged to inhabit is not inert; it is alive! And the title "To Build a Fire" utilizes the infinitive form of the verb to suggest the infinite wisdom of the cosmos which, along with the infinite capacity of archetypal unconsciousness, has access to all that wells up from unknown depths.

In my view, Jack London has created a new myth of warning for a culture that considers itself advanced but which ignores the world beneath its bubbling surface, a world which as I write witnesses the bubbling surface of the gushing oil from the British Petroleum "spill" in the Gulf waters off Louisiana. London's "To Build a Fire" shows precisely the error that comes to modern "man" when, to his peril, he avoids bowing to other bases of consciousness found in the ancestor, the animal, and the wilderness–be this the frozen tundra or the ocean bed.

THE MORE OF LESS

In college I had a wonderful course on W.B. Yeats, thought I was clever in my essays, impressed my brother with my understandings, and loved my professor. She was the divorced wife of Randall Jarrell, the poet. Mackie Jarrell was her name. I loved her for encouraging me with my work, the word "encourage" meaning "to give heart to." My college text on Yeats' collected poems (1959), revisited now after fifty years, is well fingered. I turn to the poem "Among School Children" about Yeats' visit as "a sixty-year old smiling public man" (stanza I) to a classroom of children who see him only as a "scarecrow" (stanza IV). My pages contain many marginal notes, dutifully taken in class so I could decipher who the names were, what the references meant. Now, with my own seventy-year old white hair, I re-read Yeats' poem and wonder if my college understandings were those of the "best modern way" (stanza I), rather than the best postmodern way or perhaps the best premodern way. Now I see Yeats disparaging the world famous Greek thinkers—Plato, Aristotle, Pythagoras—by his word "fiddle-stick" (stanza VI), making a damning comparison between them and school children. He implies that earnest thinkers are like dutiful children, both childish in their disdain of nature's ways, which include the natural process of aging. Plato, after all, "thought nature but a spume"; Aristotle "played the taws" (birch branch)/ Upon the bottom of the king of kings"; and Pythagoras "fingered upon a fiddle-stick" (stanza VI). These Yeatsian images suggest that even key Western thinkers could no more cipher nature than could schoolchildren cipher an old man, although the children's nun teacher is proud that they "learn to cipher" (stanza I). It now seems to me that "Among School Children" stands as Yeats' Celtic rebuke to the Western dualistic tradition that separates old age from youth, when indeed the two are "yolk and white of the one shell" (stanza II), or an old chestnut tree, "great-rooted blossomer" (stanza VIII).

This is a book about images, so I want to focus on the old chestnut tree that yet blossoms. The tight phrasing, of course, is Yeats' way of demonstrating nature's paradox. Out of a very old tree comes new life, webbed in such intricate fusion that it is hard to decipher the sourcing of the life energy: is it "the leaf, the blossom, or the bole?" (stanza VIII). As James Fitzgerald (2008) puts it, probably referring to Yeats' question, Celtic consciousness sees "no distinction between branch and blossom" (p. 23). The boundary between opposites is thin; therefore, the opposites, age and youth for instance, are in energizing tension, such that "celebrating the life-affirming energy that can only be born out of a perpetual tension between opposites is the key to the genius of Ireland" (Flannery, 2008, p. 51). So intermingled are the intricate parts of that old chestnut tree that we cannot know "the dancer from the dance" (stanza VIII).

The way of thinking presented by the poet missed my college eyes, even I dare to say the eyes of professors such as the venerable Helen Vendler from Harvard, whose line by line elucidates but does not illuminate (Vendler, n.d., athome). Putting a Celtic lens into the reading completely changes what the professors teach. Into the pause of that change I place two thin images that almost slip under the eyes unnoticed: Yeats describes a woman's face with a hollow cheek as though it "drank the wind/And took a mess of shadows for its meat" (stanza IV). Here he references an unnamed fourteenth century painting of an old woman, very old, so old that her diet is wind for water and shadows for meat. The synaesthesia is startling, illuminating. By joining together that which seeks to be held asunder, like wind from water or shadow from meat, Yeats turns the forward-seeking mind around. It makes of the old woman someone magical. And magic is what Yeats, in his occult period particularly, was seeking to bring to modern audiences, transforming the way people saw things. In a letter to Yeats on this point, the poet "A.E." wrote of the changes a Celtic consciousness could bring: "A purple sheen in the inner air, perceptible at times in the light of day, spreads itself over the mountains.... Out of Ireland will arise a light to transform many ages and peoples" (in Flannery, 2008, p. 65). This is what artists and poets and musicians and mythmakers and curriculum theorists do: they transform consciousness.

Synaesthesia is one way of transforming the usual into the unusual, the more into less. This is not simply a "device"; it is a way of being in the world, surrounded by what the world offers to the senses. Philip Glass' minimalism is a ready example. I remember attending an afternoon program at Johns Hopkins University in the 70s when Glass first came on the scene. The room was packed, people standing against the walls. This was an opportunity to hear someone new. Glass sat at the piano; the notes went around and around, dizzyingly, confusingly, maddeningly. There were sudden strident silences. I had never heard anything like it. I was mesmerized. The music spoke to me on a deep level. Then I heard a stir in the room. A few minutes into the piece people started looking at one another, not in amazement. There was snickering. Rude guffaws. The audience was insulted. They began to leave loudly.

My experience long ago was not unique, in that Glass' music has often been misunderstood, called dismissively "music to climb the walls by" (in Kostelanetz, 1997, p. 89). The repetitions seem to the linear-minded Westerner simply repetitions, boring repetitions. But his musicality is mysterious: it bores down and it is charged. Speaking of the fragmented sonics of Glass' music, Marla Morris (2009) writes, "Minimal music allows one to float off into the vast inner space of memory, image, dreamscape" (p. 114). And Richard Kostelanetz writes: "It is a synthesis of sound, mind, and body achieved by placing equal importance on tone or timbre of instruments, harmonies, and rhythm (like that of a heartbeat)... [it] strikes a chord in the human unconscious" (p. 89). It seems that people in the academy are not used to floating off into image or thinking with their heartbeat.

Allow me then to step into the void these spaces and repetitions make. Allow me to step back into myth and re-introduce a strange figure poised on the periphery of Norse legend. Heimdall is the trumpeter for the gods whose job it is to warn them of imminent doom when the giants begin their rumble. There he stands on the edge of the Bifrost Bridge, in between heaven and earth. Another version of the story has Heimdall born at the edge of the world. His place is the boundary, no place for literalism (Miller, 1986, p. 71). His birth from nine mothers and nine sisters suggests birth comes from such borders. One story has him related to the giants (his mother source) while another has him associated with the waves of the sea (his sister source). Is he frost or is he fluid? He is both. The most interesting aspect of the gods' trumpeter is his unusual hearing and his far-sightedness: "He needs less sleep than a bird. Night and day he sees a hundred leagues away; he also hears it when grass grows on the earth or wool on sheep or anything else that can be heard" (in Lindow, 2001, p. 167). For these extrasensory powers, Heimdall is an important but enigmatic god.

How Heimdall acquired his powers is also intriguing. The source for this story in the *Voluspa*, stanza 26, suggests that, like Odin, Heimdall sacrificed a body part, his ear, and in return received special powers: "Heimdall's hearing is hidden/ Under the holy tree" (in Lindow, p. 170). It is this hearing from below that interests me. His hearing wool grow on sheep connects Heimdall intimately to the ram, "Heimdali" meaning "ram" (in Lindow, p. 171). Possibly the long horn that Heimdall blows to warn the gods of their doom is similar to rams' horns. These teasing fragments of story suggest a cluster of ideas connected with the image of the man with a horn.

Mythically, I think that the interstices are where we should look for the wisdom of this and any story. Heimdall hears what we cannot. If we are to hear the deeper sounds that connect with the unconscious or the heartbeat, we should "look" to what lies beneath and between. We should hear what isn't immediately apparent on surfaces: under the earth where grass grows, under the skin where wool grows; between the beats, within the silence. The ram's exceptional hearing is like other animals of myth whose animal powers are greater than humans'. This is the more of less, since the average eye or ear cannot perceive the many thrummings that lie below surfaces until we turn the dial down or let the silence speak. Hearing in the interstices allows synaesthesia to blossom. Hearing in the interstices, with Heimdall, strikes responsive chords in the human unconscious, if we have ears to hear.

The subtleties and wisdoms of myth, found in the interstices, are what this chapter explores. Besides the cracks of the in-between, so many other "littles" offer themselves for exploration, like little creatures, little actions, and little spaces that paradoxically are manifold in meaning. Take little creatures. One of the delights for me in reading these *fabula* is coming across the small creature that can easily be overlooked. Fairy tales are full of such creatures. Tom Thumb, Thumblina, dwarfs, toads and frogs are some of the little creatures of fairytale. Little people delight thrill-seekers or teach acceptance; little creatures reward the virtuous. But fairy tale, as David Miller (1976) explains, is a genre with a message, unlike myth. Fairy tale's message is not *sotto voce* but clear and unambiguous:

> The fairy tale strategy may symbolize a life experience in which there is a strong wish to remove the warring ambivalences and the fundamental ambiguity, to make the life-story one-dimensional, replacing the ambivalence of the concrete images of daily experience with abstract ideas. (pp. 162–163)

Children reading fairy tales will learn to decipher morals but not cipher meanings.

The tiny creatures that help Psyche complete her tasks are other mythic examples of the more of little. Psyche's helpers are ants, a green reed, an eagle, and a speaking tower (of stone). All these creatures direct Psyche, the soul, to attend to the natural world and in that attention to see or hear beyond the obvious. The soul's way is nature's way and involves careful separation, one species from another, as in the ants sorting seeds and grains into their spartacles. I imagine Psyche appreciating the help but also discovering the wisdom behind the task. Psyche, the soul, proceeds by distinguishing one thing from another, this from that, bean seed from poppy seed; giving to each its due, what James Hillman (1996) calls its "daimon." In his quirky brilliance, Hillman captures, if that is the right word, the particularity of the daimon:

> The daimon motivates. It protects. It invents and persists with stubborn fidelity.... It is out of step with time, finding all sorts of faults, gaps, and knots in the flow of life—and it prefers them. It has affinities with myth, since it is itself a mythical being and thinks in mythical patterns. (p. 30)

I enjoy the challenge of teaching this myth of Psyche and Eros because it always sets apart the subtle from the unsubtle students. The latter want big. They hate it that Psyche despairs. What a wuss, they say. They ridicule her tasks, which are nothing like he-man Herakles. But many (not all) subtle students see something little going on and like it that our reading eyes are directed downward into such small, tiny helper creatures. This prime myth of the soul's connection with love, Psyche with Eros, turns discussion away from the grand gesture toward a process of seeing through, seeing in to the inwardness of things (Hillman, 1975). And the distress of Psyche is all part of the psychologizing of the story, which is wetted by tears.

Another little creature of myth is from a strange Brazilian story about the flood. A god in disguise visits a humble cottage. He is covered in sores, disgusting to look at, his head surrounded by bees. This last detail of the bees is a telling image of the guest's divinity (Hillman, 1996, p. 277). The father, Wainkaura by name, welcomes the stranger, perhaps intuiting his divine status, and brings him into the hut. Wainkaura not only washes the guest's sores, Jesus fashion, but invites the stranger to sit on his virgin daughter's lap. This moment in the tale is the virgin sacrifice. In exchange for the kindness shown him, the stranger god rewards the host with news of an impending flood, telling the host to go kill a dove. In the meantime, the god impregnates the daughter, a deed which the god confesses upon the host's return but which the host presumably expected. Thereupon the god does a remarkable thing: he "took the dove's fragile carcass and turned it into a boat large enough for Wainkaura's entire family" (in Hathaway, 2002, p. 40).

The image of a fragile dove transforming into a large boat is richly suggestive. As my students and I ponder the many images, we remark on the bones of the carcass which serve as the ribs of the boat. We remark on the dove's traditional symbolism with purity, and its connection with the virgin daughter. We remark on sacrifice and reward, traditional mythical motifs of honoring the gods. We remark on traces of Christian iconography, with the daughter's virgin lap recalling Mary, the dove re-calling the Holy Spirit, the motif of humility by the host washing his guest's sores recalling Jesus; and further, the guest-host dynamic that reflects foreknowledge and promise. And all the action is inside a small space where very large mysteries take place. The wonder of the tale, to many of my students, is the dove-boat transformation. This suggests a subtle but very important mythic motif of the interconnection of all: bird, bone, boat. Surely, this mostly unknown flood myth focuses on the more that emanates from the little.

Other little creatures that inhabit the cosmos in small but big ways are spirits that live in the Other Place, variously called the Fairy Mound for the Celts, the Unconscious for depth psychology, the Underworld for the Greeks, or the Afterworld for the Chinese. Most cultures grounded in nature worship have stories of visitations by dream spirits, ancestors, or subversive spirits; clearly, not all these visits are pleasant. Something is wanted by the visitor, who must be propitiated in order to keep the cosmos in balance. Novelist Lisa See (2008) writes of such ghost visitations:

> Ghosts, like women, are creatures of *yin*—cold, dark, earthy, and feminine. For months I made things easy on myself by staying in Ren's bedchamber, where I didn't have to worry about the suddenness of sunrises or strategize as to how to navigate an impossibly tight corner. I was a nocturnal creature. I spent my days nesting in the rafter or curled in a corner of the room. When the sun set, I became more brazen, lounging like a concubine on my husband's bed, waiting for him and his second wife to come to me. (pp. 152–153)

This ghost's sensuous needs are met vicariously as she, with wile and humor, haunts the bedchamber rafters of the man who should have been her husband. She is weightless and outside of time but full of the weight of emotion.

To think of two worlds so opposite in every dimension except intention is not so strange when we consider the findings of quantum physics or the discoveries of the unconscious. What myth does is to personify these deep-level energies, giving them intelligence. Life exists everywhere, even where we cannot see. Jerry Wright (2008) offers a Celtic explanation for these other "wheres," calling them highly-charged places "known as *thin places* and *thin times*" (p. 3). These are the twilight places, between dusk and night; the threshold places, between two sides of one portal. On one side stands the right foot; on the other, the left. Stepping with the left foot into a thin place releases one from the constraints of time and space, matter and spirit, within and without.

Some of us are more open to the experience of dimensionless places through dream, intuition, or synchronicity. One night long, long ago I was a guest in an ancestral Scottish home; the high-ceilinged living room, they said, was frequented by a ghost. That night, late, as I got up from my bed, I felt a chill go clear through me in that vast dark living room. I knew I was in the presence of the house ghost. I shuddered but was not afraid.

As the above personal example might illustrate, invisible forces prefer darkness, so what is "less" to the literal eye is "more" to the imaginary eye or ear. As Jung said, "An unseen presence is suggested, a numen that lives its own life and in whose presence man shudders" (in Mogenson, 2006a, p. 144). Indeed, subversive spirits dwell in all aspects of the natural world: forest, mountain, desert, water; and in the habitations of the human world: domicile and psyche. Water is the chosen medium for mirages of or visitations by mermaids, mermen, Kelpie, Tikoloshe, Rusalka, Munuane, Nuckelavee, Bunyip, Vodyani, or Merrow, as well as a "host" of others. If ever one has seen the rough waters of one of Scotland's lakes, one knows that the waves just might be the scales of a Kelpie or the Loch Ness monster! To the skeptic, one can only say, "Deny away, friend. Deny away. But throw some salt over your shoulder." Or, as James Hillman (1983) puts it, "Superstitions keep the world alive for us" (p. 91).

An example of a little being that inhabits the water unaware to day consciousness is the Nixie. Jung (1977) charmingly describes this creature:

> Whoever looks into the water sees his own image, but behind it living creatures soon loom up; fishes, presumably, harmless dwellers of the deep—harmless, if only the lake were not haunted. They are water-beings of a peculiar sort…. She can be a siren, mermaid, wood-nymph, Grace, or Erlking's daughter, or a lamia or succubus, who infatuates young men and sucks the life out of them. Moralizing critics will say that these figures are projections… nothing but worthless fantasies… An unlimited amount of what we now feel to be an integral part of our psychic being disports itself merrily for the primitive (sic) in projections ranging far and wide. (pp. 24–25)

Some of my myth students actually prefer the book we use in class on demons and subversive spirits (Mack and Mack, 1998) to that on the myths. While the tendency is to bluff superiority, there is an amazing openness to the wonder of the named creatures of the dark. That the spirits are named and have a lore gives to them a certain credibility among the undergraduates. Several final projects, in fact, are student modelings or stories gleaned from these spirits.

Lacunae, vacuums, gaps, loss: these are some of the little spaces that yet offer much. I confess: I was going to conclude this chapter with a final twig on my outline tree. But. In the mail I received Hongyu Wang's recent co-edited book (2009) which she inscribed to me: "Thanks for your inspiring teaching, Mary!" Chapter Three in her book is written by one of her students responding to my published account of life with my dying mother (Doll, 1995). I am reminded of that time in my life, so many years ago, the past that is always present nonetheless. I am reminded, through the student's loving commentary, of my finally finding communication with my mother through non-speaking ways. I wrote then that my mother and I had never really known each other, I felt (she left my father's house when I was four), so the only language I used to share my life with her was the language of my father, the alphabet. The many words we exchanged over the years, my mother and me, were the superficial words of doings and dates. "We have to plot and plan," my mother would say dramatically as we would rush to a party in the back seat of a cab. Plot and plan: the formula useful for keeping things straight on my mother's busy appointment-filled calendar. But mine was a circuitous route with my mother, filled with as many holes as the cashmere sweater she gave me to wear, riddled with moth holes, my moth-er sweater.

Thankfully, I finally learned not to imitate the father way of language and literacy when I shared last days with my mother. This is odd, since my mother was a literate person, an editor of some note during the 40s and 50s in literary New York City.

But my fondest young-year memory of her was her reading voice. She was an excellent out loud reader, which she did faithfully of a summer holiday night: reading *Master Skylark* and *David Copperfield* and Shaw. And her voice took on energy, like her laugh that was streams and streams and ripples of sheer enthusiasm, god-filled energy that could be heard down the hall. But to talk was another matter. I needed to find another way to communicate, other than the way of the word, the curse of the word (Shlain, 1998). Sue Rankin, Hongyu's student, reminds me of my own learning "lessons in an unspoken language" as an avenue for reconnection with the lost mother (in Wang and Olson, 2009).

I am put back in mind to my discovery of little actions like gesture and repetition as ways to convey meaning. I am reminded that I put on my mother's clothes as a mirror of my affection for her, just as she wrapped herself in an afghan I had knitted her. I am reminded that I substituted music and color in her dying room, rather than chatter and daytime soaps. I am reminded that dream and silence were new avenues for communicating in an older way, a way of Inanna disrobing the self from all of the accoutrements inherited from the outside world. And most surprising to me is the gift of this student's writing, reminding me that it was not just I who learned to unlearn, but my mother, too, who was all there in her dying bed, the full matter of her body unashamedly there, waiting and passive but also strong and resistant. What is there to learn in unlearning? asks Sue Rankin. "First, to be limited by the patriarchal image, a fairy-tale, fantasy image, is to be isolated within femininity and to fear what which mother offers" (in Wang and Olson, 2009, p. 23).

Here within the denials, regrets, and forgetfulnesses of my own past, those great lacunae of memory, lies more than can be expressed in words. I believe that my mother and I celebrated her life through her dying and we came up with our own unspoken ritual of celebration. The space that no-talking opened allowed for a new growth of respect and obligation to the process we were in, the larger process of the dying. These were secular moments turned into sacred moments, "the ceremonial aspect of life that bestows sacredness upon persons, acts, and objects which have a role in the performance of ceremony" (Fingarette, 1972, p. 76).

The finale of this chapter concerns the more of less space as witnessed in a performance of *Dogugaeshi*, traditional Japanese puppet theater. The word "dogugaeshi" means "tool" or "method of exchange," referring to a set of screens folded, flipped, or pushed aside to reveal an evermore opening of ever more screens. Experiencing these opening screens gives a sense of space as Vine Deloria, Jr. (2009) describes it in Native American Indian ceremony: endless, engaged, flexible, offering gifts from within its energy field (pp. 85–89). I was fortunate to spend a mesmerizing hour in a darkened theater with this experience of Japanese puppetry, brought to American audiences by puppet master Brian Twist. The stage is small (puppet theater size), the screens are small, the theater is pitch dark. But what goes on inside the small space is nothing less than wondrous, an emptiness that is full. As one critic wrote, "This is more than a beautiful display; it is an invitation to actively lose yourself in simply paying attention" (Santiago, 2009, p. 30).

The screens, eighty-eight of them, are intricately painted in a variety of styles and moods. Some are traditional renderings of wind and water, waves and flowering trees.

One image of a dragon opens before our eyes, then divides down the middle to reveal another image, a golden carp curving in on itself. The images replace one another with differing paces, some jerky, some fluid, some slow, some rapid. An audience is kept off guard, an expression I experienced in my body since I could never guard myself: so much whiz of movement together with the smorgasbord of visual display, concealing, revealing kept me guessing. All is constant surprise and utter confoundment. I think of the image of a bread loaf that string theorists say is one way to envision our eleven universes, divided into separate slices but all united within one loaf (Greene, 1999).

Beside the obviously traditional screen images, there is a mix of other designs: American pop art, abstract geometrical patterns, waves of color and waves of sound. Not all the sounds are comforting; there is the sense of collapsing worlds as one screen unfolds next to another, cycling into images of falling debris. The sound at this point is loud, insistent and frightening. I had the urge to flee but the room was too dark. I think this brief moment in the piece is a reference to the dropping of the atom bomb on the tiny island of Japan. The live music we hear offers a counterpoint to the near-destruction of Japanese culture by the bomb and is performed on a lute-like instrument called a *shamisen*, played by Yumiko Tanaka. Seated on a rotating platform and dressed in traditional garb, she looms over the audience, rotating mysteriously at intervals. Her human size seems enormous, two or three times bigger than actuality, compared with the tiny screens and retreating images. Possibly her presence is the assurance that no bomb can completely obliterate the traditions of Japan.

All is not serious. The magic continues with the appearance of a single fox puppet, like the Japanese Kitsune but painted with Disney eyes. She/he peeks around disappearing screens and reappears impossibly from other directions, inviting us to view his/her palace that stretches back and back, a distance of great depth. When the Kitsune is seen with candlelight, we know we are in another space, "the realm of dreams, myths, and imagination" (Spangler, 2007, nytheater).

The more of less might be summarized by the small prefix *syn,* meaning "together" and "with." The given examples of poetic language, mythic creatures, non-speakings, and artistic performance show a variety of things that live together and with one another, differently. Synaesthesia brings together aesthetic senses in unusual combinations; synchronicities bring together times that defy chronology. I am grateful to old wives for their tales of creatures that disbelievers scoff at. And to experience the magic of theater or music, not knowing what to expect, seeing with all ears open: such is the syncretism that unites opposites in little spaces of much moreness.

PART III:
MYTH AS COSMOLOGICAL PEDAGOGY

ARTWORK "THE KEY GARDEN" BY ALEXANDRA C. SCHAUWECKER, SCAD 2013.

DANCE AS LIFE FORCE

The summers I spent in New Mexico I remember for the smell of pinon wood after a rainstorm, the narrow sidewalks on dusty Canyon Road, a Shubert piano concert, Indians wrapped in blankets in scorching midday heat, and my mother's ramada where, as the sun set behind the Sangre de Cristo mountains, we cooked out and smoked cigarettes. Best of all I remember the Indian dances we witnessed in the hot summer sun: the anticipation, waiting in the empty plaza of Taos pueblo, the sun beating down, Anglos like us lining the walls, waiting. Waiting. Then, faintly, the sound of drum beats. Then from a far off corner, the procession, slow; women in headdresses and black ornamental dresses, barefoot, solemn, waving boughs first with one arm then with another; Kochari dancers with their lavishly expressive bodies taunting the tourists, weaving in and out, sometimes taking away cameras, punctuating the solemnity with clowning; men coming out of the kiva, coming down the ladder, joining the dance. Elders, a chorus of men, beating drums and chanting to the rhythmic drum beats, a rhythm my Anglo ears can not comprehend; the chant low and punctuated; the dancing steps of the dancers anticipating the beat exactly: one, one, one; pause; one, one; pause; one, one, one, one; pause; one. I can not keep count. The Indian children, as solemn as their elders, do not miss the irregular beat.

Winter dances may have been even more magical. Again at Taos, in the freezing cold, a small boy dances with his elders. He can't be more than six. It is freezing cold. He has nothing covering his upper body. I am shivering and he is dancing. Later, Christmas Eve, we take the bus to Cochiti pueblo, where in the Catholic Church there we attend mass, along with the Indian congregation. After the priest blesses us, he departs; people remove all the chairs in the downstairs, the dirt floor left as open space, the altar stripped of chalice and cross, replaced by pine boughs. We stand in the balcony, waiting, waiting. Hushed anticipation. Waiting. Then the drum beat. One, one, one. Pause. One, one. And through the door the dancers, lavishly painted, dance the deer dance in a sacred ritual older, more primal than the Catholic mass: the whole thing a dance of opposites.

Dance is perhaps the best expression of myth. Myth gives us the experience of being alive. Myth is lively actuality, "an experience that shakes the innermost structure of being" (in Adams, 2001, p. 14). Dance is vitality itself: "this is the / text of the body/ dancing torsos/ back to the/vowels of the heart" (Snowber, 2008). It is vibrating sounds, rhythms, energy, movement. It is freedom expressed primally without conflict of difference. If these descriptors sound like the new science of string theory, that is intentional; for string theory strikes me as very like dance, with emphasis on tiny vibrations of energy all pulling together the fabric of different universes, or cultures. Different patterns, different vibrations of strings "dance" in elegant, undecipherable patterns to form the fabric of the universe (Greene, 1999). What annoys physicists delights mythologists. Myth celebrates difference, mystery and magic. For the physicist, these words– "mystery," "magic"– are anathema: that which cannot be observed or tested cannot be called "science." While some would shrug and say, "All right, then: these strange attractors of vibrating strings cannot be measured or calculated. The phenomena are murky, monstrous even. In that case, if not science, what we have here is philosophy." No, I demur. What we have here is myth. The vibrating strands of energy that cannot be measured are what myth and primal cultures celebrate precisely because they defy precision. Myth honors, rests upon, darkness (Fox and Sheldrake, 1996, p. 147).

Dance occupies space differently from what science demands. What Indian tribes share with myth is the notion that space is experiential. It is "the sacred theater of ... life and the ritual, umbilical cord that forever connects... to... [the] divine parent, the Earth" (Highwater, 1982, pp. 131–132). Discussing the Booger dance rituals of the Cherokee Indians, Jamake Highwater (himself part Cherokee) describes how the purpose of that dance is to rid the tribe of its fear of the white man. By employing obscenity and aggression, their bodies and facial expressions can neutralize the invasive tactics of outsiders. Dance becomes "a metaphor for an entire experience," Highwater writes, by summoning feelings without actualizing them (p. 147). Because of the holistic acceptance of all dichotomies, the dance-body of the tribal performer does not feel itself existing in a uni-verse but, one could say, in multiple hidden dimensions of parallel universes, each with its own cycle of nature, "body wise—the/ cell's knowing" (Snowber, 2008).

The science-myth equation I am suggesting has been anticipated by James Lovelock (2006), famous for his Gaia hypothesis:

> Life, the universe, consciousness, and even simpler things like riding a bicycle are inexplicable in words. We are only just beginning to tackle these emergent phenomena, and in Gaia they are as difficult as the near magic of the quantum physics of entanglement. But this does not deny their existence. (p. 38)

Would a mythologist deny the existence of Gaia? As the oldest of the Greek divinities, the mother of Earth (inclusive of the biosphere, atmosphere, oceans, and soil), Gaia was revered long after the patriarchal Olympians took over her ancient shrines, the gods still swearing binding oaths by invoking her name because her name was synonymous with the laws of nature (Walker, 1983, p. 352). Recalling her importance to the Greeks, Lovelock "legitimized" myth to some in the scientific community by using such words as "system," "order," "feedback," "homoeostasis," "self-regulatory," and "chaos." His most important word, however, was to insist that the Earth, like Gaia, is "living." We should not have dominion over Mother nor subdue what creeps upon her.

The Greeks also honored Chaos. For them, Chaos breeds life and is never destroyed, like Einstein's law of the conservation of mass energy. Chaos is nothingness but yet contains a mix of materials in one big soup. When opposite entities fuse, these create seeds of life. I am thinking that myth calls seeds what quantum science calls "sparticles" (Greene, 2005): those tiniest of particles beyond the scope of scopes, which are the matter out of which energy creates itself.

Myth, of course, configures the workings of the cosmos not through laws and equations but through metaphor and image, one such being the image of Eurynome, a Titan daughter of Ocean. In the pre-Hellenic Pelasgian creation myth, Eurynome emerges from Chaos. Because she has nothing to put her feet on, she dances atop the waves. She turns south and north, her motions wheeling new energy with each turn, spinning faster and faster, more and more wildly. What further energizes the emergent cosmos from Chaos is the serpent Ophion, formed from the rubbing of Eurynome's hands. He wraps himself seven times around her, her form now becoming one large cosmic egg that gives birth to the primal elements of life, and together they ascend to Mount Olympus to watch the unfolding world of all the creeping things they have created.

So far, the dancing, rubbing, wrapping, and birthing have emitted vibrating energy. One further aspect to this creation involves violence, for when Ophion challenges the rule of the Creatrix Eurynome, she banishes him from the mountain, bruising his head, kicking out his teeth, and casting him down into the dark caves below (Graves, 1955). In typical Greek fashion, one set of creators is upset by another, such that Eurynome fades into the background of subsequent Olympian storytellings, although her name lives, hidden in the names of both Aphrodite and Eurydice (Kline, 2004, p. 161).

Chaos, snake, seven swirlings, banishment: these are the elements of cosmic birthing. A watered down version is seen with the Genesis story, as Milton (1936) inferred, calling Eurynome "the wide/Encroaching Eve perhaps" (Book IX, line 581). Eve, even though her name means "Life," does not dance in the Bible. Dancing, rather, is the ritual action of tribal cultures and myth, as we may see with another dance, this one performed in one of the oldest cultic practices even today, the Eleusinian Mysteries, so named because they take place in Eleusis. These rites honor the grain goddess Demeter, whose distraught searching for her lost daughter Persephone involves several clues to the bodily nature of danced despair. Demeter searches for nine days, neither washing nor eating, finally demanding of her brother Zeus that he oversee the return of the daughter. This return is accomplished at Eleusis, where great joy follows great despair.

I ask my students to reflect on the meaning of the mystery of Persephone's return and on the dyad Demeter-Persephone. It is important to recall that this twosome is really a threesome, since the other older goddess of the underworld, Hekate, is involved in the search and rescue. She functions as the necessary hidden third that keeps the twosome in active engagement. Students reflect on the cosmic dyadic pattern of winter/spring, mother/daughter/, grief/joy, life/death/ youth/age, and movement/stasis as underlying impulses of the reunion of Demeter/Persephone. And, naturally, they are prompted to wonder what it is that the celebrants of the Eleusinian Mystery seek on their journey from Athens to Eleusis. What is the meaning of the mystery? While no one presumably knows the answer, since mysteries are to remain secret, I think Samuel Beckett (1981) suggests a cryptic answer in his reworkings of the mythic impulse to search for what is lost (a basic theme for him): "Know happiness" (p. 59). Happiness comes out of the great No. One "knows" happiness by not seeking it. Seeking will only find trouble. Happiness would seem, in this myth, to come from the crypt; thus it can never be translated, since each reemergence is always different, birth from death. Just as Persephone emerges from her underground palace to rejoin her mother, so too must she return to the underworld to rejoin Hades, only to reemerge and return again and again: each reemergence different, each return the same.

My dance around the pin of a conundrum is, I think, something of the impulse of the Demeter initiates. In imitation of Demeter's search, they do circle dances. But instead to moving the circle in a clockwise direction, they move counter-clockwise in a left-turning direction, the sinister realm of left-footedness; that is, "in the direction of death" (Berry, 1975, p. 198). Consequently, the left-footed quester would be the one most likely to achieve transformation, the purpose of the dance.

Thwarted transformation, however, could be one way to describe Samuel Beckett's themes. In his play *Footfalls*, I have written on his mother-daughter pairing which is hauntingly similar to the Demeter dance (Doll, 1988) The play features a daughter wheeling in circles of nine paces, obsessively, while the mother off stage recalls scraps of stories about the daughter, obsessively. The viewer is most struck by sound, since May the daughter paces, counting out her steps as if the wordcounts will help track her obsession more accurately: " seven eight nine wheel........ seven eight nine wheel" (Beckett, 1976, p. 43). Following the word "wheel," which the actress accentuates, May turns. It is as if the wheel is some sort of torture device, holding the daughter into her circle, like a spoke. Buddhists teach that the point of life is getting off the wheel: that which conditions existence (Boucher, 1993). But in *Footfalls* the tracing of "wheels" become one big Mobius strip. The dance is both excruciating and tantalizing in its effect, since clarity is just beyond reach. Beckett captures for me what it is to be caught inside a circle that never stops vibrating, as in negative action or active inaction, as in the frantic dance of the quantum world.

"Frantic" would be the accurate word to describe the Dionysian dances. Dionysus, as the god of wine and theater, evoked ecstasy in his followers, mostly women who for a short time could be released from their status as housebound inferiors: they could be *ex stasis*. Known as Maenads, these followers of Dionysus engaged in ritualistic frenzy, in sheer, wild celebration of joy that knows no bounds. They danced, fornicated, ripped apart small animals, ate flesh, drank blood. Theirs was the expression of discontent when too much civilization is felt. Theirs was also an origin of the sacred rite known as communion, eating the body of the god and drinking his blood. By ingesting the god into one's own body symbolically, one is doing theater, reenacting symbolically the literal words of the command "Eat my flesh, drink my blood."

The Dionysian rituals were extra-ordinary, indeed. Their id function can be seen as compensatory to the rigid requirements of super-ego norms. As such, they allowed followers to become other than themselves for a while, to engage in enacted fantasy. This is the basis of what Armando Rosa (2006) calls "archetypal theater." Tracing its roots back to Ancient Greek drama, and to Dionysian ritual by extension, Rosa writes that this type of theater "seeks to awaken an inner spark beyond rational conscious-ness by tapping into the symbolic imagination" (p. 56). Admittedly, the classroom is a testy place to try out these ideas. Many undergraduate art students, surprisingly, are avid church goers, some of fundamentalist persuasion. Some openly express dismay at my introducing such material. After one class a few years back, I received a note from a student who suggested that it would be better if I didn't touch on such matters. Nevertheless, another student had this to say about theater and excess:

> My fascination with Dionysus not only stems from the idea that even through his death he is creating life and vegetation (which brings life within itself) but also with his theatrical ways. It seems as though everything he touches turns to inspiration: the trees breathing life into humans, the theater breathing character into actors. It is all so amusing. Dionysus seems to have an aura, a personality that is intoxicating and makes everything he touches turn to joy, excitement, acting. His drunkenness affects the people by seeping into and letting loose and living through their own inhibitions. It's exciting, freeing, memorable and flourishing with life—just like Dionysus! And that legacy is extraordinary.

I am always amazed at my students' reactions. They sit there, some of them, poker-faced, the curtain pulled down, impossible to read. These are the ones, some of them, who seek to curb my enthusiasm. But others, through class discussion and written comment, are truly opening the door of the mind, able to avoid drunkenness while yet feeling intoxicated by the sheer energy of ideas.

Perhaps it is easier, then, for students to understand what is being conveyed by the Hindu dancers Kali and Shiva. I wonder if those brought up with such images have an easier time with symbolism, since it is impossible to see the familiar Hindu image of a four-armed god or goddess literally. I think of the beloved god Ganesha with his elephant head. I think of Krishna with his blue skin. So with Kali. The symbolic nature of her nature has to challenge the literal-seeking eye of the Westerner. For there she is: four-armed, black skinned, dressed with a serpent skirt and adorned with skeleton heads. And her tongue sticks out. All of this exoticism is foreign to the Protestant Ethic or the Western rational tradition. Yet, thinking of Coatlicue, "Serpent Skirt," the earth goddess of the Aztecs, I must wonder if in fact the monstrous image breeds not symbolism but its opposite, literalism, noting that Aztec priests fed the goddess by sacrificing human flesh. Like Kali, Coatlicue was a terror to look at, with two fanged serpent heads, a necklace of human body parts, and a skirt of writhing snakes. Up until the late fifteenth century, sacrificial rites continued by the offering of as many as 60,000 human hearts to the ravening maw of the Aztec goddess (Hathaway, 2001, p. 76). Hardly symbolic.

Even though human sacrifices were also offered for a while to the gruesome Hindu goddess Kali, she is more often worshiped for her powers of regeneration under the name Kali-Ma. To see her symbolically is to focus on her dance. The most famous of Kali's postures is the odd juxtaposition of her grimacing face and menacing body with her dancing energy atop the corpse of her consort Shiva. Part of her energy is attributed to her birth in anger, from the forehead of Durga: anger energizes Kali's powers to destroy demons who threaten the cosmic order. But she also creates life, since her dancing reanimates the dead Shiva. The ambiguities inherent within the image and action of this ancient goddess remind me of the wisdom of ambiguity itself, of the earth goddess herself, of the both/and combination inherent in mythic iconography.

The earth goddess is not like the Christian Madonna. Rather, the earth goddess is the embodiment of primal energy and the combination of all opposing forces: male and female, dark and light, good and evil. She is what David Adams Leeming (1990) calls *both* "the matrix of forms, the mystery of the unconscious world" *and* "the primal energy that impregnates the matrix and allows forms to be realized" (p. 135).

The archetype of the great goddess can be thought of as a celebration of dance as life force. For it is the pattern of this archetype to bring back to life that which disappears in death. It is the pattern of regeneration, life from death. From Demeter searching for and united with her disappeared daughter; to the goddess Isis, searching for and resurrecting her disappeared brother-lover Osiris; to Kali, whose dance re-erects her consort's penis: the necessary death and the necessary dance of life combine to re-energize the cosmos.

No discussion of dance as life force would be complete without mention of two more figures, one known and one not so well known. The well known dancer would have to be Shiva, Lord of the Cosmic Dance, but also The Destroyer. How, one wonders, can violence be dance-like? One response is to look back on Eurynome, dancer from the primordial chaos, who violently threw her consort Ophion out of Mount Olympus. Another response is to consider how nature's violence—earthquakes, tsunamis, volcanoes—create new life once their dancing destructions wipe the earth clean. Whoever has witnessed a violent storm might attest that words used to describe dance, such as swaying, flashing, thrusting, leaping, might also be used to describe the terrible forces of nature. Shiva, one of the three forces in the Hindu cosmos, is as necessary a part of keeping the cosmos balanced as is Vishnu or Brahma. Once the cosmos becomes unbalanced, it must be destroyed to create a new order of balance. This is Shiva's function. His iconography shows him in the center of a circle of fire. He has four arms, two legs, and streaming hair that contains both a skull and a moon. Right/left symbolism is evident in that his right hand holds the drum beating out the ticks of time. His left hand holds the flame that burns away illusion. The left lifted foot symbolizes "release," while the right foot stamps on a dwarf named "Forgetfulness" (Campbell, 1974, p. 359). Joseph Campbell's understanding of each of the symbolic points of the dancing god allows us to appreciate the vast wisdom and complexity of ancient religion.

Finally, I want to share a lesser known dancer of religion. During research for this chapter I could not help but wonder if Jesus was a dancer. Imagine how thrilled I was to discover, indeed, in the apocryphal literature there is an omitted section in an account of the Last Supper. It has to do with what has been called the Round Dance of the Cross, found in the Acts of John. On that final night, it is written, Jesus invited his disciples to dance and sing:

> Before he was arrested... he assembled us all, and said, 'Before I am delivered to them, let us sing a hymn to the Father, and so go to meet what lies before us.' So he told us to form a circle, holding one another's hands, and he himself stood in the middle and said, 'Answer Amen to me.' (in Pagels, 2004, p. 123)

This fascinating passage shows Jesus in the manner of the Buddha equating suffering as a cosmic dance: "Whoever dances belongs to the whole. Amen, Whoever does not dance does not know what happens. Amen" (in Pagels, 125). That Jesus is viewed in so many different ways, some of these ways secret, point to a similar mystery of the universe. What is known is only partially known.

If we think through, which is to say imagine deeply, the implications of the cosmic dancer we are left breathless by the energetic power of the life force. Kali, with her primordial energy, is so vast that "the series of universes appear and disappear with the opening and shutting of her eyes" (Avalon, 1978, p. 396.) Or, as Maud Oakes observes about Shiva's dance, "its deepest significance is felt when it is realized that it takes place within the heart of the self" (in Henderson and Oakes, 1990, p. 80). Dance unites body, soul, and mind with the vibrating strings of the cosmos. A theatrical aspect of dance brings us out of ourselves into space. "This is poetry; but none the less, science" (Oakes, in Henderson and Oakes, p. 82).

CHAPTER 11

SHAPE SHIFTING

"We are ... amphibious animals caught on the hop between angel and beast."

— T. Eagleton

The summer of 2009 might be remembered for the death of Michael Jackson, tormented genius. Was he angel or beast? I am struck by my own caught-upness in the swirls of rumor surrounding his sudden death, by the emotion flooding out from his memorial, by the sordidness of his life story, slowly emerging, dripping, we could say, like the drops of Diprivan into his body (hand? neck?); by the news of his seeking seventy-two hours of induced coma: release, relief from his demons, his fleshliness; put under with anesthesia for three days into a no-dream state. And yet, Michael was a dancer! If, as Michael Gard (2006) asserts, dance has the ability to change "'who you are' in unpredictable ways" (p. 194), then this most unpredictable story, this man, this Michael Jackson was the dancer who could change himself both in his body and inside the public performances of his body – but not in his soul. He was America's trickster shape changer, neither angel nor beast.

I am struck by how split off Michael was from who he was, and that, of course, is the problem. As his producer commented, Michael was two persons: the private Michael, soft spoken and shy; the public dancer, flamboyant and bad. Who was the man in the mask? Changing his skin was one action that seemed to allow him to escape from his skin (both his blackness and his maleness), to remake himself into a— what?—white woman? ghoul? panther? machine? Another action he took was to perform on various stages, perhaps trying to feel something, to have a sense of control, to construct his subjectivity, to forget his father. As the Michael Jackson saga unfolded, we witnessed the fact that identity, anything but stable, can undergo constructions to nose, lips, eyes, chin, cheek, skin, hair; but without an energy exchange with the inner demons, the angel can never fly.

The summer of 2009 also witnessed the furor over the "identity politics" of Supreme Court then-nominee now Justice Sonia Sotomayer. Frequently, in the Senate confirmation hearings and in the media ramblings, we heard repetitions of her comment that a wise Latina woman could make better decisions than a white male. To me, that remark is perfectly reasonable. Obvious, even. Experience matters. It shapes who you are and changes how you think. Just ask Michael Jackson. But it is as if the white male senators who drilled her on this eight-year-old comment had never been called to account for *their* white male privilege, how it blinds, how it deafens. Instead, they wanted her to submerge her ethnicity, and most certainly her gender, to what they considered more appropriate (white, male). That she actually had to apologize for what she said is the problem of identity politics when a melting-pot illusion holds sway.

Caught as we are in such strident (politically correct) times, the idea of shape changing challenges the sense of correctness. This chapter takes up that challenge. I admit to having difficulty getting my mind around mythic stories of nymphs, satyrs, shamans, gods, and tricksters who disappear into trees or become animal. But let me shed my inhibitions for a while to explore what these various shape changes suggest, not just about identity but about forces that vibrate our planet.

One premise of this book is that myth and new science are on a similar wave length: what myth says in metaphor is what science says in theory. Vibrating strings are what keep the planet spinning. Energy exchange is what balances the cosmos. When myth introduces twins, one good the other bad, that is a metaphor for balance. When myth introduces nymphs merging into trees, that is a metaphor for the living organism we call "tree." Nothing is stable. All is flux. From the smallest atom to the human body as a whole, all is flux. As Deepak Chopra (1989) puts it, "The human body also stands there looking much the same from day to day, but through the processes of digestion, elimination, and so forth, it is constantly and ever in exchange with the rest of the world" (p. 49).

What is fascinating about Chopra's above quote is its wide-reaching claim: not just does the exchange system function within an organism; it functions without, as well: the body exchanges energy with the rest of the world. This understanding corroborates what Carl Jung (1958) observed about the human psyche; namely, its sickness can sicken others: "None of us stands outside humanity's black collective shadow." One would do well, he cautioned, "to possess some 'imagination of evil,' for only the fool can permanently neglect the conditions of his own nature" (pp. 96–97).

One way to acquire an "imagination of evil," without literalizing it, is to open up to the dream state. The unconscious is like another energy system that acts to balance (Jung's word is "compensate") consciousness. What this means is that the pretension to normality and goodness is only one of the twins of the self. The upper self runs smoothly in its linear fashion so long as it keeps open the gate to the "sportive fantasy" ready to bolt from dreams (Jung, 1974, p. 17). The play metaphor is deliberate, on two levels. Jung interprets dreams as if they are theater, all figures in the dream symbolic representations of the dreamer: dreamer as actor, dreamer as director, dreamer as producer, scene, critic, and so forth. This is psychic physics, recalling the Heisenberg Principle that at the subatomic level no clear distinction exists between actor and action. Jung also sees images as playful, some not so nice, offering a totally different view from which to understand one's standpoint. While dreams can "tail off everywhere in inanity" and madden the logical left brain, they delight in a playful "free rein" of images (Jung, 1974, p. 17). Dream images shift and blend and sport with our morals, employing "numerous mythological motifs" (p. 79) that present themselves to consciousness for balance and compensation. Depth psychologists (like new scientists, like old myth) insist that all of life is flux, becoming, changing form.

Now to myth. The Celts, Native Americans, and Hindu myths were particularly fond of shape changing, symbolic of an expansion beyond ordinary confines and an intermingling of the divine in mundane existence. Jungian analyst James Fitzgerald (2008) explores the dramatic elements in an early Irish Otherworld story, "The Voyage of Bran," which offers a compelling example not only of belief in an other reality (call it the Otherworld, call it the Unconscious, call it the Sacred) twinned to literal reality but also a delight in processes of Becoming. The myth takes Bran away from his habituated place into a magical realm and back again, in a classic under-standing of Joseph Campbell's hero adventure. What differentiates this tale from, say, that of Gilgamesh is the constant use of the gerund, the verbal noun, to suggest the ongoingness of Bran's doings in a metaphorical sense. Even at the return moment, when Bran crosses the boundary from the sacred realm of the Otherworld back into the mortal world, the gerundive quality is not lost. Instead of committing the story to stone, as with Gilgamesh, the story of Bran is committed to Memory. "The men of Ireland do not know Bran, but they do know his story, from of old" (Fitzgerald, 2008, p. 29).

Bran's tale is exuberant, lush, and profound. The Otherworld is not dreary like Hades but magical like Elysium, filled with what can be found by the backward glance, openness to unknown figures, women, laughter and the aural sense. "Lulled by [the music's] sweetness, he slept, and on awaking found by his side a musical branch of silver and white blossoms" (MacCulloch, 2004, p. 114). This is a magical branch, a gift, which emerges from Bran's dream state as a talisman from the Otherworld. And the branch "leaps" from his hand to the mysterious Anima figure who beckons him to sail away on the waters. Once on the sea, embarking on his voyage to the unknown, Bran experiences the undivided nature of nature: what he sees as a sea is to Manannan (a god figure) a plain. Fitzgerald (2008) writes, "Bran's identity has become transformed into the symbolic dimension of story which the ordinary world can look to as an example forever after" (p. 29). All things visible take on qualities of becoming and shape shifting:

The speckled salmon in the sea were calves and lambs, and steeds invisible to Bran were there also. People were sitting playing and drinking wine, and making love without crime. Bran's coracle was not on the waves, but on an immortal wood, yielding fruit and perfume; the folk of the land were immortal and sinless, unlike Adam's descendants, and in it rivers poured forth honey. (in MacCulloch, 2004, p. 115)

These images sound like the Land of Milk and Honey, but certain features prevent it from lapsing into Biblical commonality. Bran, after all, upon his return is not recognized and the tales of his future wanderings are not of interest. His stay in the Otherworld seems to him "for a year, though it was in truth many years" (in MacCulloch, p. 115). And his companion becomes a heap of ashes upon setting foot on land. What we experience in this story is the meeting of time and space in an idyllic place beyond the opposites. The return to the mundane world, however, reduces the gold to ashes. The idea is that one cannot hold onto as personal possession the wonders of the fantasy land. This story of transformation is not that of a conscious construction of visibles, as with poor Michael Jackson's morphings, but of a willing participation in the dream state, world next door—and a necessary return. The story is a reminder that the return is essential; otherwise, one can be deceived into thinking that this land is Neverland. The significance of the mythic journey, as Fitzgerald (2008) puts it, is that "identity depends both on a center where singularity exists, and a peripheral area which presents multiple possibilities of being… the [I, by which we define ourselves] arises out of the multiple possibilities within the unconscious" (p. 21). Importantly, it is the margin not the center that is the source of change, and it is the return that makes the hero. In "The Song of Wandering Aengus," the great poet W.B. Yeats (1959) suggests a vision ("a fire in the head") of the effervescence of this Otherland: its "brightening air" with clear references to Celtic motifs: "the hazel wood," "white moths," "a glimmering girl," "hollow lands," and "long dappled grass" (pp. 57–58).

A feature of journeys to the other realm is often signaled by a natural phenomenon, even in my own back yard. It is dusk, it is dawn, a mist descends, a haze hovers. How thin the veil! Something magical like myth occurs for me in summer when the thrumming of insects tells me my backyard is inhabited by invisibles. The edges of my garden oscillate in the heat. On autumn predawn mornings when a heavy fog shrouds the landscape, trees assume a thinner appearance. Sounds become muffled. This, I suspect, is something like that which Irish poets experienced in the bogs of Ireland.

An equally fantastical figure as Bran is the Celtic hero Cuchulainn. He is one of my students' favorites, requiring a second read over the paragraphs describing his warp spasm, or distortion:

> He grew to an immense size and quivered in every limb, while his feet, shins, and knees were reversed in his body…. Of Cuchulainn's eyes, on sank in his head so that a heron could not have reached it, while the other protruded from its socket as large as the rim of a cauldron. His mouth reached his ears, and fire streamed from it, mounting above his head in showers, while a great jet of blood higher and more rigid than a ship's mast shot upward from his scalp, within which his hair retreated, and formed a mist all about. (in MacCulloch, 2004, pp. 154–155)

Now, Here! is a warrior! That he must die alone standing tied to a rock is another tip off that Here! is a warrior. As my student Elise sees it, Cuchulainn's death offers "a powerful image: this insane warped man fighting with the force of so many others and yet fighting alone…. this puts the thrill of fighting valiantly with one's comrades in the gutter." The text I use in class offers other strangenesses about this figure, which another student commented on:

> I found the description of Cuchulainn's appearance one of the more interesting aspects. He had seven fingers on each hand and seven pupils in each eye. I understand that the authors of Celtic myths embellished a lot to make things more exciting to the audience and I find this quite similar to their art. A term that is often used in relation to Celtic art is *horror vacui,* or the fear of empty spaces, a term used to describe the intricate line work that fills every space available.

Ben's observation connecting art and myth interests me for its additional insight into new science, with its understanding that solids are filled with gaps and spaces. Deepak Chopra (1989) explains this paradox solid/empty by referencing the human body, claiming "everything solid, including our bodies, is proportionately as void as inter-galactic space" (p. 96). Embellishing the void is one way to ward off its horrors. Another way is to so intricately work the lines of the craft of metal working into triplicates that the figure melds with the ground, a new/old idea of interconnectedness. Certainly, the body of Cuchulainn in warrior pose gives rise to these ideas. He is a veritable explosion of form, of willful superabundance.

It is easy for the skeptic to label as "superstition" that which the Celts knew as mysticism. The Celts believed in the mysteries of the cosmos, accessible to the one who entered an altered state of consciousness either through dream or vision or potion. The very prevalence of shape shifting as seen in such motifs as the Celtic knot, severed heads, and magical cauldrons, all braided together, suggests a unity beneath the forms and changing shapes. A myth of the first Welsh poet Taliesin is rife with such changing shapes of humans, reminiscent of "The Runaway Bunny" story I knew as a child. To escape the goddess Cerridwen's anger at his disobedience, the boy Gwion Bach turned into a hare; she turned into a greyhound. He became a fish; she took the shape of an otter. He turned into a bird; she turned into a falcon. Finally, when he became a single grain of wheat, she swallowed it. Nine months later, she gave birth to Taliesin, so named for his radiant head, symbolic of his visions. The name change from Gwion Bach to Taliesin is symbolic, too, of his being birthed anew as a shaman. Commenting on this wondrous tale, Tom Cowan (1993) writes

> Clearly, we are working with a complex set of interlocking symbols and images, but the classic elements of the shaman's initiation are a key to understanding them. Although they seem to defy time and space, as visionary experiences they form a coherent whole: death or near-death experiences and the resulting trans-formations of consciousness; the help of animal spirits and the ability to transform into them to receive their specific energy and knowledge; the journey into nonordinary reality; the realization that all creation is interchangeable, and, in some sense, one. (pp. 42–43)

The Celtic knot expresses just such interconnectedness.

Now, with Native American mythology various similarities can be found with Celtic mysticism. The story of Sky Woman is one such. She is the grandmother of twins, Good Twin and Evil Twin. They function symbolically as positive and negative energies that work off each other to keep the cosmos in balance. My class text describes how Good Twin dug up his mother's dead body and turned her face into the sun, the back of her head into stars and moon, and the tears of her grandmother into irrigation for plants and fruits. Thus out of death comes life, a basic mythic motif. Further, Good Twin balances Evil Twin's bad actions. While he creates razor-edged rocks, Good Twin creates soothing waters (in Hathaway, 2002). This motif of balance and creative opposition is foreign to the Western mind used to separating opposites, good from bad. But by resolving a split-off sense of things, this Native American cosmogony anticipates the dynamism of subatomic physics, where vibrating strands of energy which cannot be observed create all the different particles in nature, like a cosmic symphony (Greene, 1999).

Cosmogonies of dismemberment, such as above, provide us with the sense that all is useful in the cosmos, nothing is wasted, everything has intelligence and spirit.

For one student, this idea of ecological exchange among different energy systems is "amazing": "The idea that we are part of the earth and vice versa, is a concept that I wish was still in common practice nowadays, especially in modern religion," he writes. "It is almost common knowledge that the Indian people of North America always hated to waste anything, whether it be from their crop or from their hunt, but we Americans are a wasteful people."

Enter Louise Erdrich, of the Ojibwa tribe. She explodes the concept of the "positive primitive" with her unsettling accounts of life on the plains. In *The Antelope Wife* (1998) the reader is introduced to an Indian creation story with twins. I am comfortable with this idea until I read past the second line: "Ever since the beginning," she writes, "these twins are sewing. One sews with light and one with dark.... They sew with a single sinew thread, in, out, fast and furious, each trying to set one more bead into the pattern than her sister, each trying to upset the balance of the world" (p. 2). *Upset* the balance? The craft in question is, I thought, an honorable one of beadmaking. One set of beads is white and pale; the other is red and blue-black. But then the details get more graphic. Not only do the girl twins vie to create chaos, the beading awl is made of animal penis. There is sharpness here. Strangeness. Surely this detail of the awl is one way of to suggest that all–every organ, structure, aspect of an animal—can be used in new ways. Still, the eyes in my white skin open wide.

Turning the page my confusion mounts. Erdrich introduces the first character. He is a Calvary soldier who comes upon an Indian village in chaos. He feels contempt, then hate, and takes pleasure in aiming his gun this way and that:

> Eager, he bayoneted an old woman who set upon him with no other weapon but a stone picket from the ground. She was built like the broken sacks of hay he'd used for practice, but her body closed fast around the instrument. He braced himself against her to pull free, set his boot between her legs to tug the blade from her stomach, and as he did so tried to avoid her eyes but did not manage. (p. 4)

I am beginning to get a sense that this is a different kind of myth, what Jamake Highwater (1994) calls a "new myth" that recognizes the irrationality, violence, and chaos in the cosmos:

> The old mythologies provided us with uniformity, predictability, and a comforting orderliness. God was not a gambler. But the new myths of science and psychology, like the new visions of the arts, are fraught with inconsistency, unpredictability, and the inevitable threat of chaos. (p. 144)

I am learning to adjust my eyes, my white eyes, which are looking to see what I expect: a cosmogony of balance between good and evil, a harmony, perhaps even a Celtic romanticism about Native American experience. My white eyes are reading what my white eyes want to read. Now I have to adjust my glasses, and re-read Erdrich's opener to see what I think she is telling us: the sister twins of the prologue here have been tainted by the white intrusion of the Indian Diaspora. While one twin has a set of pale, white beads, representing the white man, the sister twin has a set of red, blue-black beads, representing the red man battered. The intricate beadwork is not creating a grand design but a war between red and white and it is a fight for the survival of a culture.

This is a culture that is comfortable with the idea of hybridity, just as Erdrich herself is a mix between a German father and an Ojibwa mother. Much of her novel centers on the idea that nothing is distinct from anything else, not past from present, not sky from earth, not animal from human. *Antelope Wife* takes its name from the woman character who is a descendant from an antelope. She is strangeness itself; that is, she is strange to human-animals not used to seeing the world from the perspective of animal. Erdrich slips in animal/nature words in the description of the wife but does not offer direct comment, as if to keep the reader at bay. The wife floats on springy, tireless legs (p. 23), has a "deer-haunch bottom" (p. 46), has hair "dark as heaven, with roan highlights and arroyos of brown, waves deep as currents, a river of scented nightfall" (p. 24) and scent "like grass and wind" (p. 107). She is of nature. And, while she seems uncomfortable in the presence of humans, her presence spooks others. Erdrich suggests that the once-close connection shared between animal and humans in Native American life has been severed, although traces of that connection remain to remind. The antelope wife "alters the shape of things around her and she changes the shape of things to come," Erdrich writes (p. 106). For a reader, like myself, schooled in Western European thought, this particular character (not to mention another one who had a deer husband) sounds bizarre. But consider this:

> The ability to transform into human or animal form might be considered highly suspicious, and one may be tempted to relegate these transformation myths as mere superstitions of a primitive people. However, keep in mind that the point of these teachings isn't whether once can actually, physically, transform into another species, but rather [of] the interdependent nature of our relationship with animals. (Lacourt, 2010, p. 82)

Clearly, the discomfort that the antelope wife causes herself and others when traversing among humans is a signal of the great divide brought about by "civilization."

This idea of unbalanced life is not new to Native American thinking. The film *Koyaanisqatsi* (Reggio, 1983) takes its name from a Hopi Indian word meaning "life out of balance." Filmed fifteen years before Erdrich's novel, *Koyaanisqatsi* juxtaposes images of the natural world of canyons, rivers, and clouds with the unnatural world of technology, commodity, and the space shuttle disaster. Without words, only employing the mesmerizing music of Philip Glass, the film indicates that we do not live in an interpreted world where understanding comes from being rooted in the earth and its bounty; rather, the canyons of our big cities form the new cathedrals for worship.

Art has always been an implicit part of the community mentality of Indian life (Highwater, 1994, p. 156). The world we find with both Erdrich and the film directed by Godfrey Reggio uses its art to express the chaos of life, where those who live close to the land must now do so in a decidedly nonromantic way. There is no Elysium here. It is probably disingenuous of Reggio to claim that his film is pure art, made without predetermined meaning, simply there for the viewer to take from it what she will. The film, built on contrast of speed, image, and musical intensity, is clearly, like Erdrich's novel, a statement about the current lack of connection between humans and the world we inhabit. What may have once been harmony and balance is now most surely interrupted.

Erdrich shows us something of what Toni Morrison reveals in her novels: the other side of the myth of the American Dream. For both women novelists it is the old women characters that refuse sentimentality while also refusing bitterness. They are hardy: "[they] believe that they have earned the right to talk about sex, birth, blood, the size and shape of men's equipment, the state of their own, even at the Christmas dinner table" (Erdrich, p. 202). A pregnant woman is advised to eat the head of a skunk in order to have an easier birth. This communal banquet is full of the grit of life, one cycle, of which death is another and rebirth a question.

Reading the new myth of Erdrich is a learning experience that challenges a Westerner schooled in "scholarly prejudice" (Deloria, Jr., 2009). What we read in her work is ambiguity unfettered. Belief that the world is ordered is challenged, and all hierarchies are thrown out the window. The unsparing lack of sentiment, the political intent, the relative humorlessness are all traits of her remarkable explosion of ideas. The new myth she presents, with its nonlinear logic and emergence of intelligences in nonhuman forms, is surely tragic, showing that humans have lost the trajectory of their destinies. But it is also convergent with the new scientific theories of complexity and chaos—long holding residence in American Indian tribal customs, habits, and social organizations (Deloria, Jr. and Wildcat, 2001, p. 34). Perhaps it is the animals that will hold the necessary beads of the cosmic design. Endowing dogs with intelligence, Erdrich writes: "We dogs know what the women are really doing when they are beading. They are sewing us all into a pattern.... We are the tiny pieces of the huge design that they are making—the soul of the world" (p. 83).

As a professor of literature, I have long felt that literary artists give us insight and theory through fiction (Doll, 2000). Fiction allows us the second look at startling ideas that otherwise we might overlook. Myth, too, is fiction in the sense that it hides in metaphor what are truths too difficult to express directly, like the necessary energy that comes from the play of opposites, like the loss of energy when one opposite overtakes the other, or like a cosmos that is enspirited. Louise Erdrich, as I have tried to show, is one artist presenting a new myth.

A different approach to the idea of change and myth is one many Southern writers tackle when exploding the myth of the Old South as a gracious, hospitable, elegant, and chivalrous place. This is the myth that life on the plantation was as serene as its surface representation would seem to suggest: big house, white columns, oak trees lined with Spanish moss, happy darkies. As the song goes, "It's a fact, it's actual, everything is satisfactual." Well, shucks, zippity doo dah. Disney (1946) exploited that myth for white America in his *Song of the South* film with no intention of looking beyond and under the white lies. But in that same decade of the 40s, Katharine Du Pre Lumpkin (1946/1997) questioned the traditional orthodoxies of Southern social conditions in her portrayal of the archetype of the Southern Gentleman. She gives a full account of the expectations of the young master, his place in the world secure. "More plainly than anything else," she writes, "he would know that in his circumstances of life on a slave plantation the white master did not do any farm work himself.... He would know as a fact beyond argument or questions that his black slaves deserved and needed their slavery" (pp. 88, 89). Lumpkin keenly portrays this sense of entitlement which necessarily accompanies a sense of privilege. It is no wonder, she shows, that the onslaught of the Civil War changed everything and shattered the Myth of the Old South:

> [The Southern Gentleman] would know he was master in all things on his plantation, everything, nothing excepted, including the life of his slaves. With it he would know that his station was secure as a Southern gentleman. It would seem it left a special stamp on men who lived this life. But more particularly in a special way it stamped their sons, who were reared to expect it and then saw it snatched away. (p. 89)

Not so fast! As my student Caleb Dorr recollects, the Old South ideas lived on, well into the 20th century. He comments:

> It was not until I read some of the works by W.J. Cash and William Faulkner that I truly understood what was behind that perfect Southern façade. Most of the Southern gentlemen that occupied my home town, Madison, Georgia, were, in fact, people "sprung for the most part from the convict servant, redemptioners, and debtors of old Virginia and Georgia (Cash, 1997, p. 76), though to my young eyes they were all rich, successful, and virtuous. I knew that when I grew up, I would own that big white house my parents owned and that I would employ our caretaker, and that I would be responsible for the wellbeing of our 'plantation.' I came to believe that the whole world was this way, and that it would remain so; that is until I left Georgia to live in the bustling city of Houston, Texas.... I found over time that people were not all kind, and that not everyone was a gentleman or lady.... When I came back to Georgia after years of traveling, Georgia to my eyes was different yet entirely the same. (midterm exam in my Southern Literature class).

It would seem that Caleb has lifted the Veil, seeing both what was now different (with one set of eyes) and yet, contrapuntally, entirely the same (with the other, old set).

So many shapes. So many changes. That is myth; that is dream for some, nightmare for others; that is the process of becoming, which tradition seeks to hold back. To see through the fog of legend, as Caleb did, is to take a very big step in changing consciousness. Life means changing form, for all is in flux. To understand the "Myth of the Old South" is also to understand how the rigidity of its forms could not withstand the wrongness of its institutions. Irish mysticism, Native American new and old myths, and the fiction of bad myths all show the rise and fall of inevitabilities as well as the futility of supposed facts. Gertrude Stein had it wrong. A rose is not (just) a rose.

THE COSMIC MOUTH

There is a carved stone head dating back to Neolithic times found in Knowth, Boyne Valley, Ireland that has spiral eyes, snake spirals on both sides and a fluted design along the forehead and chin. Most striking is the wide open mouth gaping from the center of the head. According to Marija Gimbutas (2006), mytho-archaologist, the open mouth symbolizes "the generative Divine Source." When the spout of a container was shaped in the open mouth formation, the liquid poured from it "reenacted" the Goddess function of offering sacred moisture, from which all life springs (pp. 64, 65). Gimbutas connects this type of stone sculpture, found not only in Ireland but also in the east Mediterranean and southeastern Europe, with what she has called Bird Goddess figurines of Old Europe, often placed in tombs to symbolize the regenerative power of life coming from death. One god associated with the Goddess was Hermes, also connected with fertility and life but also with the underworld and ghosts. It is said of him that "When he shines forth, the earth blossoms and when he laughs, the plants bear fruit, and at his bidding the herds bring forth young" (Harrison, 1962, p. 296). What these divinities have in common is the power of the mouth. What pours or laughs from the mouth is necessary for cosmic energies to create and recreate out of death. But such pourings-forth speak a kind of language long lost to modern ears.

Samuel Beckett (1977) may have had this inability to hear other kinds of language in mind when he wrote his short play *Not I* with two "characters": Mouth and Auditor. According to his biographer James Knowlson (1996), "Mouth's" monologue has the feel of old Ireland "evoking the life of an Irish 'bag lady,'... totally shut in on herself, speaking to no one—until something happens that releases a stream of sound, so that words flow out of her like water gushing from the mouth of a stone lion in a fountain" (p. 522). The title *"Not I"* is meant to disconnect the figure on stage from anything remotely similar to an "I"-speaking character that theater-goers would recognize. What issues forth from "Mouth" are vehement spewings, often unintelligible, with, as Beckett writes, "refusal to relinquish third person" (p. 14). Lacking the first person pronoun, the figure "Mouth" cannot be seen as fully human, for what characterizes the human condition, the notion of "character," is memory. But the figure cannot get purchase on her past, or her present for that matter: "steady stream... straining to hear... make something of it... and her own thoughts... make something of them... all–... what? ... the buzzing?" (Beckett, 1977, p. 19). The voice's clamoring does not belong to "Mouth" but occupies "Mouth's" orifice to express a stream of verbal discharge such as one might find with psychotics or split personalities.

The experience of being in company with "Mouth" is completely dislocating for a hearing-viewing audience. Beckett deliberately places us inside the territory of the unfamiliar so as to force connection back to very old, archetypal source material, with universal significance. The open mouth is a play with "blubbering lips" that works, Beckett says, "on the nerves, not the intellect" (in Doll, 1988, p. 59). We need to think at the cellular level where the memory traces lie. Although "Mouth" mouths winter and spring images, with their symbolic seasonal connections to the mythic Persephone-Demeter goddesses, there is no sense of regeneration such as the myth intends. The old myths and relics, having died, insist, however, on coming back and do so with a vengeance (Freud's "return of the repressed"). "Mouth," reduced to being a talking machine, cannot understand her own speech-acts. Her refrain "God is love... tender mercies" (Beckett, 1977, pp. 22, 23) is a mere mechanical talking point, uttered as a Christian slogan that has explained-away the life-affirming, necessarily paradoxical, old myths and mysteries. The open mouth of the stone figure that once was the source of deep memory is now inaccessible to modern ears. Like others of Beckett's female figures, "Mouth" is a tormented soul, ghosted by the dead, there but not there.

The material that causes Beckett's figures their despair would seem to issue from an Irish collective unconscious. The female figures in "Not I" and in other of Beckett's later plays act as conduits that no longer promise regenerative powers. Instead, the open mouth is a furious sputter of half-remembered pieces from various pasts. Meaning has been buried for so long, millennia in fact, that the female open mouth, while full of sound and fury, signifies nothing.

Apprehending meaning from "nothing" is one of the themes in *King Lear* (1623/ 1999), a play in which the word "nothing" rings the tragedy. Asked to tell her father how much she loves him, to earn her rightful portion of the king's land, Cordelia refuses to speak falsely. She repeats the word "nothing," to which her father responds, "Nothing will come of nothing. Speak again" (Shakespeare, I, i, l.90). "Speech is lying and silence is truth in this play" (Orgel, 1999, p. xxxiii) where, however, nothing and nonsense are full of meaning.

Shakespeare's Fool, unlike Beckett's female figures, knows whereof his "nothing" speaks. In *King Lear* the Fool has been termed the "uncanniest character in Shakespeare" (Bloom, 1999, p. 494), who makes witty use of "nothing." The Fool is an archetypal character who functions as a mediator between realms to break distinctions, reveal ambiguities, shift point of view, and see inner truths. He belongs to an occult world beyond our knowing, so riddles his speech. Like a Zen koan, the riddles of the Fool "speak the truth, which he knows not by ratiocination but by inspired intuition." He is "the impartial critic, the mouthpiece of real sanity" (Welsford, 1966, p. 269). While King Lear may represent secular authority, he lacks self knowledge—a fact that the Fool and the favored daughter Cordelia both understand. Cordelia and the Fool reflect each other and they also act as Lear's shadow, for they see into his darkness. "It is no accident," Enid Welsford (1966) writes, "that the plot of the most universal and human of tragedies [*King Lear*] should emerge from a mist of folk-tale, mythology and primitive (*sic*) superstition" (p. 272). Stephen Orgel (1999) concurs, noting "Though the story of Lear comes from the chronicles of ancient Britain, the action belongs more to the world of legend than history.... [and] momentous decisions are determined by trifles" (p. xxxii). Harold Bloom (1999) comments on the Fool's absent presence, as being "something other than a character" (p. 494). Call him an archetypal figure full of ancient memory traces.

Isn't it interesting that the tragedy *King Lear* gets its momentum from "nothing"! Is this Shakespeare's "butterfly effect" of chaos theory, as Edward Lorenz (1993) termed it, where small perturbations can render fast-growing strange effects? What at first seems like a small disturbance on Cordelia's part to refuse to flatter her father becomes, in the end, the cause of mental and physical storms "far from equilibrium," as chaos theorists like to say. And it is mouthings that cause the chaos.

For the premoderns, chaos was the prime matter out of which order could be created. Creation stories frequently begin with female symbols that remind us that it is the Goddess who gives form to life: she is the *prima materia* (first matter) without which life could not exist. Out of the darkness and the un-knowing, out of the unseen pattern of being, something gropes its way from apparent chaos into ever widening places. But to see the order forming or to hear what is as-yet unspoken is the stuff of both very old stories and very new ones. Chaos (without which there would be no creation) is not formlessness but is rather form-in-the-making—call it spirit, fluidity, energy, vital integrity. But for Shakespeare's tragedy and Beckett's nerve-drama, the open mouth speaks to deaf ears.

I chose the above two plays to illustrate a loss of the essential human. In Jungian terms, Lear's egotism is a result of a split from his unconscious material which the shadow (the Fool) represents. Lear identifies, instead, with his role as mighty king. His split-off self causes the storm in nature and the storm inside himself. "Mouth's" vocalized irruptions also represent a psychic disturbance, the result of being alienated from her instinctual foundation. The words that spill out of "Mouth's" mouth, inexplicable to her, are the result of living alone along the surfaces, thereby blocking the conduit that connects one back to the dynamism of ancestral sources. Jung (1958) explains:

> What our age thinks of as the "shadow" and inferior part of the psyche contains more than something merely negative. The very fact that through self-knowledge, i.e., by exploring our own souls, we come upon the instincts and their world of imagery should throw some light on the powers slumbering in the psyche, of which we are seldom aware so long as all goes well. They are potentialities of the greatest dynamism, and it depends entirely on the preparedness and attitude of the conscious mind whether the irruption of these forces and the images and ideas associated with them will tend toward construction or catastrophe. (p. 107)

Jung's concept of the shadow is the "nothing" that we need to know. It follows us around but is behind us: while we cannot see the shadow, others can. If the "slumbering powers" are allowed access to the upright ego, the result is a fuller, more dynamic being. Denied access, all hell breaks loose.

Myth, especially Greek and Roman myth, frequently mentions an oracle which heroes and tragic figures felt the need to consult for explanation, guidance, or prophecy. The oracle could be interpreted as myth's shadow. An oracle, accordingly, is "an utterance, often ambiguous or obscure, given by a priest or priestess at a shrine as the response of a god to an inquiry" (Webster). The priest or priestess was the medium through which the gods spoke. But because the utterance is divine, it is shrouded in mystery, riddle, or darkness. Sometimes the speaker was figured as

Sibyl, sometimes Themis, both goddesses with cosmic connections; sometimes the priest of Apollo at the Delphic oracle; sometimes the Lord, who comes to Moses in a thick cloud atop a mountain; sometimes—yes—the oracle is a dream that speaks in metaphors and images, the language of the gods. Aeneus consulted Sibyl twice, once to receive instruction about the Trojan War and once to ask to visit his father in the underworld. Virgil describes Sibyl's words as issuing from inside a cave concealed high in a mountain and echoing from 100 interior entrances. She voiced her prophecies "hiding the truth in words of darkness" (in Rosenberg, 1994, p. 138). Ovid describes the two survivors of the great flood, Deucalion and Pyrrha, as in need of help from the holy oracle. How would they repopulate the Earth? Themis took pity on them, uttering what I consider to be the first mythic riddle: "Throw behind you the bones of your great mother" (in Leeming, 1990, p. 59); in plain speech: throw the stones of Mother Earth, from which a new race of humans would be born. When Moses received the Ten Commandments, he had to climb the sacred mountain, the *mons veneris* of Mother Earth, the cosmic center nearest the sky god, "where the word—the cosmic energy—can be received" (Leeming, 1990, p. 316). These examples demonstrate the utter seriousness with which our early ancestors and myths sought connection with mouthings from unseen shadow forces.

The Greek myths, as we get them, show oracular speakings from cave or mountain that the rational mind could eventually decode in order to attain advice, direction, information. That seems logical and straightforward; safe, even. The oracles were located up high, with better access to the sky gods. What the mouth said or prophesied resulted in outward action. Very patriarchal. What about those other mouths, more like vaginas, that are located chthonically in primitive earthiness, associated with the goddess? Poet Richard Brautigan appreciated that other open mouth of the Great Mother when he wrote, "O please, my Lady, allow me to know your inner mystery. Open the door to your cave. I will try not to be afraid of your hidden dangers" (in Canan, 2007, p. 102). The goddess of non-Classical periods was often horrendous to look at and had a vomiting, ravishing, gorging mouth, sometimes many of them. I am thinking of the Babylonian Tiamat, the Egyptian Sehkmet, or the Japanese Uki Mochi. What to make of these mouths and of the fear or disgust they evoke?

Tiamat is case in point of a Mother goddess originally viewed as a neutral figure, if not a positive one. The origin of her name comes from the Hebrew "tehom," meaning "deep" (in Thury and Devinney, 2009, p. 52). Hers was the province of salt water, a necessary component for creation; her shape was that of a serpent. The water-snake combination suggests the deep, primordial, regenerative powers of Tiamat. Like the Old European Bird Goddess with her life-giving moisture, the snake goddess had a vital influence in fertility but also with the regeneration of dying plants (Gimbutas, 2006, p. 121). The snake in mythology is thus "essentially double. It arouses fear, brings death, and poisons; it is the enemy of light and at the same time a savior in animal form.... it promises knowledge born from immediate inner experience, insight, secret wisdom—gnosis" (Von Franz, 2000, p. 82). The positive elements of the quasi-matriarchal view of Tiamat, the sea-snake, changed when the patriarchal hero story of Marduk emerged. Then the relation between Tiamat and Marduk became simplified as a battle of good over against evil. To prepare for this battle,

Tiamat multiplied her serpent image, giving birth to dragons and sea monsters. Nevertheless, the hero, in typical slaying mode, defeated the "monster" by shooting an arrow into her open mouth. Her body was then split open, ensnared, trampled, and crushed—described in extensive graphic detail, one of the first action, rape dramas of the West: "He shot an arrow which pierced her belly,/ Split her down the middle and split her heart,/ Vanquished her and extinguished her life./ He threw down her corpse and stood on top of her" (in Thury and Devinney, 2009, p. 71). In later evolutions, Tiamat has become the plaything for today's youngsters as queen of evil dragons in the role-playing game *Dungeons and Dragons*.

The Egyptian goddess Sehkmet retained the goddess quality of being a both/ and figure. Perhaps for that reason she was revered for her powerful elemental solar energies, emanating from the sun god Ra. As the Eye of Ra, Sehkmet was sent to destroy humankind, but then Ra changed his mind and tried to slow down the destruction by pouring red beer on the ground. Sehkmet, thinking the beer was blood, gorged herself to fullness until she slept in a drunken stupor; then she turned into the cow goddess Hathor. Or. Sehkmet as fierce destructive power is paired with Bast, a lion-headed goddess like Sehkmet but of milder disposition (Hathaway, 2001). The stories of Sehkmet suggest her devouring mouth can break down what is temporal and burn away excess. But also she was worshipped as a healer, connecting her with Bast, a lunar deity. The sun-moon oppositions, with their corresponding elemental powers, give to this Egyptian goddess the necessary dynamic dualism found, for instance, in the Demeter-Persephone Greek myth. In other words, Sehkmet's devouring mouth is not simple destructiveness; combined with Bast, she is a regeneration goddess overseeing temporal/eternal cosmic cycles.

The essential both-and quality of the goddess is also seen with the Japanese Uki Mochi, goddess of food. She is hospitality itself, as seen by her vomiting mouth, from which come fish, seaweed, game, and boiled rice. Her bounty extends within her body, as well. Upon her death "herds of cattle and horses stampeded out of [her] head. Rice, millet, and red beans spilled out of her eyes, ears, and nose. Wheat sprouted from her genitals, soy beans ... from her rectum, and even a mulberry tree crawling with silkworms sprang from her body" (in Hathaway, 2001, p. 121).

The connection of specific body parts, notably the mouth, with goddess power replays with varying images the larger idea of regeneration. Reading these myths requires a necessary de-literalizing. How far from safe and clean are these stories! How gross! How vital! It is not enough to infer moralizing generalities. These goddess images draw our eyes down, below and into the earth: the mouth is the body's meta-phor of a womblike cave, in which and out of which new life emerges, vomits, gorges, or licks. Yes, the licking tongue of the cow, always associated with the goddess, brings to life the ice-buried giant Buri, in the Norse creation myth. In Egyptian mytho-logy the sky goddess Nut "covers the whole earth, a huge cow on whose belly all the stars are constellated" (Von Franz, 1972, p. 50). Fluid in its multivarious forms is the initiator of life: salt water (found in other cosmological birth forms as sweat or tears), vomit, spittle. The vagina as mouth is cave, the womb of the earth. These stories with their vivid images stop our clocks. The action of the mouth takes us away from noun-centeredness into the vitality of the verb, since the cosmic mouth is open to action: spewing, sputtering, issuing, licking. The gerundive, facile mouth makes us aware of how mouth does more than utter words.

I will finish this chapter on mouth metaphors with some god myths by way of both comparison and contrast with the goddess myths. First, contrast. Classical Greece recounts the stories of the patriarchal mouths of the Titans Uranus and Kronos; and the Olympian Zeus. These mouths devour not to rebirth but to demolish. The tales, so influential for Freud's Oedipal theory, recount father-son fear, a fear so strong that the fathers literally eat their sons. And the fear is generational, repeated from father to son to father to son. When in class we discuss the idea of being meta-phorically "devoured" by our parents, I begin to see a shift in student response. This simple move from literal to metaphorical, by way of negative family patterns, is a starting process in bringing mythological stories into deeper and more personal meaning for twenty-first century students struggling with their parental *imago* figures, from whom they/we never outgrow.

Now for comparison. Mouth as a generative orifice is stunningly suggested in the Egyptian myth of Atum's open mouth. According to one translation of the Pyramid texts (c. 2400 BCE), "Atum put his penis in his hand that he might obtain pleasure of emission thereby and there were born brother and sister" (in Thury and Devinney, 2009, p. 409). Another translation focuses more specifically on the moment of mastur-bation: "I had union with my clenched hand, I joined myself in an embrace with my shadow, I poured seed into my mouth" (in Hathaway, 2001, p. 19). I wonder if this male mouthing is a metaphor for creative speech. In any case, the story is immensely entertaining for students.

Male mouths may also offer themselves as fantasy receptacles for travels to strange places. The ancient writer Lucien's *True History*, for instance, tells of a sea monster that swallows a ship with all its crew. Erich Auerbach (2003) sees Lucien's fantasy of the monster maw containing woods, mountains, lakes, animals, half animals, and two humans as the prototype for Rabelais' Pantagruel, whose mouth contains many kingdoms and cities. "The fine mountain landscape of the teeth is a picture of the Western European agricultural countryside," but on the other side of the teeth "over yonder" are uncultured barbarians (Auerbach, 2003, p. 269). The point of Rabelais' satire, according to Auerbach, was to cast aspersions on the European sense of itself as a utopia, when actually "one half the world does not know how the other half lives" (p. 270). The other half, evidently, lives in the mouth beyond the teeth from which all utterance, all places, even all beings emerge.

The cosmic mouth is as various in mood and outflow as the regions of the planet and the outer planets. The desert's cold/heat, the oceans mild/fury, the forests dense/fragility, the mountains peaks/valleys, the galaxies swirl/smash—all are contained within the cosmic mouth. Think here, especially, of the Hindu blue-skinned god Krishna. Playing outside one day the child/god, incarnation of Vishnu, was scolded by his mother for eating dirt. When she ordered the boy to open his mouth, she saw there the whole universe with everything in it and around it: "heaven and earth, the constellations of the zodiac, the distant reaches of outer space, time, nature, and even her own small village, with herself in it" (in Hathaway, 2001, p. 317). As David L. Miller (1986) comments on this wondrous event, "it is as if our world is the dirt in God's mouth. Or perhaps it is that our dirt is the universe of God's mouthings" (p. 73). If we are the mouthings of the universe, then we are full of dirt. The name of the first man Adam, after all, means "dirt" or "clay," and Eve means "life" (Beneson and Rosow, 2009). Dirt contains the diversities of life, organized information, micro-organisms. Dirt, in short, is the matrix of life on earth and contains the cycle of decomposition and composition such as envisioned with the goddess religions. Dirt is the skin of the earth, the interface between life and death. The cosmic mouth of Krishna containing It All is myth's metaphor of being neither in nor outside the mouth but in transition. "One of myth's functions," Miller (1986) continues, "is to keep life in this transition, not knowing, not literal... to keep it moving, on the edge... liminal" (p. 73).

A hovering quality emanates from the liminality, call it skin, that separates the many cosmic opposites, especially the opposition between inside and outside. Feeling the body's mouth as separate from the world's mouth is the cause not only our estrangement from but especially our endangerment of the cosmos. How can we keep the hovering presences alive? In our days filled with busyness it may be difficult to find the space necessary for reflection and quiet listening. Lately, in sym-pathy with my writing on cosmic mouthings, I have taken to sitting outside at evening, listening. The experience is not just calming; it is deeply spiritual. In his mediations on silence and the desert, poet and professor Dennis Patrick Slattery (2004) writes,

> In the silence beyond words gathered an atmosphere, an intuition of grace to shift my vision so I was able to see the spider web that needed only a few degrees' rotation for its filaments to become visible. Perhaps only a couple of degrees or less separated me from the entire invisible world. (p. 125)

In another work, Slattery (2006) comments, "Our sounds are pushed out and taken in through the hollows of our bodies, the deep dark caves of our flesh, the cavity of the mouth" (p. 229). The poet knows the many mouths inside us that call for deeper listening. Salomon Resnik (2001) calls these intersections between what is inside the body and outside the body "mouth spaces" or "hole zones" (p. 116). The Sacred Pipe ceremony of the Sioux recognizes a sympathy that exists between inner and outer mouth spaces. The open shape of the pipe, viewed as a portal containing potential energy, can invite cosmic participation. When using the pipe properly and with preliminary recognition, the bowl "becomes" the universe (DeLoria, Jr., 2009, p. 85). Objects like the bowl of the Sioux pipe can have "fleshy, earthy relations" (Jardine, 2000, p. 213) that sustain us. What will happen when subjects and objects, both, lose their sustainable relations? What then?

Perhaps it takes a catastrophe like the British Petroleum oil "spill" to awaken attention to what inattentiveness has caused. Every day the paper is filled with the news of no-news from the Gulf Oil spill. As Associated Press writer Peter Prengaman (2010) writes, "Americans have been guided by fires in their bellies and a deep belief in the ability to accomplish anything" (p. 4A). Ah, but there's the rub. Accomplishing is doing, extraverting, acting out, chopping down, taming the wild. It is dredging and drilling with flawed equipment and corporate greed. But the Gulf oil spill continues to vomit from its Deepwater hole mouth. And it's not just the Gulf waters, nor even the flora and fauna along the riverbanks, that are besmirched. Archaological sites on the shore are at risk, including wooden shipwrecks, American-Indian shell midden mounds, and pirate colonies (Burdeau, 2010, p. 4A). Those who live among the ruins are beginning to wonder if we have lost our way.

What is a gulf? My dictionary defines it as "a deep hollow; any wide separation; something that engulfs or swallows" (Webster): it is the both/and of this discussion. It is a mouth. A cosmic mouth. The gulf that is besmirched is spitting back what it has been forced to swallow by the Deepwater Horizon drill. It is vehemently displaying the wide separation between economics and ecologics. Into the deep hollow we would do well to remember the words of the *Tao te Ching* (Waley, 1958*)*: "Those that would gain what is under heaven by tampering with it—I have seen that they do not succeed. For that which is under heaven is like a holy vessel, dangerous to tamper with" (p. 179).

OLD MYTH/NEW SCIENCE

He marked the marshy ground around the dock

The crawling railroad spur, the rotten fence,

Curriculum for the marvelous sophomore.

It purified. It made him see how much

Of what he saw he never saw at all.

— Wallace Stevens

I think it was about six, maybe eight, years ago that I started intuiting that myth was saying in metaphor some of the language I was reading about in new science. When I first taught myth and studied it in graduate school, the focus was on classical myth from Greece and Rome. Not even Egypt was a consideration, nor Babylonia. Subsequently, teaching at an art college that draws international students, I decided to expand my study for my students and myself to include the myths of Asia, old Europe, Africa, and the Americas. Even more recently, I have been delving into Celtic mythology. Science, of course, is less metaphor than it is process. While the process of testing and ruling out falsifiability is standard science through and through, the role of imagination does play a part of the scientific process. In that spirit I offer several mythic metaphors which reveal the wisdom of our earliest ancestors, a wisdom that saw, heard, and felt the universe as alive, energetic, and moving in ways that reveal, uncannily, a complex cosmos with many dimensions, many energies, many subatoms, and many quarks (strings).

Before I launch a discussion of myth and science, a few disclaimers are necessary. Myth, which shares with traditional knowledge certain beliefs, is different from standard science, which eschews "belief" in favor of "rationality." Myth is about experience; science, about experiment—blind and double blind experiment. Myth pictures a worldview that is cyclical, webbed, contextual, dynamic and spiritual. Science views the world theoretically, materialistically, quantitatively, and by observation. Myth is orally transcribed from generation to generation and welcomes the full range of the senses. Science works in laboratories, in isolate groups, and utilizes a method of hypothesis, predictability, testing evidence and achieving certainty. Myth is *fabula*, fabulous, fictional, funny, and weird. Science is serious, studious, stentorious and rational. Myth revels in symbiosis and synaesthesia; science demands evidence and data. While the two modes of knowing are clearly different, the very things that seem most anti-science—uncertainty and unpredictability—are the very things that myth tolerates well. Or, to put it another way, complex thinking about reality forefronts the shortsightedness of simple scientific explanations, or phrases that wax poetic. Scientists have been known to become violently irrational about a simple metaphor like "the memory of water" (Josephson, 2005, p. 2). Perhaps what is needed in science is what Edward de Bono (1991) calls "lateral thinking," which is what myth demonstrates well. Indeed, as Bill Doll and Donna Trueit (2010) write, "we are moving from a science that studies particles to the new sciences of chaos and complexity that study the interactive relations between and among particles, events, happenings" (p. 841). While traditional science delves in the "rock logic" of argument, and reason, and myth delves in the "water logic" of patterns, flow, and humor (de Bono, 1991), it appears that such different discourses can indeed surf the same wave.

Interestingly, several writers, without expanding the comment, mention or imply "myth" and "science" in the same sentence. Joseph Henderson and Maud Oakes (1990), who are archetypal mythologists, describe the dance of Shiva that sends waves through inert matter. "He sustains its manifold phenomena. In the fullness of time, still dancing, he destroys all forms and names by fire and gives new rest." The concluding sentence reads, "This is poetry; but none the less, science" (p. 82). Gary Zukov (2001), who writes on consciousness and physics, also sees in Eastern mythology a connection with new science. Citing the figure of Kali as the infinite symbol of diversity, Zukov says that she is the metaphor for the entire physical plane. "Although most physicists have little patience (professionally) with metaphors, physics itself has become a powerful metaphor.... physicists are doing more than 'discovering the endless diversity of nature.' They are dancing with Kali, the Divine Mother of Hindu mythology" (p. 346). Niels Bohr, physicist known for his concept of complementarity, wrote "The development of atomic physics, which forces us to an attitude toward the problem of explanation recalling ancient wisdom, that when searching for harmony in life one must never forget that in the drama of existence we are ourselves both actors and spectators" (in Leshan, 1975, p. 236). David Tacey (2010), an associate professor of literature and depth psychology, writes, "The mythic bonds to nature are not to be dismissed... as archaic remnants of a useless or unscientific way of viewing the world" (p. 333). Bringing together new science with the ancient science of alchemy, Jungian analyst Andreas Schweizer (2009) comments, "In alchemical thought, organic as well as inorganic matter is something vivid and transformable, pervaded by a living (divine) spirit. Today's quantum mechanics shares this concept of matter insofar as it teaches the paradox posed by the mutual exclusivity of the description of light... either as a movement of waves, or as particles" (p. 87). Curriculum theorist Jayne Fleener (2005) also hearkens back to ancient thought when she observes, "Like Giambattista Vico's *New Science*, written almost three hundred years ago, the new sciences are approaches to meaning that go beyond the myopic perspective of Modernism or the techniques of modern science" (p. 3). These writers – mythologists, psychologists, educationists and physicists, from seemingly disparate fields – are talking the language of, well, disparate fields like myth and science. Note the alchemical references (early science more interesting to myth and psychology because of intense concentration on imagination), the acknowledgement of ancient wisdom, and the specific mention of Hindu deities. We must not be fooled into thinking the word "wisdom" is soft.

Perhaps no subject matter is as aware of its connection with old folklore and myth as the shadow side of theology known as demonology. A supplementary text

I use in my myth classes incorporates a great favorite of student artists, subversive spirits otherwise known as demons or fallen angels. The book is full of small flying things and large galumphing goliaths. These creatures inhabit the various regions of the earth (water, mountain, forest, desert) including domicile and psyche. Often, the creatures are invisible. Their hovering activities defy probability (like subatoms) because they occupy a force field that embeds itself in a "more-than-human" world (Abram, 1997). Folklore warns of their power to do both good and evil, but in themselves they are beyond classification. It is in this sense that the editors of the demon text conclude their chapters on such familiar demons as the Djinn, Merrow, Yuki-Onna, and Kitsune with their own nomination: the Quantum Daimon. "The Quantum Daimon is neither alive nor dead, it is neither particle nor wave, it is neither fortune nor misfortune, neither good nor evil. It is not one thing or another" (Mack and Mack, 1998, p. 272). With this inclusion in a book dedicated to folklore, the editors suggest that what once was superstition can open up horizons even on the scientific front.

Interestingly, the neither this-nor-thatness of new science (different from traditional science) is analogous to mythology, which cannot be understood normatively. When we apply terms that imply a "versus," like "good versus evil," we are in an ethical rather than a mythical domain. While we might be comfortable with "versus" or "shall not"—so! Ten Commandments—this is hardly what we experience with old myth or new science. In fact, new science sheds the oppositional stance that pits things against humans, humans against nature, in favor of relationships and shifting perspectives. This newness, while some would call it so, is really mythic, as I hope to explore. But myth is not "versus" new science; it shares a similar con-fusion of complexities and dynamisms: the two can be considered a hybrid of scien-mythic understandings.

Or take the correspondence between myth and science another way: a study of insects. As a reviewer recently commented, the book *Insectopedia* by Hugh Raffles, combines science with history with fantasy in a "multi-eye-opening journey into another existence." Once again, as myth and new science agree, this insect study reveals the fullness of emptiness: "another world filled with an ever-moving, airy regiment, where "a lone ballooning spider was floating on its filaments, its body borne up on unseen currents. It was evidence of an aerial plankton, an ocean over our heads" (Hoare, 2010, p. 18). But what is even more scien-mythic is the existence of locust swarms seen, now, in North Africa and the Middle East that has been the stuff of Biblical lore for eons. Indeed, as I fumigate my house for the thirteenth time against a gnat invasion, I am experiencing the iterative dynamics of an annoying chaotic population that has invaded my own back yard.

Nevertheless, and by way of introducing further myth-science correspondences, we must not overlook indigenous North American spiritual insights into a meta-physics of place and power. While new science is moving away from a mechanistic reductionist model, called by some the "matter myth" (Davies and Gribbin, 1992), to a physics of open, dynamic systems, the indigenous experience has always embraced such. Daniel Wildcat (2001) explains: "When we start examining issues of complexity, emergence, the principles of self-organization, the biological phenomena of morpho-logical or structural change within species, all of that knowledge is perfectly and completely consistent with indigenous worldviews" (p. 36).

Indigenous worldviews propose the idea of an all-pervasive spirit that sings, moves, pulses, and weaves. This is what Annette Gough (1998) honors as "aboriginal science," contrary to the Eurocentric bias of Western science. Sometimes the spirit "thinks" creation, sometimes she "sings" creation, and sometimes she "weaves" a world into view. One name given this spirit is Spider Woman, called variously Grandmother Spider, Old Spider, Earth Mother, Thought Woman, or Water Spider. We can sense a reverence in this naming for ancestors and those of old age, as well as for the craft of weaving. As metaphors, weaving and spider precede the new science metaphors of the universe as "fabric" or "web," one worldview calling back to another. The ancient view that all is interconnected by a web of relations is as scientifically true today as it is spiritually beautiful. Break that web and the cosmos suffers. What the Hopi Emergence prophecy foretells is that earth-sky-human-animal-plant relations are the web, which has always been "read" in the earth itself: "Plant forms from previous worlds are beginning to spring up as seeds. This could start a new study of botany if people were wise enough to read them. The same kinds of seeds are being planted in the sky as stars... [and] in our hearts" (in Leeming, 1990, p. 85). The wisdom of the prophecy depends on an ability to read the textured world, not just to smash atoms. When discussing mythic cosmologies we should recall the very strong words issued by Michel Foucault (2003) who speaks up for "subjugated knowledges" –those knowledges thought of as lesser or antiscience because they are not hierarchical, organized, or filtered "in the name of a true body of knowledge, in the name of the rights of science that is in the hands of the few" (p. 9).

To connect old myth with new science, specifically, I will propose several ideas from science that resonate with metaphors in myth. While the word "theory" carries more weight than the word "myth," it is time to honor two different ways of seeing/conceiving the worlds we inhabit. These scien-mythic ideas include force fields, invisibility, time travel, extrasensory perception, quantum theory, relativity theory, and string theory.

We can look to force fields as one "place" to place myth and science. Michael Conforti (1999), a pioneer in the field of matter-psyche studies, defines force fields as "preexistent domains that, like frequencies on the radio, can be tuned into and accessed." Accessing these fields, he cautions, is a spontaneous occurrence, by no means to be thought of as "casual" (p. 45). This cautious approach suggests what Rudolf Otto (1958) means about facing the gods: the experience should be awe-full, meant to inspire awe because, in many ways, it is beyond our ken. Speaking of natural processes, long before new science was being theorized, Alfred North Whitehead (1978) wrote this, in language that suggests the dynamic processes of nature: "Nature is a theater for the interrelations of activities.... of the forms of process" (p. 36). Christopher Bache (2000), professor of Religious Studies, has personal experience with force fields in the classroom. He calls these, variously "course fields," "learning fields," and even the "mental field of a university" (p. 198). Process forms. Force fields. Learning fields. Force theory is process itself and depends on at least three elements: fields exist before forms, fields are inaccessible to sight, and fields are activated by an outside force (Conforti, 1999, pp. 53, 55). So now, let me introduce some mythic counterparts to science's force fields.

Enter the cosmic man. This is a well known Chinese creation myth involving an egg floating in darkness surrounded by Chaos; inside the egg is P'an Ku. Darkness and chaos swirl and churn for eighteen thousand years, as does the egg. Inside the egg P'an Ku grows broader and denser while the egg grows bigger and bigger. In one day he goes through nine transformations, each transformation enabling him to grow ten feet taller and develop in wisdom, "becoming more divine than Heaven and wiser than earth" (in Thury and Devinney, 2009, p. 111). At last the shell cracks and P'an Ku emerges, "his colossal body matted with hair and adorned with horns and tusks" (in Hathaway, 2002, p. 7). The horns on the head would seem to be a significant feature, an ancient Western symbol of divine potency, an outgrowth of the life substance of the brain as a procreative element (Onians, pp. 237, 238). The horned P'an Ku creates wonders with the universe, which is his divine power in action. But it takes another eighteen thousand years for him to unfold the contents of the egg into the swirling mass, separating the sky (albumen) from the earth (yolk). When P'an Ku lived out his life, he died and his body was transformed into the world as we know it with wind, thunder, oceans, rivers, mountains, soil, rocks, minerals, plants, constellations, planets, moon, and sun (in Thury and Devinney, 2009). This idea of the disembodied god forming the manifold elements of the cosmos is myth's way of endowing all matter with *spiritual* energy.

I see in this unusual birthing and dying of the cosmic man from a cosmic egg several ideas that resonate with force field theory. Darkness and chaos are the preexistent domains, in which the egg as form rests. The inside of the egg contains incipient life, alive but inaccessible to perception, since the process takes so many thousands of years. It is the inside activity of P'an Ku's growth over those thousands of years that ultimately activates the birth of the god from the shell, a result of his self-regulating, dynamic, emergent growth process which takes (the Chinese are precise on number) eighteen thousand years. Here, energy and matter combine. Besides the significance of the horns (a sign of divinity), P'an Ku's body is matted not smooth, to suggest that the energizing motion from inside the egg is jumpy. As Jayne Fleener (2002) explains, "motion, at the subatomic level, does not occur in smooth progression but in jumps or leaps.... Quantum physics is thus a study of relationships that provide us with a perspective of the universe as participatory rather than abstract, emergent rather than determinate, and discontinuous rather than continuous" (p. 69). It is noteworthy, as well, that P'an Ku's actions are described, specifically, as divinely wise, another reference to the horns and suggestive of the intelligence of immateriality. One can see in this creation story some aspects of the big bang theory of creation, which posits that the universe began with the explosion of a tremendously dense energy source expanding ever outward.

I have often pondered the strange little poem by Wallace Stevens (1919/1972) titled "Anecdote in a Jar." I see it now as analogous to P'an Ku's egg in the Chinese cosmos, expressive of the powerful relationships of two unrelated entities, each, however, capable of exerting its own force field:

I placed a jar in Tennessee,

And round it was, upon a hill.

It made the slovenly wilderness

Surround that hill.

The wilderness rose up to it,

And sprawled around, no longer wild.

The jar was round upon the ground

And tall and of a port in air.

It took dominion everywhere.

The jar was gray and bare.

It did not give of bird or bush,

Like nothing else in Tennessee. (p. 46)

The poem has excited much critical interpretation, particularly about the relationship between jar and nature. "Relationship" is the operative word here, since the poem suggests a both-and quality between two opposites that nevertheless exude their own pull. Modern physics, according to Ernst Mach, shows that material objects are inseparably linked to the environment; their properties interact with and reach out to the universe at large (in Capra, 1991, p. 209). Stevens signals the relationship, or interaction, of object with the natural environment by different sets of sounds. The domain of nature in the poem has "ound" sounds: "round" (twice), "surround," "around," "ground." The jar has its own pull with "air" sounds: "air," "everywhere," "bare," but is also physically grounded, partaking of both air and earth. What is fascinating here is the jar's dynamic quality that exerts a centripetal force, a magnetic power, taming the wilderness while the wilderness itself is the centering draw. It is the *object* that has this livingness which, like wave fluctuations, opens out to the wild, actually taming its "slovenly" and "sprawling" qualities. As John Vernon (1973) observes, this sense of object as event rather than thing endows an active quality to form—as its own kind of force field, as it were. Even in the 70s and 80s, literary critics were suggesting the very sort of ideas that characterize the new science of complexity theory, dynamic relationships, and force fields. And even farther back, in 1919, the poet Stevens gave the object (an "it") magnetic pull. I wonder if his "anecdote" owes ancestral homage to Confucius' "analect" of a vase as a holy vessel (Fingarette, 1972).

The Celts had a keen understanding of force fields. Even now, in the Dingle Peninsula of southern Ireland, you will see stone mounds in farmers' fields that date back to the Bronze Age. The government protects these mounds, called fairy mounds, in the belief that they are sacred spaces. Irish myths are full of reverence mixed with fear of these mounds, called *sidhe*, because they serve as portals to the invisible otherworld. They can properly be termed force fields since they are places where time is experienced as highly-charged energy (Wright, 2008).

One way the Celts imaged the energy that emerges from the *sidhe* was as a horse or swan, animals which were seen magically to have connection with the otherworld. In the beautiful tale of the goddess Niamh and the mortal Ossian, the horse plays an intermediary role between two worlds, similar to the role of Hermes in Greek myth. Ossian is entranced to leave Killarney, to mount Niamh's white horse, and to go live in Tir nan Og, "the land of the forever young." It is the horse that will take him across the water once to the otherworld and again back across the water to his home-land when he is homesick for his father. Always, myth has the important "yes, but" moment; in this tale Ossian may visit his father but he must not dismount from the horse. Of course, he does what he is forbidden to do, with the result that his youthful handsome body transforms into a crippled old man. The horse, however, retains is magical youthfulness and connection with the beyond: "The white horse turned, shook his head and galloped off over the glen, seeming, as he crossed the mountains, to vanish into the sky" (O'Connor, 1996, p. 86).

The horse as a magical energy force occurs elsewhere in literature. Franz Kafka's "A Country Doctor," for instance, contains several old world folktale moments that surround a magical beast. The country doctor, called to a patient's bedside in a nearby town, is whisked away out of his courtyard gate by two horses, only to be already there at the patient's cottage. He had gone ten miles distance in no time. Then the horses slipped their reins loose, "pushed the windows open from outside, I did not know how; each of them had stuck a head in at a window and, quite unmoved by the startled cries of the family, stood eyeing the patient" (Kafka, 1979, pp. 162–163). The horses defy time and space, knowingly, and take an interest in the wounded youth. Jungian analyst Eleonora Babejova (2009), drawing on her background in Slovakia, comments on the horse as a mediator between worlds and shapes, "so that the boundary between the human/horse grows transparent" (p. 133).

"Force fields" is understood metaphorically by imaginative literatures as "egg," "jar," or "horse," either organic or inorganic forms. These are not simple forms. And I find it significant that the above examples credit a knowingness to the forms, an intelligence that shares divine qualities. I think here of the wise horse-man creature of Greek myth, Chiron, who tutored Asclepius, Achilles, Herakles, and Jason. This ancient understanding of the rich complexity of non-human animals once again throws into question such stable (pun) anthropomorphist oppositions as human over against animal. The mythic Chiron, like the mythic P'an Ku, had "wisdom"— a word delibe-rately chosen by the ancient texts. With new science, we are learning to re-think relationships, or rather to re-member them, and to pay attention to the words the poets and storytellers use. Possibilities are opening out, relationships are complex, actions are self-enacting, the world speaks. We are learning (once again) to see the insides of things. As Jacques Derrida (1991) put it, "if one reinscribes language in a network of possibilities that do not merely encompass it but mark it irreducibly from the inside, everything changes.... These possibilities or necessities, without which there would be no language, are themselves not only human" (p. 116).

Of course, there need be no speaking for speech to be felt. I teach eight o'clock morning classes and often am met with silent students, stubborn in their sleeplessness. Is this what is meant by aura? For surely, the stubborn silence casts a negative spell around the room which saps me of my energy. This sapping is not unique just to early morning classes, unfortunately, no matter how experienced a teacher one may be. Aura can also be felt as charisma. Certain people exude charisma, a quality felt even from people like Hitler and Ahmadinejad. Without opening their mouths, their personage emits an energy that draws people to them. Aura was depicted in early Renaissance paintings by halos around the heads of saints, suggestive of a special kind of force field. These examples are felt in addition to being seen.

Another way to consider energy forces other than speaking is the effective use of sound as vibration. Whistled speech is a form of communication done purely with the lips. It occurs among people who live in mountains and dense forests, in such places Mexico, the Canary Islands, China, and Papua New Guinea ("Whistled," 2009, p. 25). In the American South there is a tradition of ring shouting, which is a spiritual dance-like practice rooted in slave ceremonies. A true ring shout beckons the spirit of God and consists of a series of call and responses between a songster and a baser. Female shouters shuffle their feet in a counter-clockwise direction while singing (Felty, 2010, p. 1C). Going against the clockwise direction is especially mystical, similar to the Eleusinian Mysteries, since what is being beseeched is the ear from another domain.

Humans, then, can have this animal capacity to sense what is not "there" and to communicate in unspoken ways. I like to think of Herakles less as a Tarzan figure and more as a human-animal (a new form of the post-human) when he wrestles with the Nemean lion and puts on the lion skin. One Greek vase pictures Herakles in a dance with the lion, probably suggestive of the manner in which Herakles killed the lion—by strangling it. The donning of the lion skin can be read not as fetishizing the lion but more as putting on its knowledge with its power, as Yeats said of Leda's swan (1959, p. 212). All of Herakles' twelve labors involve various regions and creatures of the world, including the domain of death. Herakles, a human-animal, is able to see how much of what we saw we never saw at all (to paraphrase Stevens). The human-animal form, at the very least, suggests a return to the thick intelligence of animality (Wolfe, 2010).

To penetrate, draw out, enter, or participate in the invisible world or the world of other forms is the very stuff of old myth, science fiction, and new science. It is as well the stuff of *re-ligio* understood in its root form as a linking-back. Perhaps what is needed is not evolution but devolution, of stopping thinking that humans are the only subjects capable of thought and action, and of stopping thinking hierarchically. It now appears that the move to study the interiority of subatoms and particles, as in quantum physics, is a move to reconsider all assumptions that what isn't there isn't there. "There" calls into question categories of thinking about reality. As Marla Morris says (2001), "There is no out there or in here. It is all mixed up in a noisy way. Scientists who are wedded to positivism might be uncomfortable with this ambiguous way of looking at lived experience because one can no longer say that what is out there is out there in-itself" (p. 101).

Words, then, can fool our thinking, make fools of our thinking (Note well: the Irish word for shaman is "fool"). Words like "then," "until," "soon," "ago," and "tomorrow" imply a linearity to time, like an Aristotelian drama of three satisfying acts—a beginning (past), a middle (present), and an end (future). But when we enter a more magical "once upon a time," the sense of time chopped into disparate, neat sections evaporates into not-so-thin air. And that is what the behavior of electrons demonstrates: electrons can seemingly be many places at the same time (Kaku, 2008, p. 59). This notion is what Kafka described when his horses transported the doctor many miles in a nothingth of a second. Fantasy, yes; chemistry, yes; scien-mythic, yes. The quantum world is a fool's paradise, with no before and no after. Similarly, Einstein's relativity theory showed that time is like a river, now speeding up, now slowing down. One second on Earth is not absolute. Traveling at the speed of light would enable a time traveler a mere minute to reach the nearest star, while four years would have elapsed on Earth. This is traveling into the future. Einstein's theory further proposes "closed time-like curves" or paths for time travel into the past. Following the curve would be something like entering a wormhole, where journey into the past is conceivable (in Kaku, 2008, p. 222), although no one has yet found such a thing as a wormhole.

Nestled by his mother's knee, a child enters "once upon a time" without blinking. And there, in the open space of relativity, he hears stories about the Celtic otherworld and stories of voyages. Oh, not just journeys, and certainly not just trips. Voyages! a word that implies something magical, as in the Voyage of Bran, a Celtic giant. Just as he was losing his life by a poisoned sword in battle, Bran ordered his men to decapitate him before the poison destroyed his soul. "Once you have cut off my head, I shall remain with you until you have completed your task," he said (in Ellis, 1999, p. 284). The task is the voyage from Wales to London, where the head was to be buried facing east so as to protect the British Isles from invaders. The voyage took many years, for the men were in the company of Bran's living head. For seven years they feasted and chatted with the head. For eighty more years they voyaged with the severed head, lingering and entertaining it in a spacious hall with three doors, two of which were open but the third of which remained shut. The warriors were forbidden to open the third door. When one of the warriors opened the third door, consciousness returned to the group and they resumed their voyage and completed their burial task. Being in the presence of Bran's living head (his soul) enabled the men to lose track of time, to enter a deeper world of the unconscious. This is one version of time travel, which anyone who dreams can relate to.

Another version of the voyage into deep space concerns the tradition of the shaman. Thomas Berry (1990), eco-theologian, speaks of the power of the shaman then and now:

> More than any other of the human types concerned with the sacred, the shamanic personality journeys into the far regions of the cosmic mystery and brings back the vision and the power needed by the human community at the most elementary level. The shamanic personality speaks and best understands the language of the various creatures of the earth.... The planet Earth and the life communities of the earth are speaking to us through the deepest elements of our nature, through our genetic coding. (pp. 211, 215)

This shamanic speaking from the elemental level is old myth, new science at its most profound. While the Celtic myth of Taliesin seems pure *fabula* to the skeptic,

I am not interested in entertaining a skeptic's viewpoint. Rather, in my mind's eye I see another child at her mother's knee listening dreamily to the magical tale of the poet Taliesin, who voyaged to a place where he gained total knowledge of all that had started from the very beginning of time. In one second Taliesin knew the secrets of the ages, all the meanings of the universe, the stars and the moon—of everything (in Matthews, 2002, p. 39). The dreamy girlchild hearing this story may grow up to be a nuclear physicist who yearns, even today, to discover the "theory of everything" known as the "code of the universe": "the capacity to explain every fundamental feature upon which the universe is constructed.... all matter and all forces unified under the same rubric of microscopic string oscillations—the 'notes' that strings can play" (Greene, 1999, p. 16). This Faustian desire for "all" is uncannily echoed by two mythic figures, Taliesin and Orpheus. So, back to Taliesin, the voyager. It would seem that the story of the shamanic poet is based in part on the druid (shaman) tradition that teaches the mystical unity of all things and all beings, where all is inter-related and nothing is isolated. "This level of consciousness, like a gigantic telephone exchange, affords access to all other realms of awareness.... [and requires] a suspension of normal awareness. An empty mind allows an alternative level of transpersonal experience" (Matthews, 2002, p. 39).

Taliesin's voyage is recounted in several poems using the first person narrative to add relatability. The backstory, referred to earlier, involves Cerridwen; her ugly son Afagddu whom she wanted to change; a magical cauldron; the boy Gwion Bach tending the cauldron for one year and a day; three drops from the cauldron that fall on Gwion Bach's thumb (giving him the "thumb of knowledge"); the chase of the boy by Cerridwen and all their myriad, subsequent shape changes until finally the boy becomes none other than Taliesin with his seven senses:

I praise the one

Who, to keep guard over me,

Did bestow my seven senses,

From fire and earth, water and air:…

One is for instinct,

Two is for feeling,

Three is for speaking,

Four is for tasting

Five is for seeing

Six is for hearing,

Seven is for smelling. (in Matthews, 2009, p. 43)

The Taliesin material, as it is called (because so many poems are attributed to him and other druidic figures like Aneurin and Myrddi), contains lines and lines of the poet singing his knowledge in a boastful manner. "Compared with me, no one knows anything," he sings. "I am learned in the principal sciences/ And the reasoning of astrologers/ Concerning veins and solvents, /And the general nature of man" (in Matthews, 2002, p. 97). He recounts other knowings, such as when the bird of anger goes to its nest, smoke, cuckoos in summer, the briskness of ale, why the white swan has black feet, the number of fingers in the cauldron—and on and on. The catalogue of know-it-alls further includes the many shape changes of Gwion Bach (before he was reborn as Taliesin) from hare to fish to bird to a single grain. Each transformation corresponds with an element, such that hare=earth, fish=water, bird=air, and corn=fire. These elemental sequences imply that not only has Taliesin been through poetic initiation in the cauldron of Cerridwen's womb but he has also become acquainted with nature at its most fundamental level and is therefore at one with all creation (Matthews, 2002, p. 169). Along with the boast about being present at the Egyptian flood at the time of the Pharaohs is his claim that he was also present at the greatest recorded events in history: Alexander's conquest of the world, the building of the Tower of Babel, the Nativity and Crucifixion of Christ. As John Matthews (1999) writes, "Indeed, there is a sense in which he *was* present at these events—the *awen* (inspiration)-lifted spirit being capable of flights to which time or space form no boundary" (p. 111). Breath and hearing were thought to form "an integral part in the experience of inspiration; the poet breathes in the *awen*, hears it and gives it forth in musical speech or song" (Matthews, p. 112). If scientists today could access Taliesin's ear and breath, it might bring in a new way to do science.

Clearly, for scientists today, there is a missing loop in the paradigms that new science has discovered. They have worked with two pillars of cosmic laws: the large (general relativity) and the small (quantum mechanics), together with the electromagnetic forces of field theory. But they are still searching for the third thing and probably many more things. The universe, with its numerous hidden dimensions, oscillations, vibrations and patterns, beckons with its strangeness. Brian Greene pins his bets on superstring theory and its evolution into M-theory, but the "hunt" for the "unified theory" remains elusive. As Greene (1999) says, "physicists are relentlessly hunting down the elusive unified theory… [but] we are fulfilling our part, contributing our human ladder reaching for the stars" (pp. 386, 387). He continues with metaphors of scaling mountains, reaching peaks, and viewing from summits. I am wondering if a shift away from these phallocentric metaphors would help in the elusive hunt. Obi Wan Kenobi's advice, "Feel the force, Luke!" seems apt (*Star Wars*, 2004).

String theory is so named in the new science because of a strange new domain of the multiverse appearing as "loops of strings and oscillating globules, uniting all of creation into vibrational patterns… with numerous hidden dimensions capable of undergoing extreme contortions" (Greene, 1999, p. 386). Could this be the music of the spheres that haunts, delights, eludes pinpointing? If so, what then? What new hypotheses/insights/ questions would be available then? Could this music be like that of Orpheus, whose voice, the Greek dramatist Aeschylus wrote, affected "All" including all things and all beings? Or whose charm, Euripides wrote, acted not only on "all" living things, but beyond? Euripides even declared that Orpheus' music had the power to draw rocks to him. The all-encompassing magic of the Orphic lyre, however, had its dark side, since the singer-poet Orpheus had two histories, two pillars if you will: the history of his love for Eurydice, on the one hand; and the madness his music caused the Maenads, on the other hand, who tore the musician's body limb from limb. This seeming contradiction, of which he is the embodiment and therefore the living paradox, haunts the history of the bard so much that his presence in Greek writings during the Classical period remained "elusive" (Salvatore, 2004, pp. 173, 174). Orpheus, then, serves as an excellent mythic figure with which to compare superstring theory since the all/elusive quality that emanates from the strings of his lyre are as mysterious in myth as the oscillating globules and vibrating strands of energy are in science. Indeed, the whole mythic enterprise to embody and embrace paradox is perhaps the great stumbling block to new science. Diane Cousineau Brutsche (2009) explains:

> While quantum physics nowadays is increasingly adopting a paradoxical perspective on reality and discovering that mind and matter form what can be called a 'uni-duality' (the very definition of a paradox), most of our contemporaries keep adhering to a positivistic approach, blocked in a rational dead end and cut off from the symbolic realm. (pp. 110–111)

Music, of course, has this paradoxical nature, as Plato warned in *The Republic*, since it can cause emotional extremes, even oblivion. Music can charm the savage beast, a saying that is true in my living room. Our lumbering husky Blue is known for occasional violent outbursts. But let him hear Marla playing on one of her stringed instruments and he will slouch toward the musical source and curl up literally next to the pedals of the piano or the feet of the cello. Many depictions of Orpheus portray the same sort of scene of musician with birds or wild animals. In one early vase painting, Orpheus is depicted holding a branch in the left hand and the neck of an over-large lyre in the right, the lyre's huge size seemingly symbolic of music's supernatural quality. One bird, its mouth open, pecks the yoke of the lyre, as if to emphasize "the urgency and emotional grip of the musical attraction" (Salvatore, 2004, p. 179). Indeed, other paintings and writings suggest that the bard and his lyre were capable of exerting magnetic energy of extraordinary power even on the roots of trees. Today we might say this power is the wave-like undulations of subatomic particles unattainable to ordinary perception. In her "A Tree Telling of Orpheus" poet Denise Levertov writes in the language of roots, nature vocalizing the experience of rippling waves invading its tree consciousness: "language/ came into my roots/ out of the earth, / into my bark/ out of the air, / into the pores of my greenest shoots/ gently as dew/ and there was no word he sang but I knew its meaning" (in Doty, 2004, p. 47).

The mystery of science, the mystery of myth: both fields are full of dynamic forces, energizing thought as reimagined matter. Myth matters. Its root stems from the Indo-European stem *my* found in myth, mystery, muttering, and mother (Doty, 2000, pp. 5–7). The searched-for T.O. E. (theory of everything) known as M-theory also has roots: membrane, murky, mystery, magic, mother, matrix, and monstrous (Greene, 2003, DVD). Do these words sound mythically familiar? Do they belong to the same family, as monstrously mysterious as that might be? Nobel Laureate Brian Josephson (2005) welcomes the hidden potential of the mind as an avenue science should explore and remarks disparagingly on the "masculine aspect of our culture" that is suspicious of any non-logical unconventional ways of thinking (p. 3). Surely both realms of science and myth revel in paradox (myth more than science.) Both realms evoke wonder.

Curricular implications from both fields, as Jayne Fleener (2002) observed, suggest that "our understanding of the complexity of the curriculum entails a holistic, multi-perspectival, holographic approach to exploring our own experiences with schooling" (p. 3); and again, "I think of my students as relationships," (p. 95)—both ideas expressive of a way of viewing power (energy) as coming from within: within relation-ships, within the insides of the persons we teach. In his teaching of science and mathematics, Timothy Leonard (2008) connects the life discourses of scientists with the life stories of students to encourage dialogue with image, myth, and imagination. His intention is to provide insights and stretch the imagination. Like the science writer Lewis Thomas, Leonard seeks a two-fold function of the imagination between fantasy and reality that does not scoff at sending out Bach quartets to other life forms. Dennis J. Sumara and Brent Davis (1998) write about "unskinning" curriculum so as to recast self images, rename ideas, and dislodge fixities. Noel Gough (1998) uses the word "interreferencing" to study not one but different genres of texts, including autobiography, fiction, and the "manifold fictions of the world around us" (p. 111). Christopher Bache's (2000) experiences with transpersonal modes of learning unveil the classroom itself as an energy field. Since we are all vital parts of living patterns, he argues, it is not just students and teachers who have "mind" but so does a class-room with students, so does an entire course over the years: "I think that pedagogical techniques which stimulate strong student interest and participation and which invite high levels of critical reflection and the free expression of individual thought will encourage the development of strong course fields" (p. 198). These educationists are tapping into energy sources found in classroom relationships, as well as in and between texts, which suggests the exciting idea that generating interest and engage-ment does not just lighten the atmosphere but lightens up a mutually interactive "class mind." The prefix "un" or "inter" is frequently used by curricular theorists to open various ports of energy for creative discussion not usually considered appro-priate curriculum material. As Bill Pinar (1998) boldly put it, "Like physics or art, curriculum as a field cannot progress unless some segment of the field explores phenomena and ideas that perhaps few will comprehend and appreciate, certainly not at first and perhaps never" (p. xiii).

Then there is the matter of extrasensory perception, clearly a phenomenon that cannot be dismissed out of hand, although few would call this science, with the possible exception of Nobel Laureate in physics Brian D. Josephson. He observed (2005), "I did not fall into the trap of simply dismissing paranormal claims out of hand, as many scientists do" (p. 1). Call ESP a subjugated knowledge (Foucault, 2003), like myth. It was my freshman year when I received communication in a dream about my father's death. My dream took me into my father's house which was totally dark. I focused in on his study, also dark, which showed his desk piled up with dentist bills. The dream sentence that I clearly remember was "he is being dunned." Note the specifics of the dream as to dentist bills and the odd locution "dunned." At the time, unknowing to me, my father was indeed being dunned by my brother's dentist bills. My brother's name was Duncan. Those few images would not seem to have caused me such distress. But I woke up hysterical, with a terrible dread that my father would die. I remember crying down the dorm hall to the rooms of the faculty resident. We talked about my father over several glasses of Scotch for an hour or more until early the next morning. Within a few days I received word that my father had died in his sleep.

Sources that defy prediction or measurement have, among certain groups, always been petitioned. Carl Jung's *Red Book* (2009), which I saw on view at the Rubin Museum in New York, is an extraordinary collection of images and writings from Jung's active encounters with his imagination. Fearing that he might be called insane because of the bizarre images he confronted and drew, Jung and his family withheld publication. The exquisite drawings I saw included multiverses of varying unearthly activities: parallel universes containing other life forms with multiple heads, arms, and legs. The hybrid, beautifully painted figures and designs seem to have been the work of a brilliant 20th century mind in commune with 21st century science as well as with the age of alchemy. Perhaps not surprisingly, the material that burst forth from his unconscious became the source for Jung's archetypal theory and the conviction that it was the "numinous beginning which contains everything" (Henderson, 2009, p. 190).

This is not the only time the claim of seeing All or wanting "everything" has been mentioned. Space, far from being empty, is alive, dynamic. The implication these ideas have for all kinds of space—within us, surrounding us, outside our planet, outside our planet's planets—is full of dancing possibility. If we are to heal our planet soiled by gushing oil spills and human-made pollutants, waste, and greed, we must heal at the quantum level, looking not just out there in the frontiers of deep space but in our own inner spaces. As Deepak Chopra (1989) writes,

> Perhaps quantum events are not exclusively "out there" in space, but "in here" as well. Do we have "black holes" into which matter and energy disappear forever? Yes—we call it forgetting. Do we speed up time and slow it down? Yes again.... Whenever any mental event needs to find a physical counterpart, it works through the quantum mechanical human body.... both soaked through with intelligence. (p. 103)

Bringing myth together with science, bringing new awareness of quantum matters into the curriculum, should be an opening experience for those of us, like Wallace Stevens' "marvelous sophomore," who may yet learn to see the curriculum of our inner and outer worldspaces in holy different ways.

MYTH, THE NEW "M" THEORY OF EDUCATION OFFERING ELEVEN UNIVERSES

In this last chapter my intention is to bring together voices that are not commonly joined: poets, psychoanalysts, and writers; together with curriculum theorists; together with students in my myth classes as well as in my Absurdist Imagination class; along with my own riffs. There are four types of voices in each section (universe), no one voice speaking to another with any intention to contradict; rather, the voices sing their own tunes. Together what we have is an orchestration under my selection that suggests to me the kind of sweet dissonance and rhythm found in jazz. One of the key components of jazz is improvisation, which Ted Aoki (2005) says "is a way to create spaces to allow differences to show through" (p. 368). This chapter will focus on this idea of difference heard not as opposition but as "contrapuntal polyphony" (Aoki, 2005, p. 371). We need the different soundings that each voice brings. In her novel *Jazz*, Toni Morrison (1993) celebrates the city with its necessary contradictions; she calls contradiction the very essence of life. But "really," she writes, "there is no contradiction—rather it's a condition: the range of what an artful City can do" (p. 118). Similarly, I have found throughout my study of mythology that while opposites exist, they are necessary: they provide a living tension. It is this "condition" that offers a new sense of *things* and *ideas* not as separate entities. "Motor cars become black jet boxes gliding behind hoodlights weakened by mist. On sidewalks turned to satin figures move shoulder first, the crowns of their heads angled shields against the light buckshot that the raindrops are" (Morrison, 1993, p. 118). Call it a mosaic, call it a montage, the picture that Morrison paints is life presenting itself musically. Jazz is unique in that it was born from sadness and despair but rises above the problem without eliminating problematics.

So I offer the following eleven universes, which new science says surround unseen our small planet. Let the universes swirl around one another, sometimes repeating, sometimes jarring, but always expressing, syncopating, riffing, soloing—together in one sonorous jam session. Let us dance to the dancing energy that is the world, celebrating not opposition, which the Buddhists tell us is a false distinction, but the jazz of paradox.

Universe 1. "Take a thing for what it is and let it talk" (Hillman, 1983, p. 14).

Now there's an idea: substituting thing for person. Things, objects. Not subjects, not even "English 123," not even "student." Shift the perspective from me to it. Take the phenomenon at its face value, without putting subjective valuation on it, without submerging it to MY interpretation. Object reality. Objective consciousness. Placing our ideas onto things does not give its itness a living quality. As we read, view, listen, the world of the thing may be more interesting, which is to say different, from first glance. We are too much with seeing, too little with hearing, especially when what needs to be heard speaks in a different way.

This shift in focus allows several "things" to happen in the classroom. Perhaps first is the attention to text. Surely we know that students approach the text with all ideas firmly in place in their brainpan. If a strange thought is expressed in words, the tendency is to skip that strange thought and move on, ignoring the rumble in the back of the head. If a strange image appears in words in the text, a similar strategy is invoked: let the words blur a little so that the strangeness does not have time to disturb the already-known and take shape. To do otherwise is to engage in close reading. To do otherwise is to stay awhile in discomfort, allowing the thing to "talk."

Petra Munro Hendry (in press) refers to this attention to thing as an engagement with images. She writes, "We must suspend a sense of linearity, of permanence and duality, as we engage with the images of the wisdom age. Curriculum as image transcends time and space." The stranger and older the material, the greater opportunity for engagement–if we let our students dare the engagement. Recall Eliot's prudish Prufrock: "Do I dare to eat a peach?" (in Mack et al., 1992, p. 1750, line 122).

Teaching mythology I have ample opportunity to introduce the strange or weird image. I am always interested how long it takes for the weird image to actually become a serious discussion, not just a dismissal of those crazy folks' superstitions "back then." But when the spark of re-cognition occurs, a seeing as if having known this in some before-time, wonderful "things" happen. The following is the sense of itness Corey Vaughan expressed in a Beckett write-alike assignment:

> That time it rolled to a foot of a tree live oak eucalyptus pine and stopped as though asking to go on stopped and surrendered to forces unseen to you the brown and wrinkled skin from weathers that couldn't go on but the kids in the four square court shouting and you said you promised yourself you'd never forget this day and you never have despite the warm warnings of growth and growing up greater good that call your name from the other courts in other times.

The world opens to us as we await the many different speakings in the cosmos, but, of course, these speakings may be no more than murmurs or babbles. We must bend down low and listen, listen. Hovering presences await us.

Universe 2. "I would love to see the death of the expert" (Robinson, 2008, p. 224).

Here is an invitation to consider just what an expert is telling teachers what knowledge is of most worth and how to measure that knowledge. Measurement, accountability, assessment, total quality management: these are the abstractions used by experts to determine what is learned, what taught. If the teacher can state with precision what goals have been taught and what outcomes achieved, then according to the experts, that teacher can chalk up her success factors and get a merit raise, and students can march to graduation. How dry. Can I measure a flower?

I just read my student evaluations, this set from three sections of Composition 123, the basic requirement for incoming students. My students appreciated the work we did and expressed how much they had learned. Fine. I was particularly grateful for the comments that remarked on my humor. She is a funny woman, they said. But they also said, many of them, that I was not "clear." I needed to give better direction to my assignments. I have often been told that by students wanting me to outline my expectations, and of course the administrators echo this requirement. Hmm. Then, wouldn't students be following my instructions and the administrators' demands, not their own intuitions?

This emphasis on clarity is one I observed with horror in some of the classes I attended once. In one memorable class, memorable because I couldn't actually believe I was seeing what I was seeing, the teacher distributed detailed (clear!) directions for how to do a particular assignment. There were several pages of instructions, all numbered, all clear. Several minutes of class time were taken up with having different students read the instructions out loud, one by one. Is this a new way to do power point?

The increasing insistence on clarity and lock-step-by-lock-step is really a throw-back to the old factory model, which encouraged teachers to keep students "task on time" so that they can "produce" more, quicker. Bill Pinar (2009) offers this riposte:

> Education, unlike manufacturing, is not a business. However much politicians would like us to turn out "products" to be sold in the global market-place, how-ever much some parents would like their children to be clones, in confor-mity with their "values" (as they rename their preferences and prejudices), our students, as we know, are not products but singular subjectivities.... Intellectual work is psychological labor. Rather than being "noise" in the system, under-mining its efficiency, what we feel, how we think, our relations to others configure our curiosity, animate our interests, drive our desire to explore and discover. (p. 52)

Yes, the point here is that education should animate not automate. My student Chrystin Garland, an animation major, explains. "Animation is the art of movement. The word comes from the Latin word *anima*, meaning *soul* or *spirit*. Whether through a series of intricate drawings or as a computer generated puppet, it is the animator's duty to breathe life into their character" (Artist Statement, 2009, spring). For her final project she created a goddess which she named Anima and which she described as follows:

> Anima floats across the painting in three separate poses in order to emphasize the constant need for movement. In fact the goddess herself has never been caught standing still. She is always running about busying herself with any activity she finds enjoyable and exhilarating. Her many arms also help illuminate this fact, while the dark shadows under her eyes suggest that the ever-active goddess gets very little rest. Anima wears not a hat, but a light table upon her head, as well as a stunning robe made entirely of twelve field paper. These are iconic tools for the traditional animator and a necessity for such a goddess. The painting is void of color in order to emphasize the "soul" qualities of Anima. Though a goddess, she is more recognizable as a spirit darting this way and

that between and within the realms of human imagination. (Artist Statement, 2009, spring).

I am intrigued with the light table on the head of goddess Anima, who is colorless. We can then put our own colors on her as we wish, I imagine. But catch her if you can, for she is darting, probably fleeing from the experts who want to box her in.

Universe 3. "It is terrifying to be alive and awake" (Reis, 2008, p. 254).

The comfort zone is shattered, old regimes jolted asunder, biases and prejudgments thrown out the window when one awakens. To what? If one is fully alive and awake, one no longer can take for granted the occurrences around one, or within one. This can be terrifying if one has lived with pleasant lies or with an over-saturation of feel-goodness that can be deadening (same thing as boring). If one is witness to the drying up of lakes or the extinction of animal species, one is alert to life out of balance. If one is faced with irreconcilable relationships, it does no good to pretend that all is well.

So much pretense goes on in institutions the agenda of which is to deliver a passport to excellence. Nothing wrong with excellence except if error, bad starts, self-estrangement, vulnerability, grief, and shame are not also a part of the journey. I have noticed that when a different track is taken in a discussion, say of a particular image or line of poetry, examining its darkness, there is a quiet in the classroom. There is a sense that, finally, some truth of lived life is seeping in through the white walls of learning. A ho-hum lesson suddenly becomes charged.

Paula Salvio (2007) speaks to these issues that are "cast beyond the pale of the curriculum and replaced with the language of excellence and mastery" (p. 70). In her study of Anne Sexton, a brilliant but disturbed poet-teacher, Salvio introduces a terrifying figure whose dilemma gives us pause. She was a true paradox: beautiful but haunted, successful but mentally ill, liberatory for her students but confined within her own obsessions. Her life is the example Salvio offers for the terrifying awakenness that can occur when we are invited to explore our own disturbances in the public arena known as the classroom. Salvio (2007) writes:

> Why are particular figures ignored in education while others are recognized? I've often thought that Sexton was not only too excessive a figure to use as exemplary in teacher education, but too ordinary as well. What educators often forget is that the normal is not the same as the ordinary. The norm signifies nothing more or less that the prevailing standard while the ordinary, the every-day lives we lead, an ordinary pedagogy if you will, one that is opposed to the standard or normal varieties, can indeed be strange, polychromatic, and contra-dictory. The ordinary fears and anxieties that face teachers and students recede further and further into the background discussion in education. (p. 3)

In her ground-breaking study, Salvio refuses to romanticize illness or fetishize excess; rather, she offers a challenge to the notion that standards of excellence, mastery, and good teaching must exclude terrifying ordinariness. Calling Sexton "a teacher of weird abundance," Salvio suggests that by flattening out the kinks of lived experience, administrators and system-makers seek to cleanse the curriculum of very real issues, such as personal failure, not-good parenting, concealment, abuse, and ingenuine speakings. What is needed is more weirdness in the classroom if we are to recognize our own weirdnesses instead of casting them onto the Other.

Enter the weird. Myth, understood correctly, is weird. Myth is full of contradiction. From the first day of class I attempt to disabuse my students of the notion that contradictions are out of place. "You just contradicted yourself," a student said to me recently, as if that is the worst thing a teacher can do in front of the classroom because in our system contradiction *is not rational*. "Can you hold these two ideas together," I asked, "without worrying about contradiction?" I do not think my answer solved her problem.

To see a student embracing contradiction is rare, but in my Absurdist Literature class, the whole point of Absurdism is to crack open the too-firm notion that contradiction keeps things logical, right, and separate. Sihaya Harris wrote in the manner of Ionesco when she offered this amusing one-sentence spew of words that brings the opposites together:

On Tuesday morning just about an hour after the sun came up, on a morning damp and foggy just like many mornings previous, and only moments before a thunderstorm began, a storm not meant to come until later that night according to the weatherman on the radio, but which would last through the better part of the week which was the third week of June in midsummer, in a summer that had turned out to be extraordinarily rainy compared to subsequent summers and often in direct contradiction to the predictions of that same radio station's weatherman, although not particularly cooler than average summers in that particular region of the Midwest, which received an immoderate seventy inches of rain, yielding a multitude of dissatisfied complaints to a particular station the latter end of July, just before the tornedo season picked up, the rain becoming of secondary importance to an onslaught of destructive wind and hail storms, which occurred around the same time as a topical storm which crawled menacingly up the edge of the east coast, but which was addressed marginally more accurately by the radio station's weather forecasts, likely due to the firing and replacement of a particular weatherman much to the relief of a handful of residents of the broadcasting area, as they were far more at ease with the irreparable damages sustained to their homes in light of the accurate forecasting offered by the new and exceptionally more spritely weatherman, passing relatively pleasantly into a calm and ordinary autumn, during which nothing in particular happened.

Thus spake an Ionesco write-alike on ordinariness.

The terrifying aspect of being alive and awake, unafraid of inherent differences that occur, then, is that which we must dare to unlock from within: a truism psychoanalysts know for sure but which educationists are reluctant to admit through the mighty doors of academe because of what David Smith (1999) calls the "absolutely reductive way [of] Learning Theory" (p. 81).

Universe 4. "Realism is the corruption of reality" (Stevens, in Moore, 2004, p. 116).

Here is the great caution against thinking that reality is only presentable through the visual, which is the literal. What is in front of our eyes, particularly, can be

125

only half, or a third, of what is "there." To mistake reality for visual observance is to lack imagination and kill the vitality that can be expressed in other means with deeper sonar depth. The poet Wallace Stevens knows this. Do we?

I want to take this idea "reality," which Stevens suggests is a corruption of the real, and apply it to a fond notion of classical Western thinking: "development." This word is loaded especially when it is connected to the word "child" or "adolescent." Child development is what Jean Piaget (1999) outlined in his stage theory, suggesting that as a child moves out of animistic thinking, where a sympathy exists between creature and universe, that child will begin to "develop" in the sense that she will see herself as separate from the living world around her. That separation begins a new stage of rational thought in adolescence. The sun no longer follows the child around, magically, as the child moves through her mornings. Magic vanishes when rational thought emerges.

Somewhat on these grounds is another critique of development, this from post-structuralist Nancy Lesko (2001) who links adolescent development with the Great Chain of Being. This is a very interesting observation. The Grain Chain of Being is highly patriarchal, which means it is also hierarchical, which means some things are better than others, some people (men) are better than others (women), some species (human) are better than others (animal), some races (white) are better than others (black, red, yellow), and some patterns of living (civilized) are better than others (primal). Lesko's critique sees that privileging "civilized" behavior brings with it a host of other Western ideas, notably imperialism, progress, and capital: "In addition to imbedding hierarchies based on race and gender, adolescent develop-ment also spoke to the context of building a nation with an international reach... Building a nation and an empire put a positive valence on developing human capital and producing useful citizens" (2001, p. 92).

Lesko situates her considerable critique within social programs of male youth control:

> Adolescent development became a useful way to talk about and strategize for racial progress, male dominance, and national strength and growth. The new experts on adolescence identified particular problems to watch for and offered active, supervised activities, especially team sports, as the prescribed path toward national progress and functional elites. (p. 6)

Her study focuses on adolescent males, connecting the outgrowth of school shootings in the past ten years with a serious misunderstanding of "masculinity" that has carried forward from earlier decades. The association between masculinity and primitive energy, she says, is at least a century old. "Primitive energies were gathered by being in nature, by hunting, by competitive games, and through righteous wars" (2001, p. 219 footnote). No room for dreamers here, if all is to be monitored in the name of development and civilization. Where do artists go if all activity is programmed, supervised? Michel Foucault's panopticon looms over this scenario, as does George Orwell's *1984*.

Just as Nancy Lesko troubles the concept of adolescence, I continue to trouble the notion of the mythic hero, which is also expressive of a masculinity program to equate "civilization" with control over natural forces, be they hormonal or cosmic.

My male students usually choose to portray male heroes for their final projects, drawn usually from either the highly patriarchal Greek or Norse cultures. The projects are easy, in the sense that the agenda is one familiar to the Western imagination: the idea of power means subduing natural forces, winning, and re-asserting "civilized" values. In contrast, my female students often choose a goddess figure for their project. The difference between the choices and the genders might as well be the difference between "reality" and "the real." "Reality" is that which keeps the differences distinct; "the real" is that which is inherently, tensively, alive with contradiction.

The goddess figures two students chose allowed contradiction to be a living part of the figure. This, I think, is the single most important aspect of "the real." It shimmers. Reality that corrupts "the real" is ironclad. Let Madeline Patel explain. She selected for her final project both Eve and Lilith, opposite characters. She recognizes each as "personifications of how women should and should not act." That is why she wants to bring them together. She writes:

> They are complete opposites; if combined together they might represent how one woman might act. For example, a woman can be shy but outgoing, or kind but conniving. Eve is seen as the subservient goddess to her husband. She is innocent but curious. Lilith, on the other hand, was Adam's first wife, wanting to be seen as an equal to her husband. When she was denied this, she left him, deciding she would rather eat her demon children than return to him. The only reason she is considered evil is that she chose to be independent. I see one characteristic these two figures share: disobedience. They disrupted the ordered state of affairs defined by men and actually used their free will that neither God nor man could control. (Artist Statement, 2008, spring)

This observation is very sharp, in my view, and echoes Lesko's concern with the "ordered state of affairs" otherwise known as "civilization." To disrupt the order, the goddesses disobeyed. That word "obey" is embedded in the Girl Scout motto ("to obey the Girl Scout laws") and used to be, maybe still is, embedded in the wedding vow that women promise to cherish, honor, and obey their husbands. Something about obedience is pure reflex, "no more a product of the conscious mind than the bark of a dog" (Frye, 1963, p. 63). Madeline's project was an illustration of two goddesses, Eve and Lilith, at the moment they come face to face with one as other.

What is it to face an other's face when that other is one's face, too? This is not identity as similarity but rather identity as mixed, a very different notion.

Universe 5. "Fear only the red-gold sun with the fleece of a fox/ Who will steal the fluttering bird you hide in your breast" (Sitwell, in de Castillejo, 1974, p. 175).

The too-bright sun of the intellect is a thief to the not-yet-fully realized image that precedes thought and lies fluttering. The fluttering of a bird is a felt image, commonly connected with the soul, often caged. This warning against over-intellectualizing is apt for a Western way that prides thought over image, mind over soul.

There is, too, the sun of a too-bright phrase, as in "the educated imagination" (Frye, 1963). I have heard of administrators who encourage faculty to subscribe to mainstream newspapers like *The Wall Street Journal* or *The New York Times*, with the intention of introducing well written daily pieces for student observation. This is a noble idea. But the preference for the *Times,* say, over my daily paper *The Savannah Morning News* suggests an elitism of big city liberalism over small city regionalism. Not to read my local paper would mean I would not know about events featuring local and as-yet not-known names in the music world; or, indeed, announcements about my own lecture at a local historic house; or, indeed, a free exhibit at our local museum featuring little-known American artists painting their versions of a Dutch Utopia (critiqued smartly by the curator). It sounds so innocent, "the educated imagination." But John Willinsky (1998) in his award-winning book *Learning to Divide the World* examines assumptions that lie beneath the noble intention to educate not just the mind but the imagination. He takes to task English literature, particularly the classics of seventeenth, eighteenth and nineteenth centuries, which had as their primary educational objective a colonizing agenda. There is, he finds, "the continuing play of the colonial imagination within the literary landscape" (p. 230). His study of various writers including Shakespeare, Milton, Defoe, and Conrad is undertaken as part of a larger study of Northrop Frye's lectures entitled "Educating the Imagination" (1983), in which Frye uncritically nominates English literary "master"pieces as the means by which students will become educated. The problem for Willinsky is "a colonial imaginary of island paradise, plantation economies, and evolutionary hierarchies. This imperial legacy lives on today as a trace element in our educational lives, not necessarily toxic in itself but worrisome as it goes unspoken and unexamined" (p. 214). This imperialist literary agenda sounds like what Nancy Lesko (2001) sees in education's mandate for excellence: both carry traces of teacherly texts meant to civilize the savage youth, who can then lead us onward and outward. The genius of literature, Gauri Viswanathan wryly observed, is that it has found "the men who are to extend her empire to the ends of the earth, and give her throne a stability that will be lasting as the sun" (qtd. in Willinsky, 1998, p. 219). Where is the bird to wing us inward?

I had glimpses of the problem of English department elitism when I attended a Modern Language Association meeting a while back and listened to learned men (mostly) expounding sophisticated and well-reasoned arguments in three piece suits. I heard the modulated voices and witnessed the chumminess with which professors from elite English departments offered to meet with one another over martinis. Yet when we clambered onto buses to take us to the airport, after all was said and done, I was stunned with how rude these erudite ones were to the bus driver. The brilliance of their explications of texts notwithstanding, these professors were enclosed in their own privileges and texts, paying no heed to what a post colonial critique offers to close reading or, as with my above example, close meeting.

For the student segment of this "universe" of sun, I present a student understanding of the Hindu figure Purusha, whose body becomes the entire world. Many creation myths have this notion of a god's body forming the structure of the cosmos, an early understanding of the divinity within the natural world as well as the interdependence of all on all. But as this student reads the story, he sees it also as an explanation of the Indian caste system, which he says is little more than "propaganda":

> The highest and ruling caste came from Purusha's head, the warriors from his arms. The lowest order of people, the workers, was made from Purusha's feet. These are propaganda symbols, used to make people believe that they belong

where they are and not to question the system. It also demonstrates how ancient cultures commonly used myth and gods as an excuse to make their exploits legitimate. (N. Taylor, 2008, spring)

Substitute the word "literature" for "myth" and this student could as well be echoing what Willinsky says about the problem of education when its political agenda goes unspoken or unrecognized. Here the hierarchical arrangement of Purusha offers a perfect example of dividing Us from Them, upper from lower, so as to legitimatize the exploits of the ones with the upper hand, as it were. The word "propaganda" applied to myth gives me pause. Well, yes. Of course. Consider how the goddess cultures were obliterated by the marauding hunter-gatherers. Consider what the Romans and the Christians did to discredit the Celts. What was so threatening about goddess and Celtic nature worship that each had to be discredited at best, all-but-extinguished, at worst? What is the agenda, we must ask ourselves, of every text we read, of every image we see. Why must difference be obliterated? Is this the kind of "reality" we sanction?

The other "universe" in the Stevens quote refers to "bird." The bird is an ancient symbol of the soul: flutterer, occupier of the day sky as well as the night sky, of air as well as of land. Who hasn't wanted to fly, like a bird? My flying dreams are pure ecstasy, and for those brief moments when I am aloft I feel freedom and thrill. I can zoom and I can hover. Susan Edgerton (1996) recounts the mention of a bird in the Nobel Prize acceptance speech of Toni Morrison:

> The woman is visited by some young people who hope to test her reputation of wisdom. They tell her they hold a bird in their hands, and ask her if it is living or dead. After a very long pause, and some giggles from the young people, the woman replies, 'I don't know. I don't know whether the bird you are holding is dead or alive, but what I do know is that it is in your hands. It is in your hands.' (in Edgerton, 1996, p. 173)

Edgerton comments "language is the bird, and the responsibility to use it is "in your hands" whoever you are—teacher, student, reader, writer" (p. 173). Yes, our words can destroy the bird, a cautionary tale for those of us in power positions. Literalism crushes. So do definitions. So do facts. These are pointers only. Facts can be disproved; literalisms are the rocks people throw at glass houses. The word has a limited ability to express, which is why metaphor is the poet's preference.

Writing his "memory shot" for an assignment based on Beckett's autobiography, Francis Fave remembers as follows:

> You see yourself at that last outset arching your feet waiting for the word from you to go. To be gone. Then the radiant sand. You lie in the dark with closed eyes and see yourself there as described hesitant to make your way across the swath of fire. You feel your feet arching up your toes pulling back before the journey begins. You are hastening across the white sands taking to the shadows to let your feet cool. Your course appears erratic from obstacle to obstacle resting at each for a moment before continuing on. Unseeing unhearing you go your way. Day after day. The same way. You lie in the dark with closed eyes and see the scene. As you could not at the time. The dark cope of sky.

The words "cope" and "swath" are deliberate, poetic, and perfect: little birds of an idea. His use of the second person pronoun, in the manner of Beckett, is an achievement of distance on the self, seeing himself from a far-off vantage point. I think this is incredibly empowering for the writer and powerfully poetic for the reader.

Universe 6. "The way that can be expressed in words is not the eternal way" (Lao Tzu, in Downing, 2006, p. 129).

Head's up, professors! The texts we teach: that's not where all meaning lies. Words on the page, words exchanged in classroom discussion may not be where real meaning lies. Take a moment to picture yourself in front of the classroom, seated on a desk, perhaps; standing by a podium, perhaps; over there by the window. The light may be on or off. You are talking. They seem to be listening. They are politely silent. I reverse the scene and picture myself fifty years ago watching the professor at desk, podium or window, me looking oh so interested. I was drifting in my head. I know this because I was a bad student in college, practically flunking out my sophomore year after my father died. I turned the pages, dutifully, and took notes laboriously, but I was not caught by the words. Not at all. I did not even know I was depressed, since I was doing what they told me to do, a punishment for my low grade-point average. As Marla Morris (2008) says, the death of the father crumbles a world. I felt crumbled but kept on turning pages.

In her chapter "Soul-Speaking: The Ill Body," Marla offers a meditation on different kinds of speaking, other than words, that relate with the soul. She is addressing the wounded soul and the ill body, showing a connection that exists between suffering and soul, as if the soul "speaks" most when we suffer. She writes, "Educating through the wounded body is soul-speaking through colors and sounds" (2008, p. 129). But she also acknowledges that the soul speaks in silence (p. 122) and in common places. "On stairwells. In elevators. While sweeping the floor. Talking on the phone. Going to the zoo. Flying. Dreaming" (p. 126). In this unusual list Marla is suggesting that the soul needs relation because the soul "intends an Other" (p. 127). This idea of the soul being the One in Many is very old and to our ears very strange. But listen to the song of the Welsh bard Taliesin, singing of his unity with all of nature, both animate and inanimate:

> I have been in many shapes before I attained a congenial form. I have been a narrow blade of a sword; I have been a drop in the air; I have been a shining star; I have been a word in a book; I have been a book in the beginning. I have been a light in a lantern a year and a half.... I have been the string of a harp; I have been enchanted for a year in the foam of water. There is nothing in which I have not been. (in Squire, 2001, p. 124)

How appropriate that I find this litany of the mystical Celt on the day Christians celebrate the birth of the magical Christ child. How appropriate, too, that I read this from a book gifted to me by Marla Morris. Synchronicities of this kind are wondrous. However much one can talk about soul-speaking it somehow eludes representation because of its depth. It is a puzzle, it is animation, and it is a mystery. Most of all, the soul is that where compassion is felt.

The mystery of the dying god evokes compassion, as one sees upon entering any Catholic church. There, many images of the suffering Christ can be found in The Stations of the Cross, which tell the story of the events leading up to Christ's crucifixion. As well, the image of the half-naked body of Christ, hanging on the cross, is what one sees over the altar, placing before our eyes in a very public way a graphic example of extreme suffering. But did Christ die for our sins, as the Church insists? I have never found that acceptable dogma since it relieves humankind from personal responsibility, which also means the "ability to respond." If I have no responsibility, what do my seeing eyes tell me about Christ? Rather, the passion/suffering of the dying god is also our passion/suffering when we are compassionate.

Marla Morris' illness was a body suffering that connected deeply with soul. She talks of soul-speaking in unusual ways that force one to "make sense of the terrible" which is "the negative" (2008, p. 120). The territory of the soul is in the negative, the empty spaces, the not-experienced-as-usual. She offers a very strange image for our contemplation: "The soul is the moon of the body" (p. 128). I am caught by the metaphor. The meaning here is not that the soul is LIKE the moon of the body, but IS the moon of the body. The moon comes out in darkness and changes over time, ripening, emptying. It is most commonly thought of as female because of its periodic changes and because of the connection with darkness. These ideas resonate deeply with Marla's felicitous metaphor but do not capture its full meaning. Good. Let the metaphor shimmer just beyond our reach. Words are not the way.

Thirty spokes converge on a single hub,

it is in the space where there is nothing

lies the usefulness of the cart. (Li, Trans., 2008, p. 203)

Writing this memory shot for the Beckett assignment mentioned above, Haley Ashkenas offers this:

Alone on your back in the dark you dream of swamps. A faint lapping of water at the shore's moist earth can be heard. It gently slaps then ebbs. At each slow ebb your chest rises and falls filling with breath then releasing.

Darkness, water, the ebbing of the tide as with breath: here is the language of a moon child.

Universe 7. "Conflict is the beginning of consciousness" (Harding, 1975, p. 5).

If conflict is thought of as the opposite of agreement, as in disagreement, it becomes disagreeable. But think of the times consciousness was awakened by a prick, blow, itch, wound, or jolt to the forward thrust of thought. The mind circles back as in astonishment. For there! in the conflicting moment, a new direction opens. A possibility like a gift arises from that which conflicts with what was previously thought and accepted. This kind of conflict can be the chink of light needed to open the mind.

Some of us in higher education have long thought it our duty to enlighten our students, show them the light, bring them out of their cave of ignorance. What a hugely absurd notion! Light according to whom? According to what regulator or agent of state? I have sat in on classes where this Platonic ideal of lighted goodness was taught uncritically. Students really tried to grasp this foreign notion that the professor so adored. "What do you admire about Plato's argument?" the professor begged his reticent class. Instructed classically and abroad, the professor could only be the apologist for Platonic essentialism, failing utterly to engage the students in healthy critique. Without problematical discussion, the class dragged on.

John Weaver's (2009) exploration of popular culture takes us to the other side of the podium and offers a serious study of the style, music and subcultures of modern youth. Our students are a generation or more removed from us, which means that if we are to "teach" we should also "learn" about our audience. Our students are sitting right in front of us, but they are not blank slates:

> Hip-hop has done more to define youth cultures than anything dominant cultures have constructed. Hip-hop has defined fashion, sports, advertising, television, films, magazines, and language. Certain people within dominant cultures have tried to regulate and sanction it, but their failures to control hip-hop have demonstrated how inept and impotent dominant cultures are and how powerful subcultures can be. (p. 44)

I expect my well-meaning professor cited earlier, so earnest, would be appalled (as would Plato) at the most un-Platonic use of forms most artists play with today. The acts of recovery, reinvention, and iteration are all means through which hipsters take the wheel in new directions. But there the student-artists sat, many half-asleep, while my professor enjoyed her own explication of text.

As curricular theorists, particularly those engaged with *post* or *re* theories (as in poststructuralism, postmodernism, postcolonialism, posthuman, postformal; or reconceptualization, retranslation, reimagining), power is a dangerous position to be in as a teacher. Consequently, an examination of one's own teacherly position needs to be foremost. How do I position myself with regard to my students and to the texts I have chosen? What position does the text take with regard to its assumptions about readers? How can I translate these assumptions, often hidden, to myself and to my students? And what about my own hidden assumptions, what Susan Edgerton (1996) calls "the self that is not master of the self" (p. 170)? Am I able to translate myself to myself? These are questions Edgerton raises in what she calls the "power relations of translation" (p. 54), a process which must come when one comes into conflict with one's self, which is why autobiographical study is so key to curriculum theorists. She writes

> [Rereading and rewriting have] raised for me issues around desire, guilt, privilege, and domination—issues that never cease to concern me in the classroom, in my relations to my students…. To be existentially dead—caught in the fictional register of identity formation?—is to be in no position to learn/teach. It is to be stupid. (p. 152)

Writing his memory shot for a class assignment, Jose Antonia Rodriguez-Romero remembers

> Fighting or defending is the torn feeling felt as your father rides off in the car.
> It is the superego versus the superego in which the superior is not a level of

consciousness attainable. Suddenly it strikes you: perhaps it is this that keeps you trapped in fear. It is time to walk, no, charge into the unknown and see what waits for you beyond the bars of uncertainty. You follow your father as you are born now into the newer self. The clean air outside rejuvenates your soul as you now treasure the reality you once took for granted (24 May, 2010).

Jose's felicitous use of alliteration of the 'f' sound, soft, works well with the hard strike of awareness about the f-f-father.

Universe 8. "I tell you the gods are still alive/ And they are not consoling" (Sarton, 1974, p. 259).

To think polytheistically, with a pantheon of deities alive still in the imagination, is to challenge a basic tenet of monotheism: there can be no god but me. What a shift in thought this provides: there is no one deity but many deities, not all of them kind or even rational. We ignore these to our peril. Our ignorance disturbs them. And what has caused the disturbance? One answer, which myth proposes, is that the gods oversee a balance in the cosmos and when that balance comes undone, humans will feel the effect as will all sentient beings. This is not consoling. Humans would do well to respect the unseen energy fields in the full knowledge that these fields exist even without our say so. The tipping points to the ecosystem have already been reached. Witness careless land use, animal and plant extinction, global warming. Witness; then petition the gods.

One who witnessed and petitioned was Carl Jung, in his recently released *Red Book* (2010), written during and after the years of WWI. He began the project after a series of visions prior to the outbreak of world war which Jung believed were messages from the beyond that seeped into his own unconscious. This process of accessing signs from the cosmos is what Jung formulated as his theory of archetypes: images (in this case of the apocalypse) that can be found culture to culture throughout time. Accompanying the beautifully strange mandalas which Jung recreated from his unconscious are his notes and dream descriptions. The drawings are intricate, beautiful, stunning, weird. Who knew Carl Jung was such an artist! How did the author of eighteen volumes of scholarly work, as well as countless letters, as well as world travel and consultation with patients, find time for this personal undertaking? The writings and drawings of his inner universe are an "enterprise of self-examination, a ruthless overturning of the rational Western mind, submerging [Jung] in a pilgrimage through the pagan land of his own psyche" (Rothstein, 2009, C5).

Commenting on his own dis-ease with "the sickness of the West," David Jardine (2008) writes of feeling far away from the "jeweled heart":

When you are living with war, things start to shut down, possibilities narrow, conversations cease. And in the ensuing silence, 'untruth' (Smith, 2006) is perpetrated....Untruth becomes truth because it is willed to be so.... This is not just a sickness of the West. It is the sickness of fundamentalism and the deafness, fear, and war footing it feeds upon, supports, aggravates, and declares as necessary always and only because of *the other's* deafness. (p. xiii)

Jardine points to the problem of not hearing opposite viewpoints, which causes a spiritual deafness. If we can no longer feel, or see, and we are in danger of not hearing one another, the gods have indeed left us to our own dumb devices.

Today, main stream education worships the assessment gods and their damnable NCLB agenda. Before the age of the assessment god, Edward Albee critiqued what America most admires in his *The American Dream*. Hear how Chris Weiderman discusses the point of the satire in his class critique:

> Edward Albee satirizes and examines the multifaceted concept of the title *The American Dream*, a phrase so ubiquitous and inclusive that it has become meaningless. It is interesting, then, that his definition of the Dream draws itself in a character as vacuous and hobbled by mindless consumerism, "Young Man." The Man is the twin of the boy the Mommy and Daddy mutilated; he feels the mutilations and emptiness from his brother's injuries. While he is beautiful, desirable, muscular, and masculine on the outside, he is empty, "dis-emboweled," a call back to his brother. His existence is the unconscious product of destructive consumption Albee sees a crippling nightmare in the concept of "The American Dream."

Today we experience the nightmare of consumerism in the American greed, some say obsession, with and for oil. The infamous British Petroleum oil "spill" is still not contained as I write, two and a half months into the despoilment of land, water, bird, mammal, fisheries, and who knows what else.

Universe 9. "Now speech has perished from among the lifeless things of earth, and living things say very little to very few" (Dillard, 1984, p. 70).

To accept that there are other speakings besides those of human beings is to accept a paradigm shift in consciousness toward Earth. The wise ones who inhabited this Earth before us revered a cosmos that "spoke" in ways that are similar to the speakings of dreams. This speech is imagistic and non-literal. To consider the things of Earth as lifeless is to ignore even further what hurricanes, tornadoes, and summer weather in winter climates are "saying" about global warming.

There are dangers here for teachers who are "deaf" to students, also. If teachers stand and students sit, a discrepancy exists between standing and sitting, standing being the more powerful stance. Surely, too, a discrepancy exists between male and female teacher or professor, the former usually credited with more prestige and (certainly) self-importance. How much more problematic, then, is the discrepancy between tall and small when the small is a child.

A critique of the construction of the child has been a consistent project of the several writings of Gaile Cannella and her co-researcher Radhika Viruru since 1997. Characterizing the child's written identity as "uncomplicated, marginalized, and even non-existent," Cannella and Viruru (2004) remark that such an attitude "is deeply implicated in the creation of technologies of power that continue to colonize and subjugate both the children and adults" (p. 117). They suggest that "the universal child" has become an essentialized, manipulating construction by institutions, ideo-logies and forms of representation. What it means to be a child, they write, has little to do with what the biggies say. Rather, they argue,

Children (and by implication all of us) have become the literal representatives of hypercapitalism as they have been reconstituted as political tools, objects of moral theorizing, and the unified, universal, yet nonexistent, identity that is used to justify adult discourse and actions.... within the adult mind and constitution, the colonization of childhood is complete and without question. (p. 118)

Writing her memory shot for an assignment, Jennifer Braunstein thinks back to when she was a child:

You are six. The heat has died with the onset of night. Onyx pigtails flounce against your earlobes, and bare toes travel lightly over the grass, into the air, and back on the ground as you capture another yellow spark that has managed to suspend itself in the soupy summer, idly unaware of the prowling girl with the crayon mask. Number twenty-one. A cicada sings you a triumphant screech as you let the firefly tickle your finger with its toes and launch solemnly back into purple space.

Here is a child, remembered from a distance, aware of the living "purple space" surrounding her prowl.

Universe 10. "We are not living our own lives; we are paying the debts of our forefathers" (Jung, 1972, p. 320).

If we are not living our own lives but the error-filled lives of our ancestors, does this mean we are condemned to repeat, repeat those same errors? Jung implies this. It is a psychological fact that the doom of the unfulfilled life may lie with the background we inherit. I think of my father's drunkenness, my mother's shortness of temper, my grandfather's anti-Semitism, my father's anti-Catholicism, my mother's bitterness, my father's bitterness. "You've got to be carefully taught," the song goes, "to hate the people your grandparents hate." Ah, the tune is so lively but the idea, deadly! Those folk whose genes we have in our own bodies clearly are part of what makes us who we are. But we are not, in fact, doomed to repeat, repeat, especially if we take a wider, broader view of parentage and of grandparentage.

The idea of the extended family has a wide connection with both personal and cosmic kinship. If, as expressed above, the individual is a composite of psychic traits from the ancestors, it is possible to think that thought backward and say, as myth does, that the individual's life is not just kin with people to whom we are connected but with symbols of the universe with whom we connect, as well. Forefather or fore-mother, in myth, is the original ancestor out of whose body is carved all the aspects of the cosmos. The extraordinarily interesting cosmologies of myth relate various ways in which the first human form (be it giant or god or goddess) provides the substance of the world above, below, and in the middle. Just so. The giant Ymir is dismembered so that his body becomes the corpse of the cosmos. His flesh becomes the earth, his teeth becomes stones, his hair becomes the forests, his brains become storm clouds, his blood becomes the ocean, and his skull becomes the sky. This is re-membering the world we live in. We should remember this so as to live our own lives more deeply and less in the shadow of the personal parent. Memory itself may be older than our ancestors and contained in nonhuman forms, then. The writer Amy Tan (2006) thinks the latter is particularly so. "It could be that we exist in all ten dimensions of a string-theory universe," she writes, "and are seeding memories in all of them and occupy them simultaneously as memory" (p. 493). Far out!

While his project is not mythically oriented, Bill Pinar (2004) is careful to connect the curriculum in its root form *currere* to the work of memory. Understanding the self is the focus of autobiographical study, and rightly theorized the self critiqued and self-reflected awakens one from dumb surrender:

> This autobiographical method asks us to slow down, to remember even re-enter the past, and to meditatively imagine the future. Then, slowly and in one's own terms, one analyzes one's experience of the past and fantasies of the future in order to understand more fully, with more complexity and subtlety, one's submergence in the present.... Not only intellectually but in our character structure, we must become "temporal," living simultaneously in the past, present, and future. (p. 4)

Living temporally, as Pinar urges, avoids nostalgia or repetition compulsion if we examine critically the "debts" of our forefathers. By being fully present to our emerging selves we can come into authenticity, freeing ourselves from past distortions. I think such critical examination is what Brian Casemore (2008) means by resuscitating the significance of "place" so as to "work through personal and historical trauma" (p. 9).

Writing on Beckett's play *That Time*, Sihaya Harris comments,

> The character seems to be questioning selfhood, uncertain of his connection with the biblical Adam as well as with his own skull. In light of this doubt, he tries to separate himself from the religious figure, to disconnect from the first man. He questions the nature of his existence as a physical being and how that would relate to his identity. Are the brain and self really one? There is a difference between thinking and feeling; we might need to feel more so as to think less.

Beckett's style has jolted my students in important ways. The memory work I ask of them is intended to disrupt their own senses of themselves as unified entities, which is, of course, a great misconception (pardon the pun). The language of contradiction, so prevalent in Beckett's work, is the necessary interruption that allows something other to break through to skulls hardened by personalistic belief.

Universe 11. "When a tree blossoms, death blooms in it as well as life; every field is full of death" (Rilke, 1946, p. 256).

This idea of the interrelation between life and death is so central to myth that, without an understanding of its meaning, myth's truths are meaningless. Perhaps death is seen as the absolute opposite to minds schooled in rational thinking. But death "blossoming" is a wonderfully mythopoetic way of expressing this idea of regeneration. Death is not the end (my friend). Burial in earth is sowing the seed into earth, readying a process for rebirth. This wisdom, culled from the early goddess cultures as well as from the vegetation deities, is also the very basis of Christian belief—but with clear differences. Christians believe that Christ died for us so that sins may be forgiven. Christ's blood is the blotter for the stains of our trespasses. This is a childish notion. The death of the Christian god understood this way is not regenerative; it is a palliative. But death mythopoetically understood is cyclical and transformative and has nothing whatsoever to do with sin. Death is a natural energy exchange: death and life, life and death. Who constructed the dying Christ as the sin-taker? The dying Christ, like Dionysus, is the living vine. "Polarity, or action and reaction," Emerson (2008) says, "we meet in every part of nature.... To empty here, you must condense there" (p. 53).

The exchanges of energy occur in space, silently, allowing a drop-down for deeper thought. "Distance involves space," Delese Wear (2006) ruminates, "the road between here and there, the heavy air between persons sitting in the same room, the minutes between now and then, the airborne messages in flight between sender and receiver" (p. 70). She continues

> I grew up with an acute sense of distance, daughter of two transplanted, farm-grown parents whose attachment to the earth and its cultivation, to the ebb and flow of seasons, to the work of hands and machines, and to the beauty of both solitary and communal work was coded in their children's DNA. (pp. 70–71)

Delese's return to the farm involves images of her past, imaginings about strangers in the field, and ruminations about teaching medical students. Death is the unspoken topic for her: her students may have to tell future patients of diseases they may die from. Will the future doctors under her charge care about how patients deal with illness, with death? Can reading literature together in the classroom open the hearts of doctors-to-be, shrink the distance between doctor and patient? As Delese travels home to her mother on the farm, she ponders the solitary figure in the doorway and a lump grows in her throat. The field with its seasonal reminders gives grace and a knowing calmness to those who live in its blooming death.

Commenting on Beckett's play *That Time*, Corey Vaughan writes this for class assignment:

> Throughout the play *That Time* we see the main character and hear three separate voices. These voices present themselves as different times or feelings of the character's past. By their simultaneous bombardment of run-on thoughts the sense of time becomes muddled, to the audience and perhaps to the main character. The voices never seem to end, being a never-ending train of thought. Time is deconstructed by the filter of the three voices, each with their own viewpoint. However, it seems that these voices are serving a vital role: they are helping him to "keep the void out."

So many universes. So many thoughts, many of them similar but written differently. What a celebration of life can be found when we blend our voices and honor the silence and, yes, even the void (that dances still).

REFERENCES

Abram, D. (1997). *The spell of the sensuous: Perception and language in a more-than-human world.* New York: Vintage.

Adams, M. V. (2001). *The mythological unconscious.* New York: Karnac Books.

Aoki, T. (1988). *What is it to be educated?* Paper presented at Convocation I. Lethbridge, Alberta, Canada: University of Lethbridge.

Aoki, T. (2005). Sonare and videre: A story, three echoes and a lingering note. In W. F. Pinar & R. L. Irwin (Eds.), *Curriculum in a new key: The collected works of Ted. T. Aoki* (pp. 367–376). Mahwah, NJ: Lawrence Erlbaum Associates.

Appelbaum, P. (2008). *Children's books for grown-up teachers: Reading and writing curriculum theory.* New York: Routledge.

Assyrian and Babylonian literature: Selected translations. (1901). New York: D. Appleton & Co.

Auerbach, E. (2003). *Mimesis: The representation of reality in Western literature* (W. R. Trask, Trans.). Princeton, NJ: Princeton University Press.

Avalon, A. (1978). *Shaki and Shakta.* New York: Dover Books.

Ayrton, M. (1962). *The testament of Daedalus.* London: Methuen/Winston.

Ayrton, M. (1967). *The maze maker.* New York: Holt, Rinehart and Co.

Babejova, E. (2009). And the river swelled with horses. *Symbolic Life:Spring: A Journal of Archetype and Culture, 82,* 131–152.

Bache, C. M. (2000). *Dark night, early dawn: Steps to a deep ecology of mind.* Albany, NY: State University of New York Press.

Bachelard, G. (1971). *The poetics of reverie* (D. Russell, Trans.). Boston: Beacon Press.

Bachelard, G. (2002). *Earth and the reveries of will: An essay on the imagination of matter* (K. Haltman, Trans.). Dallas: The Dallas Institute Publications. (Original work published in 1943)

Batchelor, S. (1997). *Buddhism without beliefs: A contemporary guide to awakening.* New York: Riverhead Books.

Beckett, S. (1938, April-May). *"Denis Devlin."* Review of *"Intercessions"* (D. Devlin, Trans.). *Tenth Anniversary, 27,* 289–294.

Beckett, S. (1954). *Waiting for Godot.* New York: Grove Press.

Beckett, S. (1958). *Three novels by Samuel Beckett.* New York: Grove Press. (Original work published 1955)

Beckett, S. (1977). *Ends and odds: Eight new dramatic pieces.* New York: Grove Press.

Beckett, S. (1981). *Ill seen ill said.* New York: Grove Press.

Beckett, S. (1988). *Stirrings still.* New York: North Star Line.

Bernstein, J.S. (2005). *Living in the borderland: The evolution of consciousness and challenge of healing trauma.* London: Routledge.

Berry, P. (1975). The rape of Demeter/Persephone and neurosis. *Spring: An Annual of Archetypal Psychology and Jungian Thought,* 186–197.

Berry, T. (1990). *The dream of the earth.* San Francisco: Sierra Club Books.

Bettelheim, B. (1989). *The uses of enchantment: The meaning and importance of fairy tales.* New York: Vintage Books.

Birkerts, S. (2004). *The Gutenberg elegies: The fate of reading in an electronic age.* New York: Faber and Faber, Inc.

Bishop, P. (2009). *Eudora Welty's centenary.* Retrieved from http:entertainment.timesonline.co.uk/tol/arts_and_entertainment/the_tls/article6162731.ece

Bloom, H. (1999). *Shakespeare: The invention of the human.* New York: Riverhead Books.

Bohr, N. (1975). In L. Leshan (Ed.), *The medium, the mystic, and the physicist: Toward a general theory of the paranormal* (p. 67). New York: Ballantine Books.

Boucher, S. (1993). *Turning the wheel: American women creating the new Buddhism.* Boston: Beacon Press.

REFERENCES

Bradshaw, G. A., & Watkins, M. (2006). Trans-species psychology: Theory and praxis. *Psyche and Nature, Part 1 of 2:Spring: A Journal of Archetype and Culture, 75*, 69–94.

Brutsche, D. C. (2009). Lady Soul. *Symbolic Life:Spring: A Journal of Archetype and Culture, 82*, 101–114.

Burckhardt, T. (1974). *Alchemy: Science of the cosmos, science of the soul* (W. Stoddart, Trans.). Baltimore: Penguin Books.

Burdeau, C. (2010, July 5). Sinking oil threatens historic Gulf shipwrecks. *Savannah Morning News*, p. 4A.

Bynner, W. (1980). *The way of life according to Lao Tzu* (W. Bynner, Trans.). New York: Perigee Books. (Original work published 1944).

Campbell, J. (1974). *The mythic image*. Assisted by M. J. Abadie. Princeton, NJ: Princeton University Press.

Campbell, J. (1987). *Primitive mythology: The masks of God*. New York: Penguin Books.

Campbell, J. (2001). *Thou art that: Transforming religious metaphor*. Novato, CA: New World Library.

Canan, J. (2007). *Goddesses, goddesses: Essays by Janice Canan*. Oakland, CA: Regent Press.

Cannella, G. S., & Viruru, R. (2004). *Childhood and postcolonization: Power, education and contemporary practice*. New York: RoutledgeFalmer.

Capra, F. (1991). *The Tao of physics: An exploration of the parallels between modern physics and Eastern mysticism*. Boston: Shambhala.

Carr, N. (2010). *The shallows: What the internet is doing to our brains*. New York: W. W. Norton.

Carson, R. (2002). *Silent spring*. New York: Houghton Mifflin. (Original work published 1962)

Casemore, B. (2008). *The autobiographical demand of place: Curriculum inquiry in the American South*. New York: Peter Lang.

Cash, W. J. (1997). The mind of the South. In E.L. Ayers & B.C. Mittendorf (Eds.), *The Oxford book of the American South: Testimony, memory, and fiction* (pp. 75–86). New York: Oxford University Press. (Original work published 1941)

Chabot, K. (2003, Fall). Sacred stone healing. *Massage Therapy Journal*, 5–10.

Chopra, D. (1989). *Quantum healing: Exploring the frontiers of mind/body medicine*. New York: Bantam Books.

Cixous, H. (1976). The laugh of the Medusa. *Signs, 1*, 1–26.

Cobb, N. (2006). The soul of the sky. *Psyche and Nature, Part 1 of 2. Spring: A Journal of Archetype and Culture, 75*, 121–138.

Coelho, P. (1998). *The alchemist* (A. R. Clarke, Trans.). New York: HarperSanFranciso.

Coetzee, J. M. (1999). *Disgrace*. New York: Penguin.

Coleridge, S. T. (1964). The rime of the ancient mariner. In E. Schneider (Ed.), *Samuel Taylor Coleridge: Selected poetry and prose* (pp. 49–69). New York: Holt, Rinehart and Winston. (Original work published 1797–1798)

Colum, P. (2005). *Great myths of the world*. Mineola, NY: Dover Publications. (Original work published 1930)

Conforti, M. (1999). *Field, form, and fate: Patterns in mind, nature & psyche*. New Orleans, LA: Spring Journal Books.

Conrad, J. (1986). *Heart of darkness*. New York: Penguin. (Original work published 1902)

Cowan, T. (1993). *Fire in the head: Shamanism and the Celtic spirit*. New York: HarperOne.

Cremin, L. A. (1990). *American education: The metropolitan experience, 1876–1980*. New York: Harper & Row, Publishers.

Crossley-Holland, K. (1980). *The Norse myths*. New York: Pantheon.

Davies, P., & Gribbin, J. (1992). *The matter myth: Dramatic discoveries that challenge our understanding of physical reality*. New York: Simon & Schuster.

de Bono, E. (1991). *I am right you are wrong: From this to the new renaissance: From rock logic to water logic*. New forewords by three Nobel Prize[for physics] winners. New York: Penguin Books.

de Castillejo, I. C. (1974). *Knowing woman: A feminine psychology*. New York: Harper & Row.

Deloria, V., Jr. (2009). In P. J. Deloria & J. S. Bernstein (Eds.). *C.G. Jung and the Sioux traditions: Dreams, visions, nature, and the primitive*. New Orleans, LA: Spring Journal Books.

Deloria, V., Jr., & Wildcat, D. R. (2001). *Power and place: Indian education in America*. Golden, CO: Fulcrum Resources.

Demetrakopoulos, S. A. (1979). Hestia, goddess of the hearth: Notes on an oppressed archetype. *Spring: An Annual of Archetypal Psychology and Jungian Thought*, 55–76.

Derrida, J. (1976). *Of grammatology* (G. C. Spivak, Trans.). Baltimore: The Johns Hopkins University Press.

Derrida, J. (1981). *Dissemination* (B. Johnson, Trans.). Chicago: The University Press of Chicago.

Derrida, J. (1991). 'Eating well'; or, The calculation of the subject: An interview with Jacques Derrida. In E. Cadava, P. Connor, & J.-L. Nancy (Eds.), *Who comes after the subject?* (pp. 96–119). New York: Routledge.

Dillard, A. (1984). *Teaching a stone to talk*. London: Picador.

Dirt: The movie. (2009). (B. Benenson & G. Rosow, Producers). (DVD). Common Ground Media, Inc.

Doll, M. A. (1988). *Beckett and myth: An archetypal approach*. Syracuse, NY: Syracuse University Press.

Doll, M. A. (1990, Spring). The monster in children's dreams: Its metaphoric awe. *The Journal of Curriculum Theorizing, 8*(4), 89–99.

Doll, M. A. (1995). *To the lighthouse and back: Writings on teaching and living*. New York: Peter Lang.

Doll, M. A. (2000). *Like letters in running water: A mythopoetics of curriculum*. Mahwah, NJ: Lawrence Erlbaum Associates.

Doll, W. E., Jr., & Gough, N. (2002). *Curriculum visions*. New York: Peter Lang.

Doll, W. E., Jr., & Trueit, D. (2010). Complexity and the health care professions. *Journal of Evaluation in Clinical Practice, 16*, 841–848.

Doty, W. G. (2000). *Mythography: The study of myths and rituals* (2nd ed.). Tuscaloosa, AL: University of Alabama Press.

Doty, W. G. (2004). Orpheus: The shamanic-mantic kitharodos (singing lyreplayer). *Orpheus: Spring: A Journal of Archetype and Culture, 71*, 37–54.

Doll, M. A. (1995). *To the lighthouse and back: Writings on teaching and living*. New York: Peter Lang Publishing.

Doll, M. A. (2000). *Like letters in running water: A mythopoetics of curriculum*. Mahwah, NJ: Lawrence Erlbaum Associates.

Downing, C. (1989). *The goddess: Mythological images of the feminine*. New York: The Crossroad Publishing Company.

Downing, C. (Ed.). (2006). *Disturbances in the field: Essays in honor of David. L. Miller*. New Orleans, LA: Spring Books.

Eagleton, T. (2000). *The idea of culture*. Oxford: Blackwell Publishers.

Edgerton, S. H. (1996). *Translating the curriculum: Multiculturalism into cultural studies*. New York: Routledge.

Eliade, M. (1971). *The forge and the crucible: The origins and structures of alchemy* (S. Corrin, Trans.). New York: Harper Torchbooks.

Eliot, T. S. (1992). The love song of J. Alfred Prufrock. In M. Mack, B. M. W. Knox, J. C. McGalliard, P. M. Pasinetti, H. E. Hugo, & P. M. Spacks, et al. (Eds.), *The Norton anthology of world masterpieces 2* (pp. 1747–1750). New York: W.W. Norton & Company. (Original work published 1915)

Ellis, P. B. (1999). *The chronicles of the Celts: New tellings of their myths and legends*. London: Robinson Publishing Ltd.

Ellis, P. B. (2002). *Celtic myths and legends*. Philadelphia: Running Press.

Ellsberg, R. (Ed.). (2003). *Flannery O'Connor's spiritual writings*. Retrieved from http:www.spirituality andpractice.com/books/excerpts.php?id+14188

Emerson, R. W. (2008). *The spiritual Emerson: Essential works by Ralph Waldo Emerson* (J. Needleman, Intro.). New York: Jeremy P. Tarcher/Penguin.

Erdoes, R., & Ortiz, A. (Eds.). (1984). *American Indian myths and legends*. New York: Pantheon Books.

Erdrich, L. (1998). *The antelope wife*. New York: HarperFlamingo.

Estés, C. P. (1992). *Women who run with the wolves: Myths and stories of the wild woman archetype*. New York: Ballantine Books.

Evans, L. (2006). Developing a Jungian ecopsychology. *Psyche and Nature, Part 2 of 2. Spring: A Journal of Archetype and Culture, 76*, 129–144.

Felty, D. C. (2010, June 19). Ring shouters cling to dying tradition. *Savannah Morning News*, p. C1.

REFERENCES

Fingarette, H. (1972). *Confucius: The secular as sacred.* New York: Harper & Row.

Fitzgerald, J. (2008). Story and the interface with the sacred in Irish myth. *Irish Culture and Depth Psychology: Spring: A Journal of Archetype and Culture, 79,* 15–30.

Fitzgerald, S. (Ed.). (1980). *Letters of Flannery O'Connor: The habit of being.* New York: Random House.

Fitzgerald, S., & Fitzgerald, R. (Eds.). (1981). *Flannery O'Connor: Mystery and manners: Occasional prose,* selected and edited by Sally and Robert Fitzgerald. New York: Farrar, Straus & Giroux.

Flannery, J. (2008). Heart mysteries: Traditional love songs of Ireland. *Irish Culture and Depth Psychology: Spring: A Journal of Archetype and Culture, 79,* 43–69.

Fleener, J. M. (2002). *Curriculum dynamics: Recreating heart.* New York: Peter Lang.

Fleener, J. M. (2005). Introduction: Setting up the conversation. In W. Doll, Jr., J. M. Fleener, D. Trueit, J. St. Julien (Eds.), *Chaos, complexity, curriculum and culture: A conversation* (pp. 1–20). New York: Peter Lang.

Foucault, M. (1979). *Discipline and punish: The birth of the prison* (A.M. Sheridan, Trans.). New York: Vintage.

Foucault, M. (2003). *'Society must be defended': Lectures at the College de France, 1975–76* (D. Macey, Trans.). New York: Picador.

Fox, M. (2006). *The A. W. E. project: Reinventing education, reinventing the human.* Kelowna: CopperHouse.

Fox, M., & Sheldrake, R. (1996). *Natural grace: Dialogues on creation, darkness, and the soul in spirituality and science.* New York: Image Books.

Frye, N. (1963). *The educated imagination. Massey lectures.* Toronto: Canadian Broadcasting Corporation.

Gard, M. (2006). *Men who dance: Aesthetics, athletics, and the art of masculinity.* New York: Peter Lang.

Giago, T. (2009, July 1). Good riddance to General Custer. *The Savannah Morning News,* p. A9.

Gimbutas, M. (2006). *The language of the goddess: Unearthing the hidden symbols of Western civilization.* New York: Thames & Hudson Inc.

Gough, A. (1998). Beyond Eurocentrism in science education: Problems and problematics from a feminist poststructuralist perspective. In W. F. Pinar (Ed.), *Curriculum: Toward new identities* (pp. 185–210). New York: Garland Publishing, Inc.

Gough, N. (1998). Reflections and diffractions: Functions of fiction in curriculum inquiry. In W. F. Pinar (Ed.), *Curriculum: Toward new identities* (pp. 94–127). New York: Garland Publishing, Inc.

Graves, R. (1955). *The Greek myths.* New York: George Braziller Inc.

Greene, B. (1999). *The elegant universe: Superstrings, hidden dimensions, and the quest for the ultimate theory.* New York: W. W. Norton.

Greene, B. (2003). *The elegant universe: Superstrings, hidden dimensions, and the quest for the ultimate theory.* Boston: WGBH. NOVA. (DVD).

Gregory, E. (1995). Angels and the apocalypse: H.D.'s tribute to the angels. In R. Sardello (Ed.), *The angels* (pp. 144–166). New York: Continuum.

Gregory, H. (Trans.). (2001). *The metamorphoses. Ovid.* New York: Viking. (Original work written 8 CE)

Griffin, S. (1978). *Woman and nature.* New York: Harper & Row.

Griffin, S. (1992). *A chorus of stones: The private life of war.* New York: Anchor Books.

Guerber, H. A. (1992). *Myths of the Norsemen: From the Eddas and Sagas.* New York: Dover Publications. (Original work published 1909)

Guggenbuhl-Craig, A. (1980). *Eros on crutches: Reflections on psychopathy and amorality* (G. V. Hartman, Trans.). Irving, TX: Spring Publications.

Haraway, D. J. (1997). *Modest_witness @ second_millenium. FemaleMan_meets_oncoMouse.* New York: Routledge.

Harding, M. E. (1975). *The way of all women: A psychological interpretation.* New York: Harper & Row.

Harding, P. (2009). *Tinkers.* New York: Bellevue Literary Press.

Harrison, J. E. (1962). *Themis: A study of the social origins of Greek religion.* New York: Meridian Books. (Original work published 1912)

Hathaway, N. (2002). *The friendly guide to mythology: A mortal's companion to the fantastical realm of gods, goddesses, monsters, and heroes.* New York: Penguin Books.

Hayward, J. (1999). Unlearning the sacred. In S. Glazer (Ed.), *The heart of learning: Spirituality in education* (pp. 61–76). New York: Jeremy P. Tarcher/Putnam.

Hemingway, E. (1968). *For whom the bell tolls.* New York: Scribner. (Original work published 1940)

Henderson, J. L., & Oakes, M. (1990). *The wisdom of the serpent: The myths of death, rebirth, and resurrection.* Princeton, NJ: Princeton University Press. (Original work published 1963)

Henderson, R. S. (2008). Witness to the ancient ones: An 'enterview' with Patricia Reis. Technology, Cyberspace, and Psyche. *Spring: A Journal of Archetype and Culture, 80,* 245–260.

Henderson, R. S. (2009). The red book—Prima materia of C. G. Jung: An 'enterview' with Sonu Shamdasani. *Symbolic Life: Spring: A Journal of Archetype and Culture, 82,* 185–192.

Hendry, P. M. (in press). *Engendering curriculum history.* New York: Routledge.

Highwater, J. (1982). *The primal mind: Vision and reality in Indian America.* New York: New American Library.

Highwater, J. (1994). *The language of vision: Meditations on myth and metaphor.* New York: Grove Press.

Hillman, J. (1975). *Re-visioning psychology.* New York: Harper & Row.

Hillman, J. (1979). Image-sense. *Spring: An Annual of Archetypal Psychology and Jungian Thought,* 130–143.

Hillman, J. (1981). Silver and the white earth (part two). *Spring: An Annual of Archetypal Psychology and Jungian Thought,* 21–66.

Hillman, J. (1983). *Interviews: Conversations with Laura Pozzo on psycholotherapy, biography, love, soul, dreams, work, imagination, and the state of the culture.* New York: Harper & Row.

Hillman, J. (1996). *The soul's code: In search of character and calling.* New York: Random House.

Hoare, P. (2010, May 2). Review of Insectopedia by Hugh Raffles. *The New York Times Book Review,* p. 18.

Hogan, L. (1995). *Solar storms.* New York: Simon and Schuster.

Hopkins, G. M. (1921). God's grandeur. In *The Oxford book of English mystical verse* (p. 355). Oxford: Clarendon Press.

Huebner, D. (1999). *The lure of the transcendent: Collected essays by Dwayne E. Huebner* (V. Hillis, Ed., Collected and Introduced by W. F. Pinar). Mahwah, NJ: Lawrence Erlbaum Associates.

Jackson, D. P. (Trans.). (1992). *The epic of Gilgamesh.* Wauconda, IL: Bolchazy-Carducci Publishers.

Jardine, D. (2000). *"Under the tough old stars": Ecopedagogical essays.* Brandon, VT: The Foundation for Educational Renewal.

Jardine, D. (2008). Forward: "The sickness of the West." In C. Eppert & H. Wang (Eds.), *Cross-cultural studies in curriculum: Eastern thought, Educational insights* (pp. ix–xv). New York: Lawrence Erlbaum Associates.

Josephson, B. D. (2005). Foreword. In M.A. Thalbourne & L. Storm (Eds.), *Parapsychology in the twenty-first century. Essays on the future of psychical research* (pp. 1–4). Jefferson, NC: McFarland & Company, Inc.

Jung, C. G. (1958). *The undiscovered self* (R.F.C. Hull, Trans.). Boston: Little, Brown and Company.

Jung, C. G. (1963). *Memories, dreams, reflections* (A. Jaffe, Ed., R. & C. Winston, Trans.). New York: Pantheon Books.

Jung, C. G. (1972). *Seminar on dream analysis.* Lecture III, 23 October, 1929. Zurich, Switzerland: The Psychology Club of Zurich. (Original work published 1929)

Jung, C. G. (1974). *Dreams* (R. F. C. Hull, Trans.). Princeton, NJ: Princeton University Press.

Jung, C. G. (1976a). Individual dream symbolism in relation to alchemy. In J. Campbell (Ed.), R. F. C Hull (Trans.), *The portable Jung* (pp 323–455). New York: Penguin Books. (Original work published 1944)

Jung, C. G. (1976b). *The symbolic life: Miscellaneous writings* (R. F. C. Hull, Trans.). Bollingen Series XX. Princeton, NJ: Princeton University Press. (Original work published 1950)

Jung, C. G. (1977). *The archetypes and the collective unconscious* (R. F. C. Hull, Trans.). Bollingen Series XX. Princeton, NJ: Princeton University Press. (Original work published 1959)

Jung, C. G. (2009). *The red book* (M. Kyburz, J. Peck, & S. Shamdasani, Trans.). New York: Philemon Series & W.W. Norton Co.

REFERENCES

Kafka, F. (1979). The country doctor. *The basic Kafka* (E. Heller, Intro.). New York: Pocket Books. (Original work published 1919)

Kaku, M. (2008). *Physics of the impossible: A scientific exploration into the world of phasers, force fields, teleportation, and time travel.* New York: Anchor Books.

Kelly, K. (1980). The Orphic mouth in *Not I. Journal of Beckett Studies* (no. 6), 73–80.

Kidner, D. (2006). Reuniting psyche and nature. *Psyche and Nature, Part 2 of 2: Spring: A Journal of Archetype and Culture, 76*, 91–110.

Kincaid, J. (1992). *At the bottom of the river.* New York: Plume.

Kline, J. (2004). Erotic undercurrents in the cult of Orpheus. *Orpheus: Spring; A Journal of Archetype and Culture, 71*, 151–170.

Knowlson, J. (1996). *Damned to fame: The life of Samuel Beckett.* New York: Simon & Shuster.

Kostelanetz, R. (Ed.). (1997). *Writings on Glass: Essays, interviews, criticism.* Los Angeles: University of California Press.

Koyaanisqatsi: Life out of balance. Reggio, G. (Director). (1983). (DVD). United States: MGM Home Entertainment, Inc.

Labor, E. (Ed.). (1994). *The portable Jack London.* New York: Viking.

Labor, E., & Reesman, J. C. (Eds.). (1994). *Jack London* (Rev. ed.). New York: Twayne.

Lacourt, J. A. (2010). My father was a bear: Human-animal transformation in Native American teachings. *Minding the Animal Psyche. Spring:A Journal of Archetype and Culture, 83*, 79–98.

Leeming, D. A. (1990). *The world of myth.* New York: Oxford University Press.

Leonard, S., & McClure, M. (2004). *Myth and knowing: An introduction to world mythology.* New York: McGraw-Hill.

Leonard, T. (2008). Imagination and mythopoesis in the science curriculum. In T. Leonard & P. Willis (Eds.), *Pedagogies of the imagination: Mythopoetic curriculum in educational practice* (pp. 83–92). United Kingdom: Springer.

Leshan, L. (1975). *The medium, the mystic, and the physicist: Toward a general theory of the paranormal.* New York: Ballantine Books.

Lesko, N. (2001). *Act your age!: A cultural construction of adolescence.* New York: Routledge Falmer.

Li, X. (2008). My lived stories of poetic thinking and Taoist knowing. In C. Eppert & H. Wang (Eds.), *Cross-cultural studies in curriculum: Eastern thought, educational insights* (pp. 193–206). New York: Lawrence Erlbaum Associates.

Lindlow, J. (2001). *Norse mythology: A guide to the gods, heroes, rituals, and beliefs.* Oxford: Oxford University Press.

Lorenz, E. N. (1993). *The essence of chaos.* Seattle, WA: University of Washington Press.

Lovelock, J. (2006). *The revenge of Gaia: Earth's climate in crisis and the fate of humanity.* New York: Basic Books.

Lumpkin, K. D. P. (1997). The making of a Southerner. In E. L. Ayers & B. C. Mittendorf (Eds.), *The Oxford book of the American South: Testimony, memory, and fiction* (pp. 87–89). New York: Oxford University Press.

MacCulloch, J. A. (2004). *Celtic mythology.* Mineola, NY: Dover Publications.

Mack, C. K., & Mack, D. (1998). *A field guide to demons, fairies, fallen angels, and other subversive spirits.* New York: Owl Books.

Mack, M., Knox, B. M. W., McGalliard, J. C., Pasinetti, P. M., Hugo, H.E., Spacks, P. M., et al. (Eds.). (1992). *The Norton anthology of world masterpieces* (Vol. 2). New York: W. W. Norton Company.

Malory, T. (1961). *Le morte d'Arthur* (2 Vols.). London: J. M. Dent & Sons.

Matthews, J. (2002). *Taliesin: The last Celtic shaman.* Rochester, VT: Inner Traditions.

Miller, D. L. (1976). Fairy tale or myth? *Spring: An Annual of Archetypal Theory and Jungian Thought,* 157–164.

Miller, D. L. (1986). *Three faces of God: Traces of the trinity in literature and life.* Philadelphia: Fortress Press.

Miller, D. L. (1989). The stone which is not a stone: C. G. Jung and the postmodern meaning of "meaning." *Spring: A Journal of Archetype and Culture, 49*, 110–122.

Miller, D. L. (1995). The death of the clown: A loss of wits in the postmodern moment. *Disillusionment: Spring: A Journal of Archetype and Culture, 58*, 69–82.

Milton, J. (1936). *Paradise lost.* London: Cassell, Petter and Galpin & Co. (Original work published 1884)

Mitchell, S. (1998). *Meetings with the archangel.* New York: Harper Perennial.

Mogenson, G. (2006a). The eyes of the background: Nature, spirit, and fire-side psychoanalysis. *Psyche and Nature, Part 1 of 2, Spring: A Journal of Archetype and Culture, 75*, 43–68.

Mogenson, G. (2006b). Miller's pentacost. In C. Downing (Ed.), *Disturbances in the field: Essays in honor of David L. Miller* (pp. 142–160). New Orleans, LA: Spring Journal Books.

Moore, T. (1994). *SoulMates: Honoring the mysteries of love and relationship.* New York: HarperCollins.

Moore. T. (2004). *Dark nights of the soul: A guide to finding your way through life's ordeals.* New York: Gotham Books.

Moore, T. (2009). *Writing in the sand: Jesus and the soul of the Gospels.* United States: Hay House, Inc.

Morgan, J. S. (n.d.). *The mystery of Goya's Saturn.* Retrieved July 1, 2009, from http://www.nereview.com/22-23/morgan.html

Morris, M. (2001). Serres bugs the curriculum. In J. Weaver, M. Morris, & P. Appelbaum (Eds.), *(Post)modern science (education): Propositions and alternative paths* (pp. 95–110). New York: Peter Lang.

Morris, M. (2008). *Soul-speaking—The ill body. Teaching through the ill body: A spiritual and aesthetic approach to pedagogy and illness.* New York: Sense Publishers.

Morris, M. (2009). *On not being able to play: Scholars, musicians and the crisis of psyche.* Rotterdam: Sense Publishers.

Morrison, T. (1993). *Jazz.* New York: Plume.

Munro, P. (in press). *Engendering curriculum history.*

Myrrh & Frankincense. Retrieved August 21, 2009, from http://www.itmonline.org/arts/myrrh.htm

Nietzsche, F. (1984). *Dithyrambs of Dionysus* (R. J. Hollingdale, Trans.). London: Black Swan Books, Ltd. (Original work published 1889)

Nineplanets.org/meteorites.html. Retrieved July 13, 2010.

Nyenhuis, J. E. (2003). *Myth and the creative process: Michael Ayrton and the myth of Daedalus, the maze maker.* Detroit, MI: Wayne State University.

O'Connor, F. (1978). *The complete stories.* New York: Farrar, Straus and Giroux.

O'Connor, U. (1996). *Irish tales and sagas.* Dublin: Town House.

Onians, R. B. (1973). *The origins of European thought: About the body, the mind, the soul, the world, time, and fate.* New York: Arno Press. (Original work published 1951)

Opie, I., & Opie, P. (1980). *The classic fairy tales.* New York: Oxford University Press.

Orgel, S. (1999). Introduction. In *King Lear* (pp. xxxi–xliii). New York: Penguin.

Ortega y Gasset, J. (1986). *Meditations on hunting.* New York: Scribner's.

Otto, R. (1958). *The idea of the holy: An inquiry into the nonrational factor in the idea of the divine and its relation to the rational* (J. W. Harvey, Trans.). New York: Oxford University Press.

Ovid. (2001). *The metamorphoses* (H. Gregory, Trans.). New York: Signet. (Original work written 8 CE)

Pagels, E. (2004). *Beyond belief: The secret gospel of Thomas.* New York: Vintage Books.

Paris, G. (1991). *Pagan meditations: Aphrodite, Hestia, Artemis* (G. Moore, Trans.). Dallas, TX: Spring Publications, Inc.

Phillips, A. (1993). Introduction. In *The electrified tightrope by Michael Eigen* (pp. xiii–xvi). Northvale, NJ: Jason Aronson, Inc.

Piaget, J. (1999). *Construction of reality in the child* (M. Cook, Trans.). New York: Routledge. (Original work published 1955)

Pinar, W. F. (1991). Curriculum as social psychoanalysis: On the significance of place. In J. L. Kincheloe & W. F. Pinar (Eds.), *Curriculum as social psychoanalysis* (pp. 167–186). Albany, NY: State University of New York Press.

Pinar, W. F. (1998). Introduction. In Pinar, W. F. (Ed.), *Curriculum: Toward new identities* (pp. ix–xxxii). New York: Garland Publishing, Inc.

Pinar, W. F. (2004). *What is curriculum theory?* Mahwah, NJ: Lawrence Erlbaum Associates.

REFERENCES

Pinar, W. F. (2009). *The worldliness of a cosmopolitan education: Passionate lives in public service.* New York: Routledge.

Pinar, W. & Grumet, M. (1976). *Toward a poor curriculum.* Dubuque, IA: Kendall/Hunt.

Prengaman, P. (2010, July 5). Gulf: Spill a metaphor for what's wrong with U.S. *Savannah Morning News,* p. A4.

Quispel, G. (1979). *The secret book of revelation.* New York: McGraw-Hill.

Rankin, S. (2009). Lessons in an unspoken language. In Wang & Olson (Eds.), *A Journey to unlearn and learn in multicultural education* (pp. 19–24). New York: Peter Lang.

Readings, B. (1999). *The university in ruins.* Cambridge: Harvard University Press.

Reis, P. (2008). Witness to the ancient ones: An 'enterview' with Patricia Reis by Robert S. Henderson. *Technology, Cyberspace, & Psyche. Spring: A Journal of Archetype and Culture, 80,* 245–260.

Resnik, S. (2001). *The delusional person: Bodily feelings in psychosis* (D. Alcorn, Trans.). New York: Karnac.

Rilke, R. M. (1946). *Selected letters of Rainer Maria Rilke* (R. F. C. Hull, Trans.). London: Macmillan and Co.

Robinson, D. (2008). Paradox neverending: Psyche and the soul of the web: A conversation with Derek Robinson by Leigh Melander. *Technology, Cyberspace, & Psyche. Spring: A Journal of Archetype and Culture, 80,* 207–226.

Romanyshyn, R. D. (2008). The melting polar ice. *Technology, Cyberspace, & Psyche. Spring: A Journal of Archetype and Culture, 80,* 79–116.

Rosa, A. N. (2006). *Oedipus—The untold story: A ghostly mythodrama in one act* (L. Toledo, Trans.). New Orleans, LA: Spring Journal Books.

Rosenberg, D. (1994). *World mythology.* New York: McGraw-Hill.

Rothstein, E. (2009, December 12). Jung's inner universe, writ large. *The New York Times,* pp. C1, 5.

Rowlands, M. (2009). *The philosopher and the wolf: Lessons from the wild on love, death, and happiness.* New York: Pegasus Books.

Sabini, M. (Ed.). (2005). *The Earth has a soul: The nature writings of C.G. Jung.* Berkeley, CA: North Atlantic Books.

St. Teresa of Avila. (2002). *The complete works* (E. A. Peer, Trans.). New York: Burns & Oates. (Originally published 1946)

Salvatore, G. (2004). Orpheus before Orpheus: The myth of the magic citharode. *Orpheus: Spring: A Journal of Archetype and Culture, 71,* 171–192.

Salvio, P. (2007). *Anne Sexton: Teacher of weird abundance.* New York: State University of New York Press.

Sarton, M. (1974). *Collected poems.* New York: W. W. Norton.

Santiago, J. (2009, June 3). The sounds of two hands, clapping. Charleston City Paper, p. 30.

Schweizer, A. (2009). 'Observe nature and you will find the stone': Reflections on the alchemical treatise 'Komarios to Cleopatra.' *Spring: A Journal of Archetype and Culture, 82,* 81–100.

See, L. (2008). *Peony in love.* New York: Random House.

Sedgwick, E. K. (2003). *Touching, feeling: Affect, pedagogy, performativity.* Durham, NC: Duke University Press.

Segal, R. A. (Ed.). (2000). *Hero myths.* Malden, MA: Blackwell Publishers.

Shakespeare, W. (1999). *King Lear.* In S. Orgel (Ed.). New York: Penguin. (Originally published 1623)

Shlain, L. (1999). *The alphabet versus the goddess: The conflict between word and image.* New York: Penguin/Compass.

Slattery, D. P. (2004). *Grace in the desert: Awakening to the gifts of monastic life.* New York: John Wiley & Sons, Inc.

Slattery, D. P. (2006). *Harvesting darkness: Essays on literature, myth, film and culture.* New York: iUniverse, Inc.

Slattery, D. P. (2009). Twisting toward the kingdom: Book review of Thomas Moore's writing in the sand: Jesus and the soul of the gospels. *Spring: A Journal of Archetype and Culture, 82,* 223–227.

Smith, D. G. (1999). *Interdisciplinary essays in the Pedagon: Human sciences, pedagogy and culture*. New York: Peter Lang.

Smith, H. (2009). *Tales of wonder: Adventures chasing the divine; an autobiography with J. Paine*. New York: HarperOne.

Snowber, C. (2008). *Personal communication*.

Song of the South. (1946). (H. Foster & W. Jackson, Directors). DVD. Walt Disney Productions.

Spangler, L. (2007, September 14). *Dogugaeshi*. Retrieved June 29, 2009, from http://www.nytheatre.com/nytheatre/showpage.php?t=dogu5747

Star Wars. (2004). (G. Lucas, Director). (DVD). Lucas Productions.

Stevens, W. (1972). *The palm at the end of the mind: Selected poems and a play by Wallace Stevens* (H. Stevens, Ed.). New York: Vintage Books.

Squire, C. (2001). *Celtic myth and legend* (Rev. ed.). New Jersey: The Career Press, Inc.

Sumara, D. J., & Davis, B. (1998). Unskinning curriculum. In W. F. Pinar (Ed.), *Curriculum: New identities* (pp. 75–92). New York: Garland Publishing, Inc.

Tacey, D. (2010). Ecopsychology and the sacred: The psychological basis of the environmental crisis. *Minding the Animal Psyche: Spring: A Journal of Archetype and Culture, 83*, 329–352.

Tan, A. (2006). *Saving fish from drowning*. New York: Ballantine Books.

Tavenier-Courbin, J. (1994). *The call of the wild: A naturalistic romance*. New York: Twayne.

Thomas, D. (1952). *Collected poems*. New York: New Directions.

Thury, E. M., & Devinney M. K. (2009). *Introduction to mythology*. New York: Oxford University Press.

Turner, F. (1995). Apollo. In J. H. Stroud (Ed.), *The Olympians* (pp. 81–90). Dallas, TX: The Dallas Institute Publications.

Vanderburg, A. (1980, February). Coming back slow. *The Old Ones: Parabola: Myth and the Quest for Meaning, 1*, 20–23.

Vendler, H. (n.d.). Retrieved June 26, 2009, from http://athome.harvard.edu/programs/vendler

Vernon, J. (1973). *The garden and the map: Schizophrenia in twentieth- century literature and culture*. Urbana, IL: University of Illinois Press.

Von Franz, M.-L. (1972). *Patterns and creativity mirrored in creation myths*. Dallas, TX: Spring Publications, Inc.

Von Franz, M.-L. (2000). *The problem of the Puer Aeternus*. Toronto: Inner City Books.

Walker, B. G. (1983). *The woman's encyclopedia of myths and secrets*. New York: Harper & Row.

Walker, B. G. (1985). *The crone: Woman of age, wisdom, and power*. New York: Harper & Row.

Waley, A. (1958). *The way and its power: A study of the Tao te Ching and its place in Chinese thought*. New York: Grove Press.

Wang, H., & Olson, N. (Eds.). (2009). *A journey to unlearn and learn in multicultural education*. New York: Peter Lang.

Wardi, E. (2000). *Once below a time: Dylan Thomas, Julia Kristeva, and other speaking subjects*. Albany, NY: State University of New York Press.

Wear, D. (2006). Shrinking distance. In M. A. Doll, D. Wear, & M. Whitaker (Eds.), *Triple takes on curricular worlds* (pp. 70–74). Albany, NY: State University of New York Press.

Weaver, J. (2009). *Popular culture primer* (Rev. ed.). New York: Peter Lang.

Weaver, J. A. (2010). *Educating the posthuman: Biosciences, fiction, and curriculum studies*. Boston: Sense Publishers.

Webster's encyclopedic unabridged dictionary of the English language. (1989). New York: Gramercy Books.

Welsford, E. (1966). *The fool: His social and literary history*. Gloucester: Peter Smith.

Welty, E. (1979). *Thirteen stories* (R. M. Vande Kieft, Ed.). New York: A Harvest/HBJ Book.

Welty, E. (1980). *The collected stories of Eudora Welty*. New York: Harcourt Brace Jovanovich.

Whan, M. (2006a). Reversion. *Psyche and Nature, Part 1 of 2: Spring: A Journal of Archetype and Culture, 75*, n.p.

Whan, M. (2006b). The unsaying of stone in Jung's psychology. *Psyche and Nature, Part 1 of 2: Spring: A Journal of Archetype and Culture, 75*, 23–41.

REFERENCES

Whistled speech: An ingenious way to "talk." *Awake!* (2009, February).

Whitehead, A. N. (1978). *Process and reality (Gifford lectures delivered in the University of Edinburgh during the session 1927–28)*. New York: The Free Press.

Wildcat, D. (2001). Understanding the crisis in American education. In Deloria, V., Jr. & Wildcat, D. (Eds.), *Power and place: Indian education in America* (pp. 29–40). Golden, CO: Fulcrum Resources.

Willeford, W. (1969). *The fool and his scepter: A study in clowns and jesters and their audience.* Evanston, IL: Northwestern University Press.

Willinsky, J. (1998). *Learning to divide the world: Education at empire's end.* Minneapolis, MN: University of Minnesota Press.

Wolfe, C. (2010). Human, all too human: 'Animal Studies' and the humanities. *Publications of the Modern Language Association of America, 124*(2), 564–576.

Wolkstein, D., & Kramer, S. N. (1983). *Inanna: Queen of heaven and earth: Her stories and hymns from Sumer.* New York: Harper & Row.

Wordsworth, W. (2008). The major works. (S. Gill, Ed.). New York: Oxford University Press.

Wright, J. R. (2008). Thin places and thin times. *Irish Culture and Depth Psychology. Spring: A Journal of Archetype and Culture, 79*, 3–14.

Yeats, W. B. (1959). *The collected poems of W. B. Yeats.* New York: Macmillan.

Yolen, J. (2000). *Touch magic: Fantasy, faerie and folklore in the literature of childhood.* Little Rock, AR: August House.

Zukov, G. (2001). *The dancing Wu Li masters: An overview of the new physics.* New York: Morrow.

INDEX

CPSIA information can be obtained at www.ICGtesting.com
Printed in the USA
LVOW101944070313

323246LV00002B/15/P

9 789460 914430